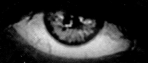
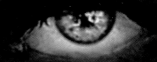

TO OBEY IS TO DIE

HEADSMASH

CREATED BY: VLAD YUDIN

STORY BY: VLAD YUDIN
SCRIPT BY: ERIK HENDRIX
ART BY: DWAYNE HARRIS
LETTERS BY: SHAWN DEPASQUALE
EDITED BY: EDWIN MEJIA

COVER BY: TIM BRADSTREET

www.arcana.com

THE VLADAR COMPANY

CEO and Founder	VP of Publishing	VP of Sales
Sean Patrick O'Reilly	Erik Hendrix	Michelle Meyers

VP of Film & TV	Senior Editor
Dan Forcey	Amanda Hendrix

Marketing	Story Editor
Emma Waddell	Mia Divac

Principal	Principal	Post Production	Development	Marketing
Vlad Yudin	Edwin Mejia	Justin Timms	Jeffrey Sutton	Rohin Katthula

ISBN: 978-1-77135-162-1   Printed in Canada

VLAD YUDIN'S
HEADSMASH

"HE WHO FIGHTS MONSTERS SHOULD LOOK TO IT THAT HE HIMSELF DOES NOT BECOME A MONSTER."

- FRIEDRICH NIETZSCHE

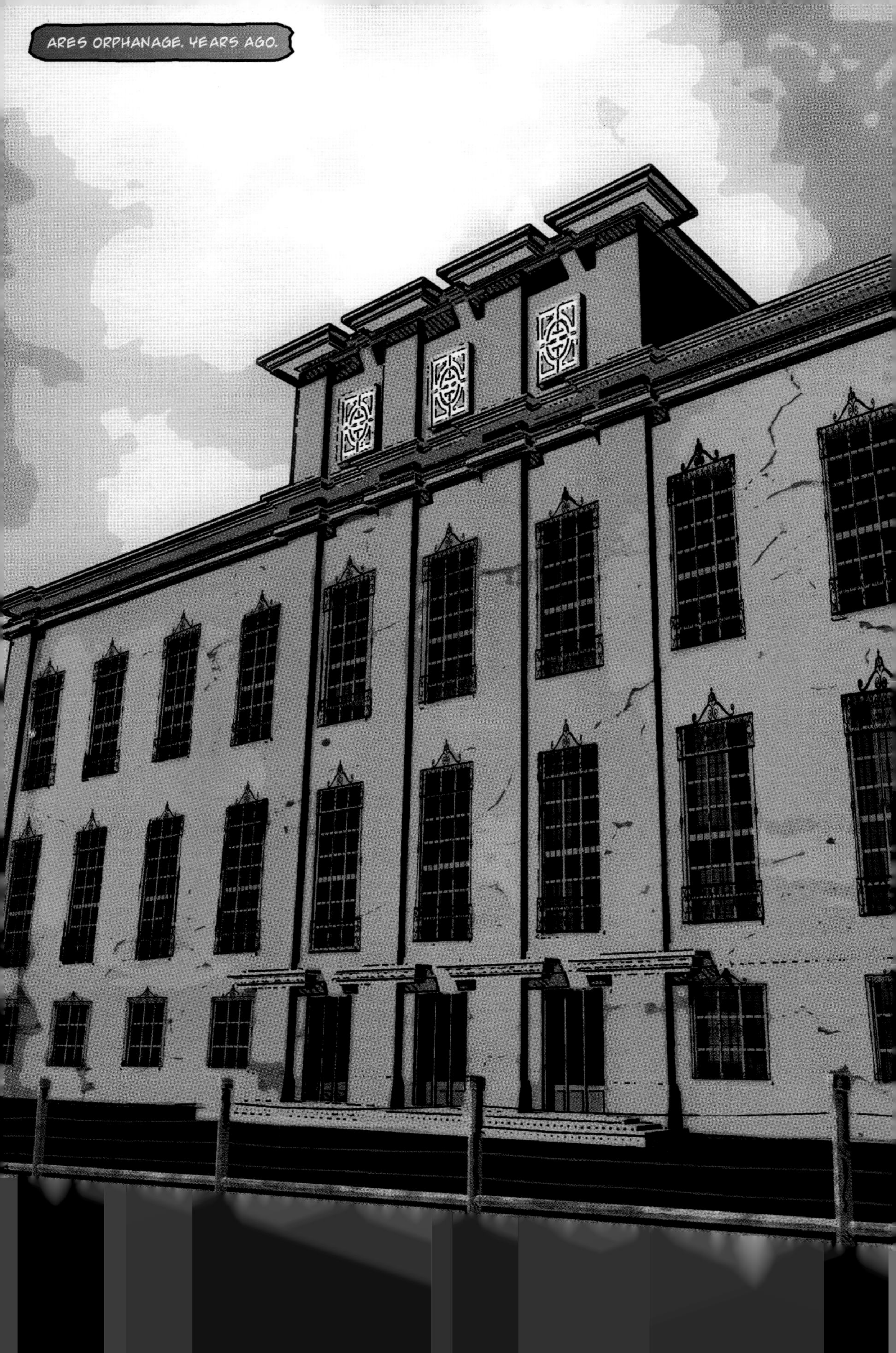
ARES ORPHANAGE. YEARS AGO.

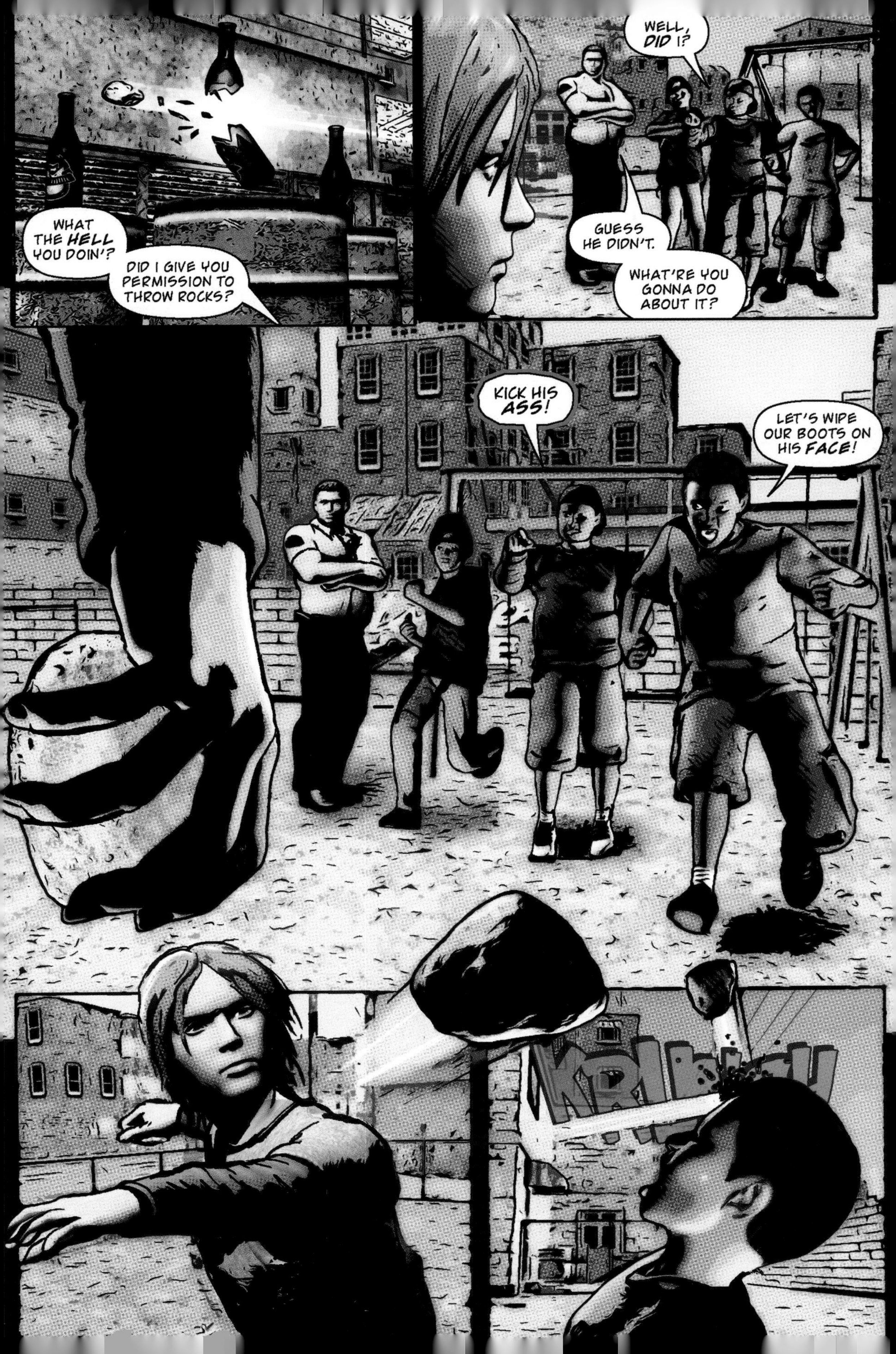
WHAT THE HELL YOU DOIN'?
DID I GIVE YOU PERMISSION TO THROW ROCKS?
WELL, DID I?
GUESS HE DIDN'T.
WHAT'RE YOU GONNA DO ABOUT IT?
KICK HIS ASS!
LET'S WIPE OUR BOOTS ON HIS FACE!

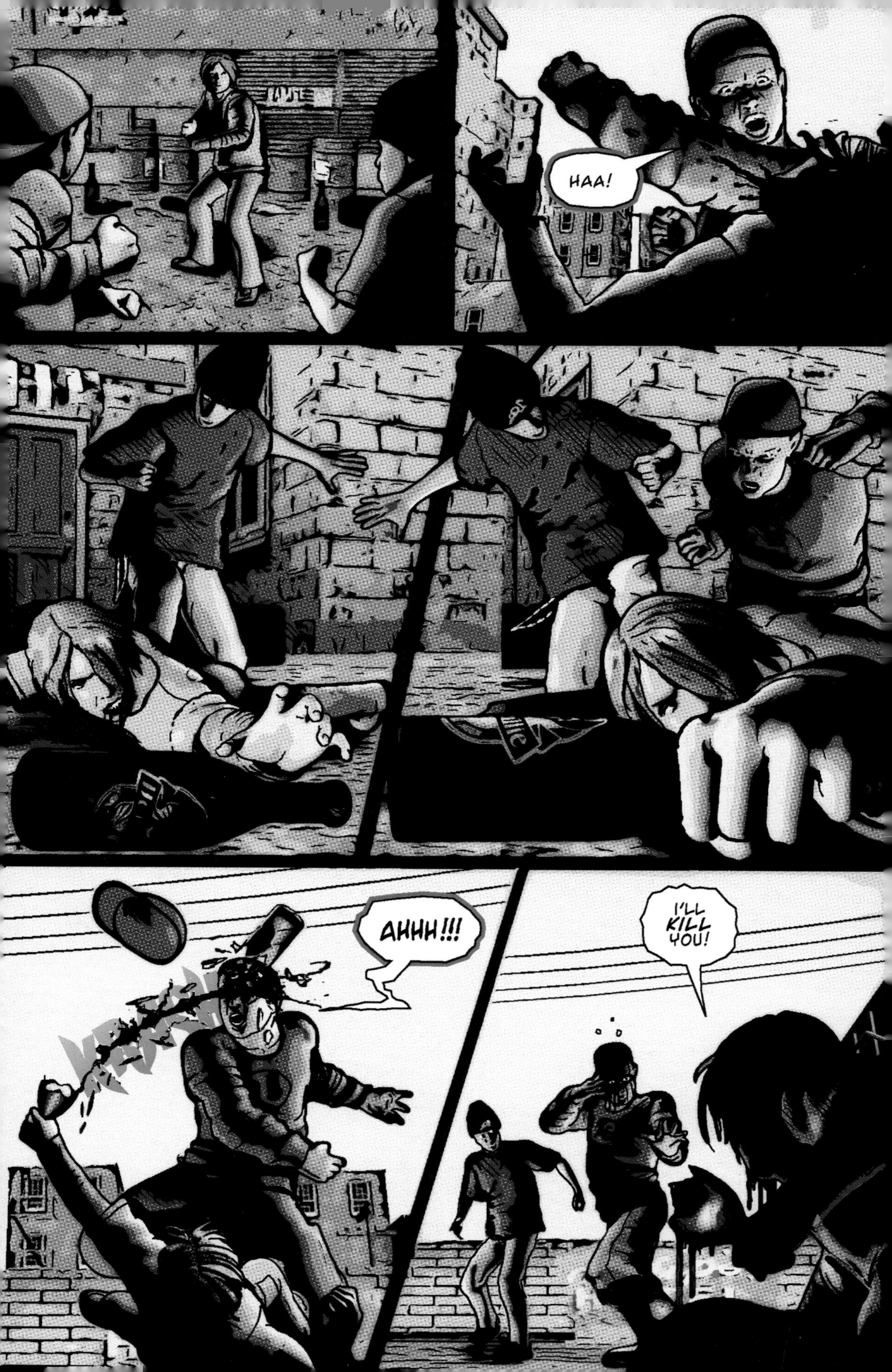
HAA!
AHHH!!!
I'LL KILL YOU!

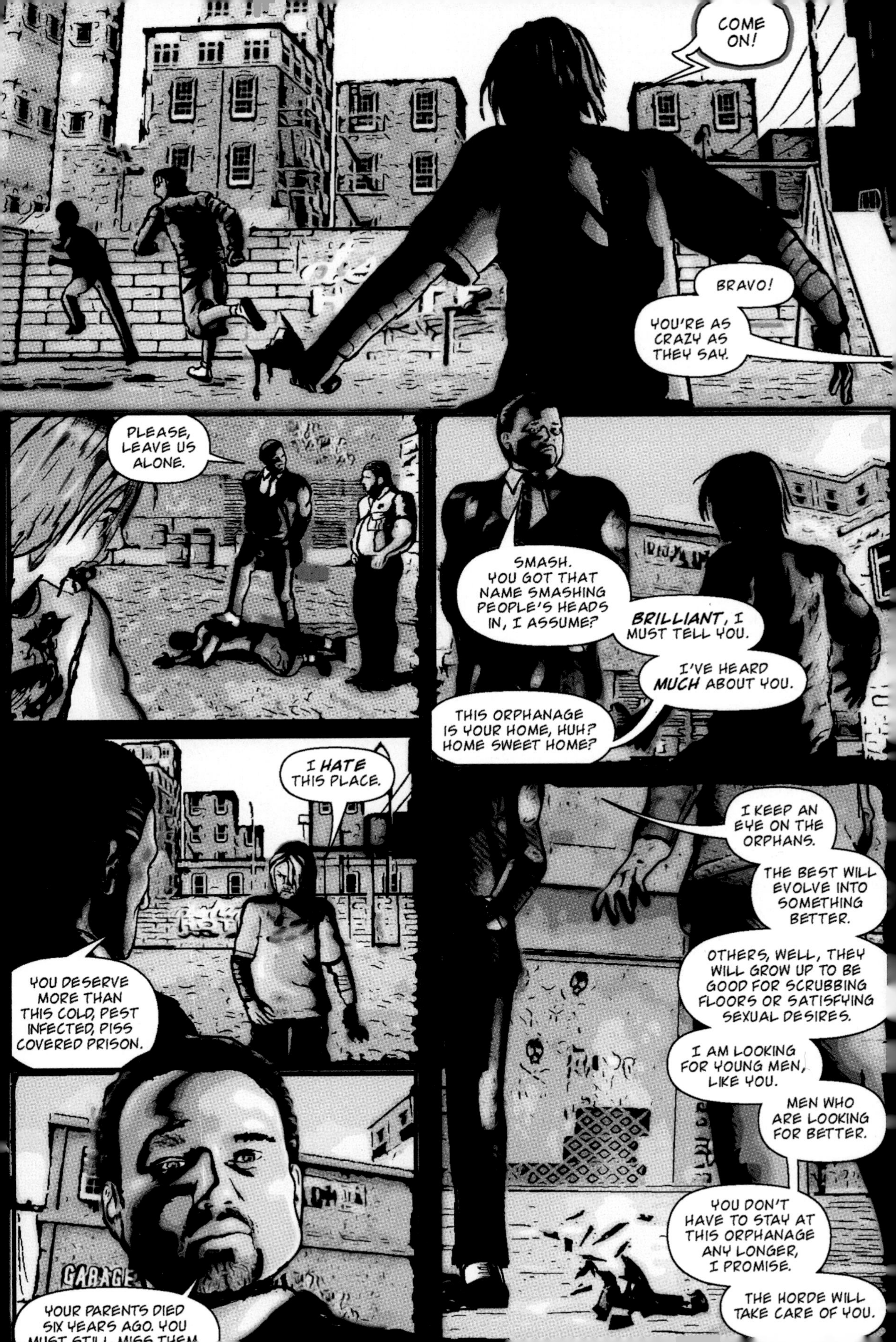
COME ON!
BRAVO!
YOU'RE AS CRAZY AS THEY SAY.
PLEASE, LEAVE US ALONE.
SMASH. YOU GOT THAT NAME SMASHING PEOPLE'S HEADS IN, I ASSUME?
BRILLIANT, I MUST TELL YOU.
I'VE HEARD **MUCH** ABOUT YOU.
THIS ORPHANAGE IS YOUR HOME, HUH? HOME SWEET HOME?
I **HATE** THIS PLACE.
YOU DESERVE MORE THAN THIS COLD, PEST INFECTED, PISS COVERED PRISON.
GARAGE
YOUR PARENTS DIED SIX YEARS AGO. YOU
I KEEP AN EYE ON THE ORPHANS.
THE BEST WILL EVOLVE INTO SOMETHING BETTER.
OTHERS, WELL, THEY WILL GROW UP TO BE GOOD FOR SCRUBBING FLOORS OR SATISFYING SEXUAL DESIRES.
I AM LOOKING FOR YOUNG MEN, LIKE YOU.
MEN WHO ARE LOOKING FOR BETTER.
YOU DON'T HAVE TO STAY AT THIS ORPHANAGE ANY LONGER, I PROMISE.
THE HORDE WILL TAKE CARE OF YOU.

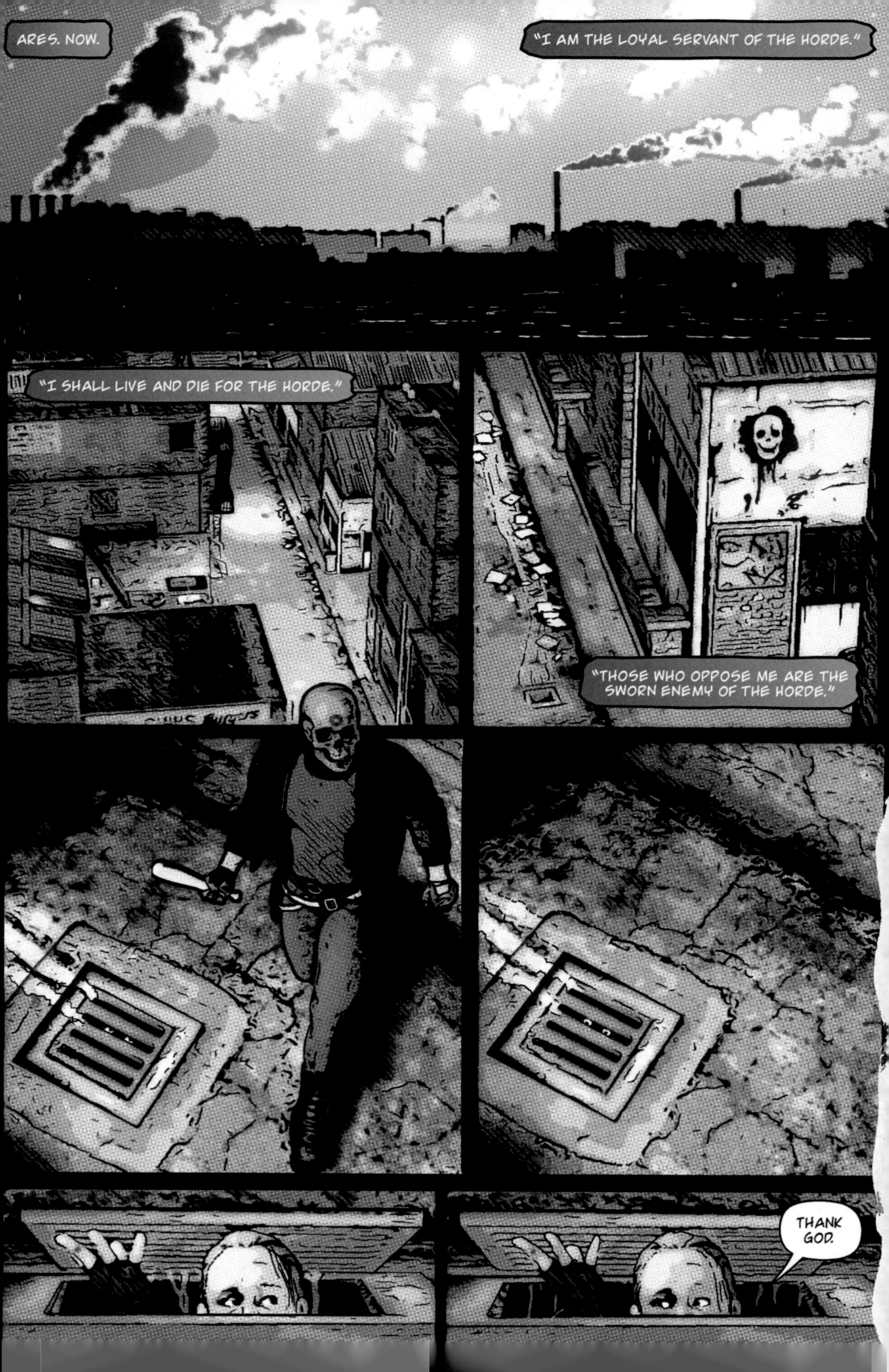
ARES. NOW.
"I AM THE LOYAL SERVANT OF THE HORDE."
"I SHALL LIVE AND DIE FOR THE HORDE."
"THOSE WHO OPPOSE ME ARE THE SWORN ENEMY OF THE HORDE."
THANK GOD.

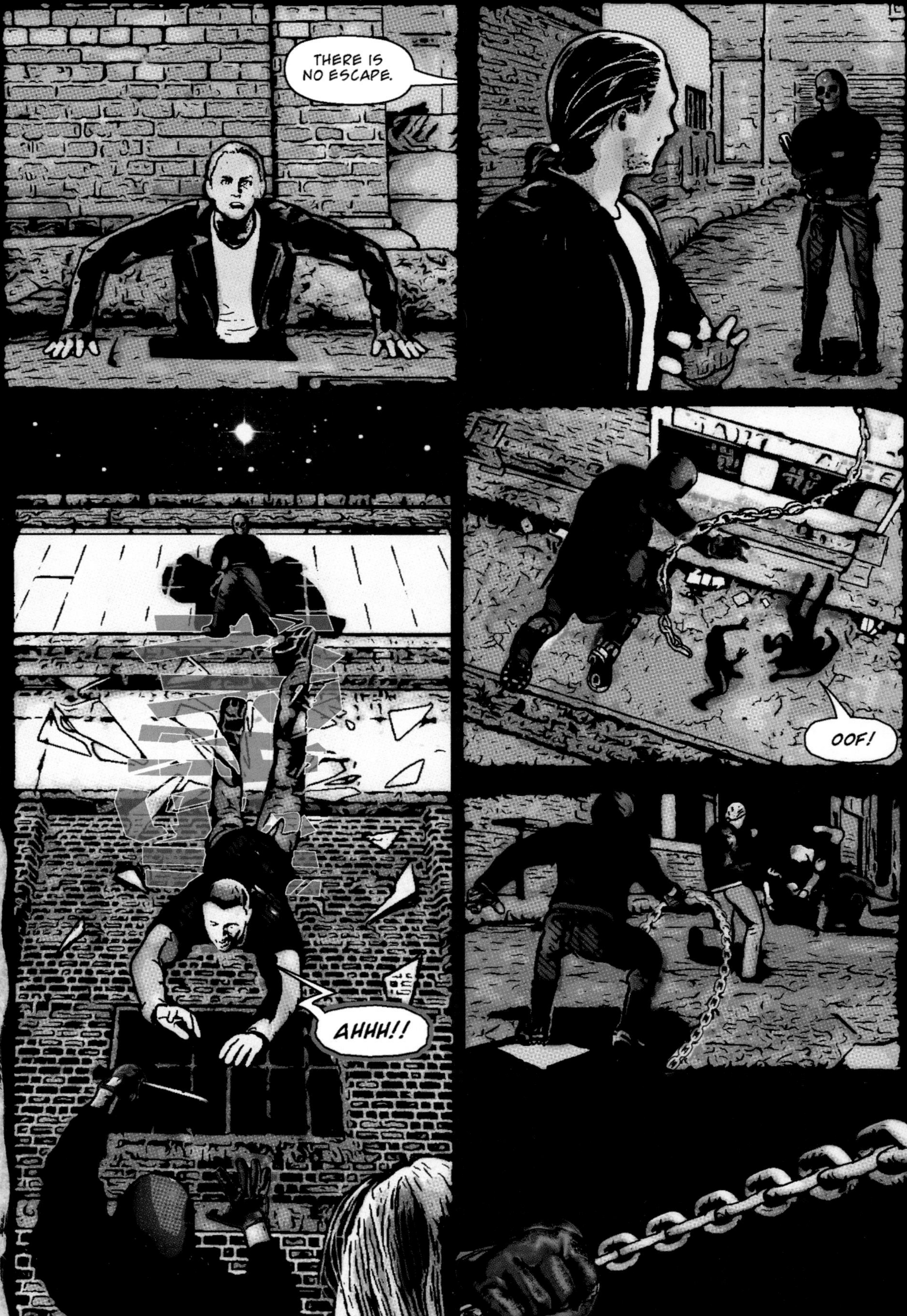
THERE IS NO ESCAPE.
OOF!
AHHH!!

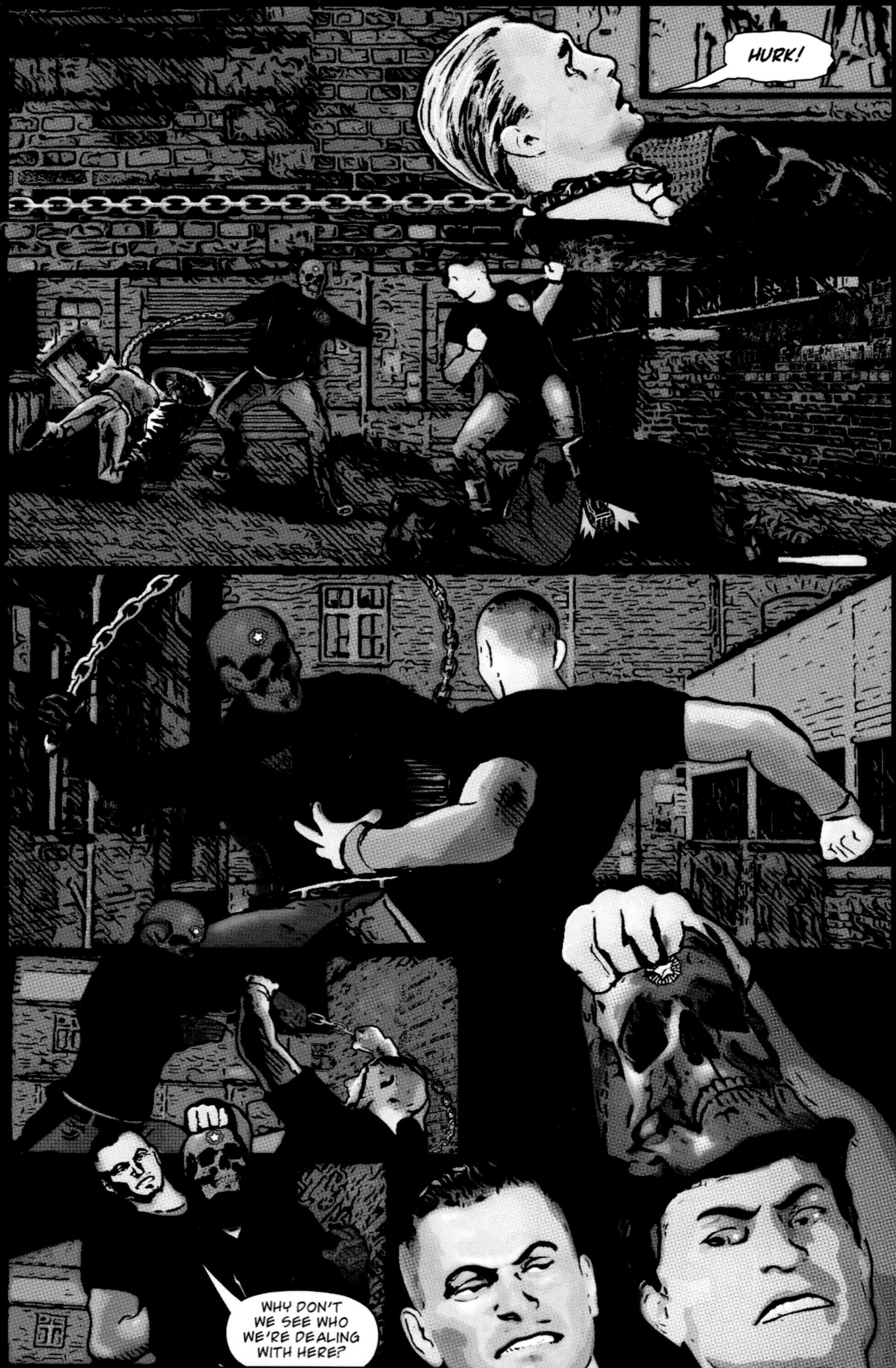
HURK!
WHY DON'T WE SEE WHO WE'RE DEALING WITH HERE?

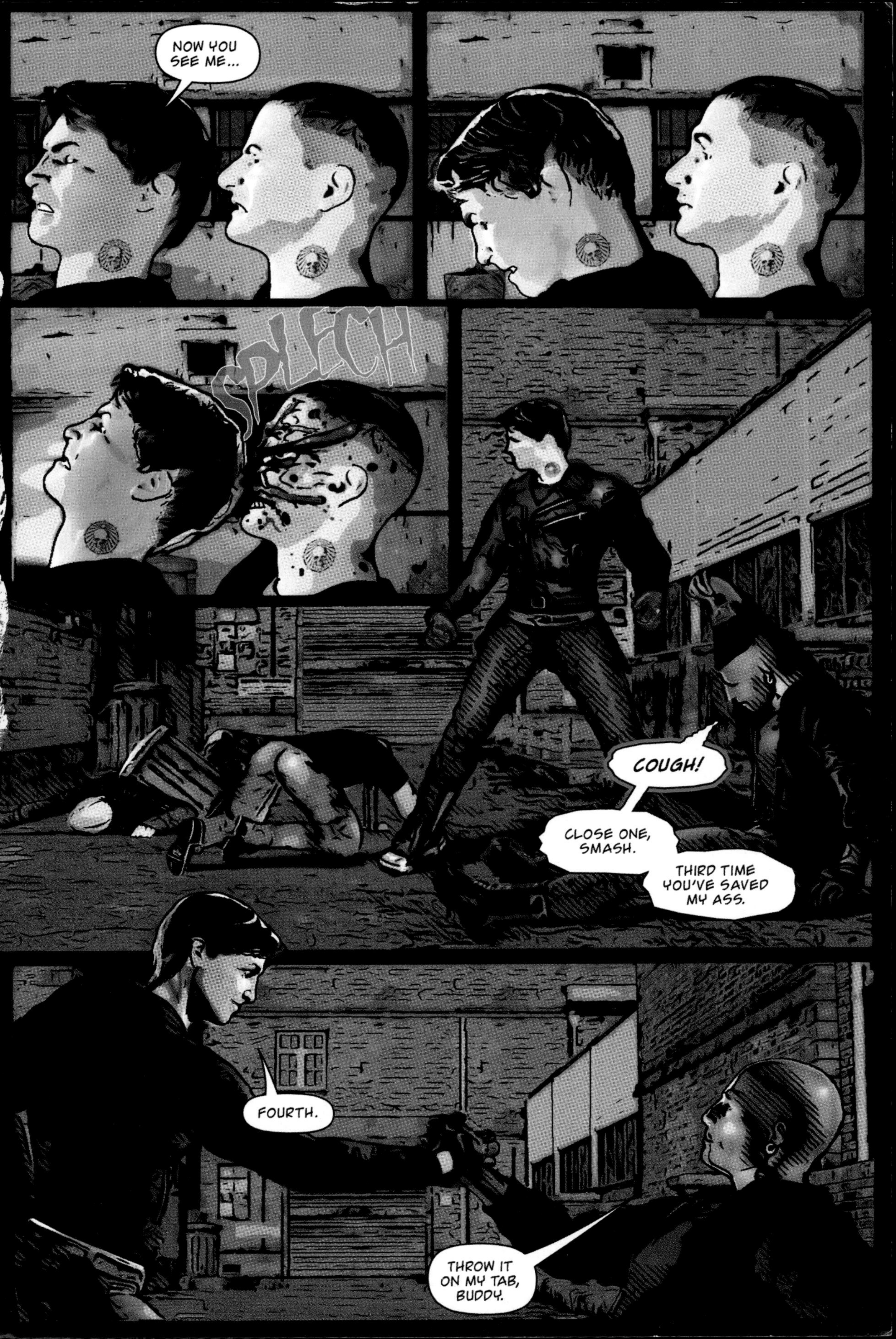
NOW YOU SEE ME...
SPLECH
COUGH!
CLOSE ONE, SMASH.
THIRD TIME YOU'VE SAVED MY ASS.
FOURTH.
THROW IT ON MY TAB, BUDDY.

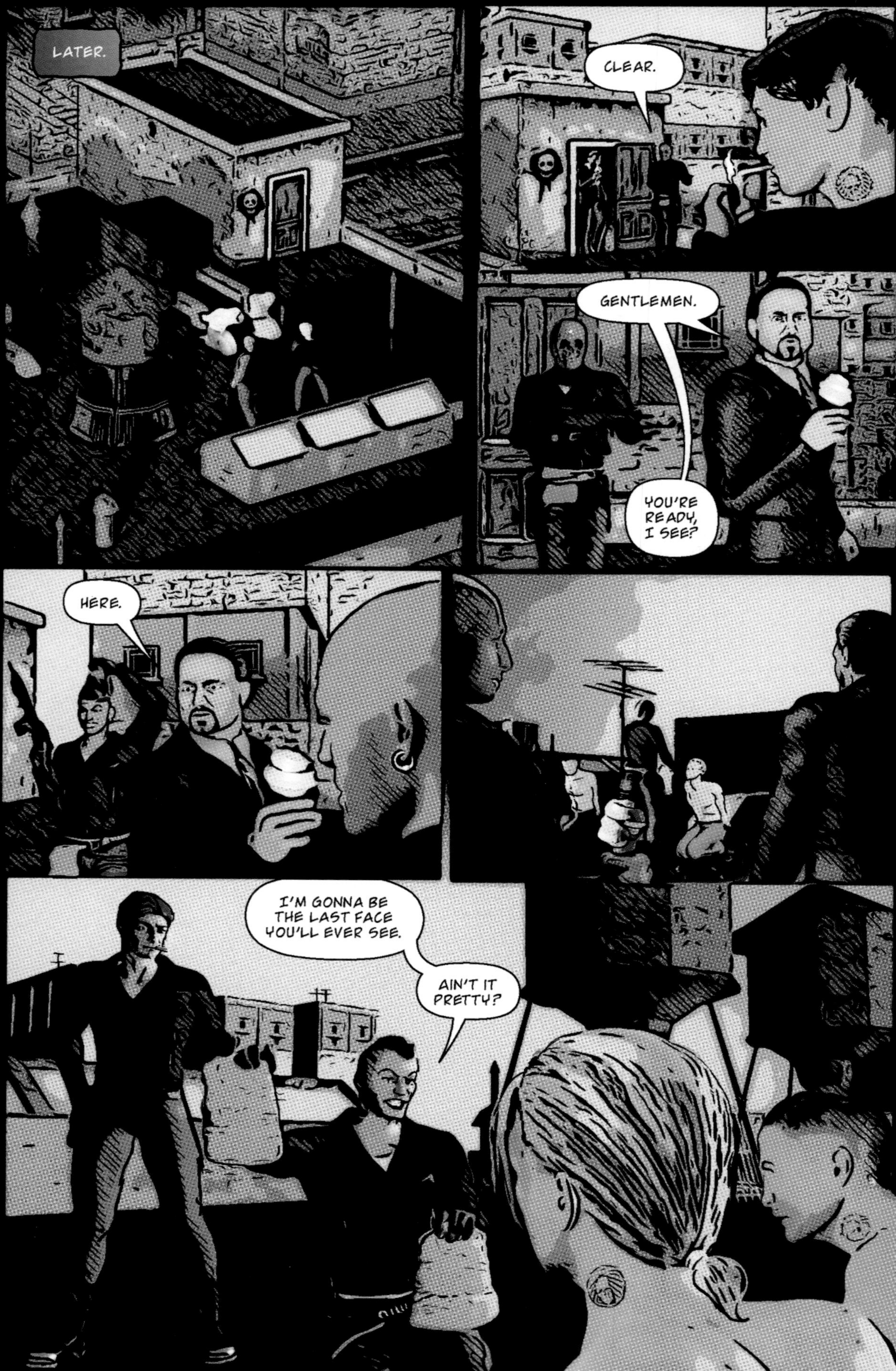
LATER.
CLEAR.
GENTLEMEN.
YOU'RE READY, I SEE?
HERE.
I'M GONNA BE THE LAST FACE YOU'LL EVER SEE.
AIN'T IT PRETTY?

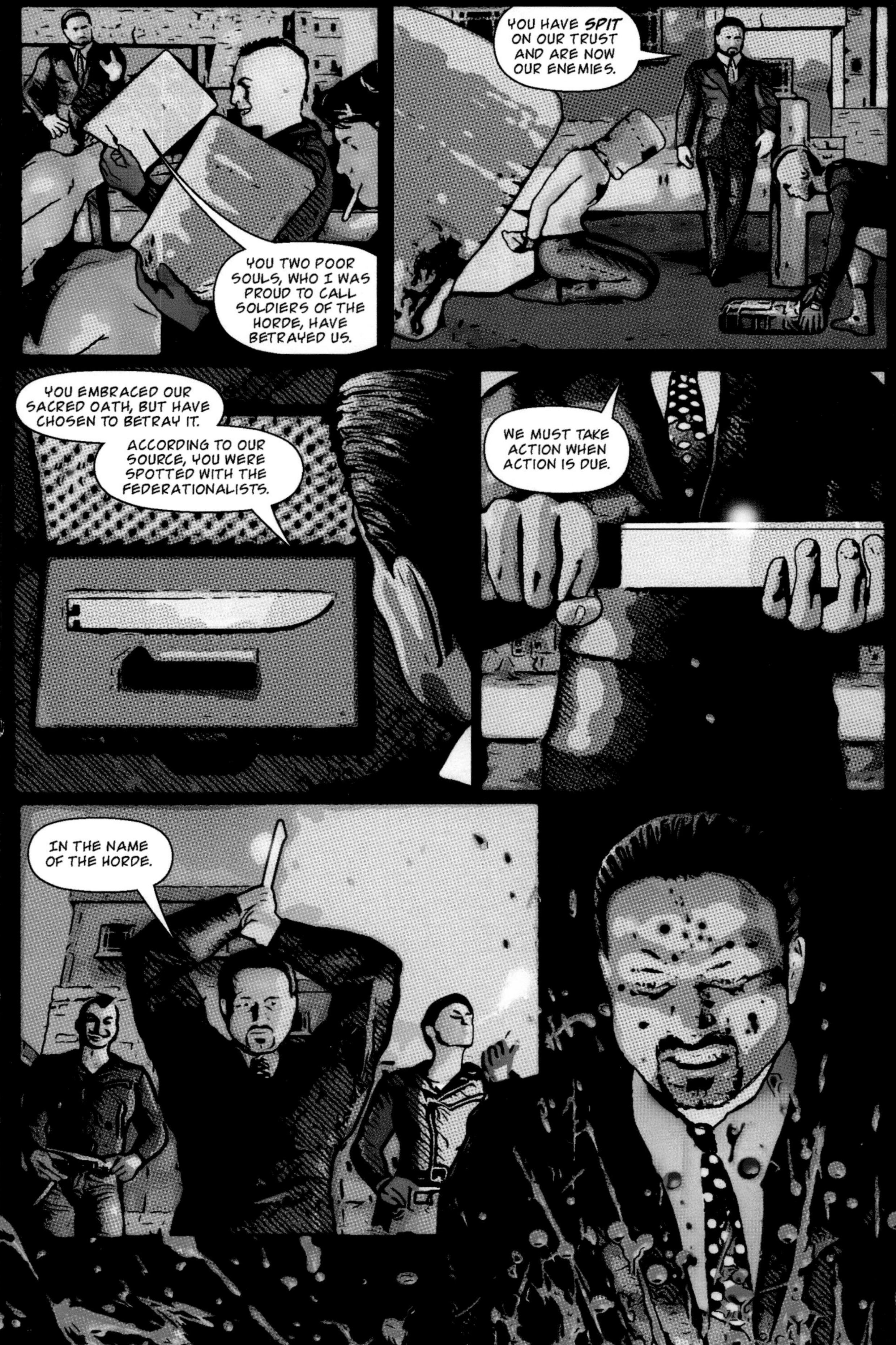
YOU TWO POOR SOULS, WHO I WAS PROUD TO CALL SOLDIERS OF THE HORDE, HAVE BETRAYED US.
YOU HAVE SPIT ON OUR TRUST AND ARE NOW OUR ENEMIES.
YOU EMBRACED OUR SACRED OATH, BUT HAVE CHOSEN TO BETRAY IT.
ACCORDING TO OUR SOURCE, YOU WERE SPOTTED WITH THE FEDERATIONALISTS.
WE MUST TAKE ACTION WHEN ACTION IS DUE.
IN THE NAME OF THE HORDE.

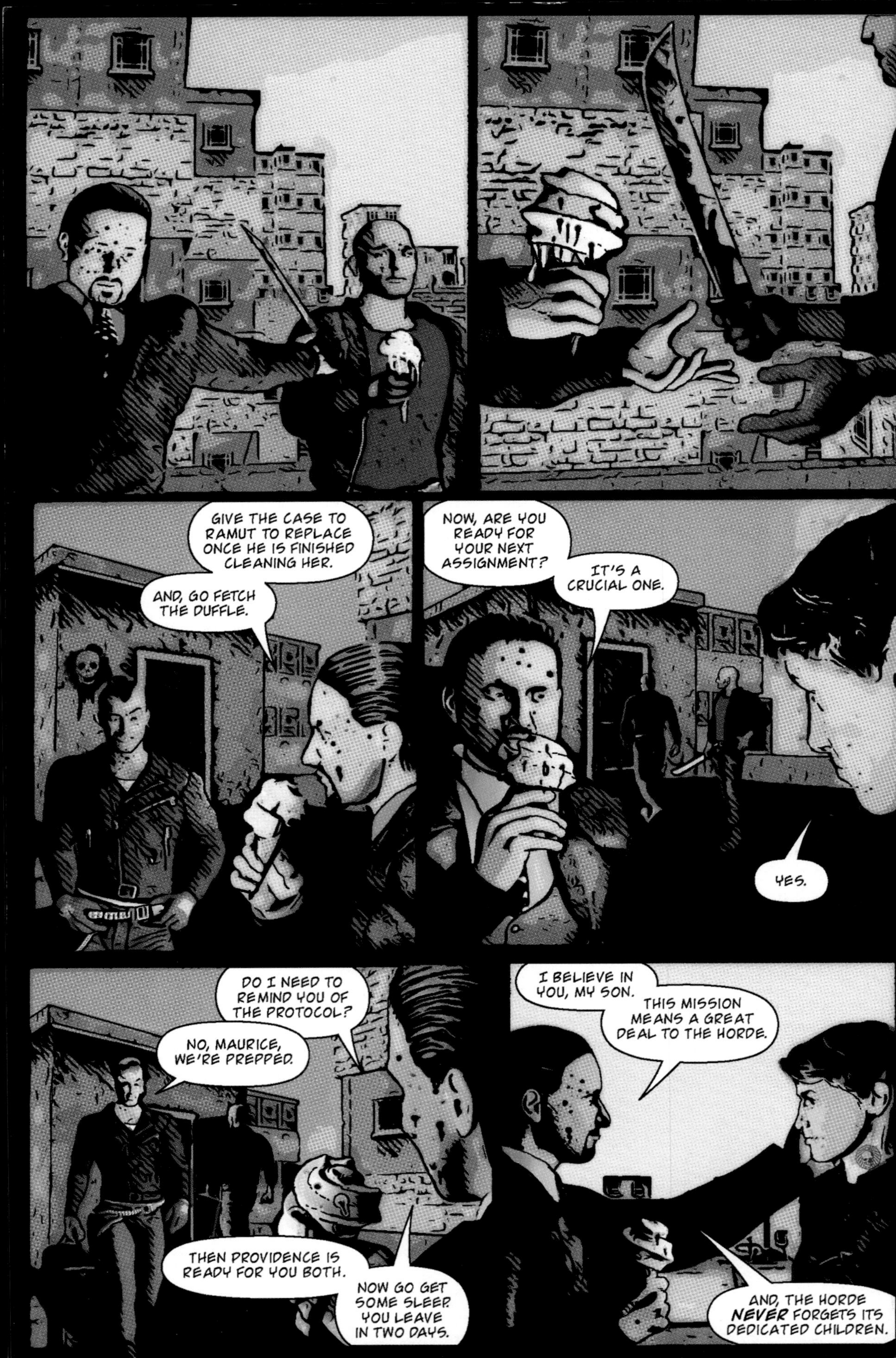
GIVE THE CASE TO RAMUT TO REPLACE ONCE HE IS FINISHED CLEANING HER.
AND, GO FETCH THE DUFFLE.
NOW, ARE YOU READY FOR YOUR NEXT ASSIGNMENT?
IT'S A CRUCIAL ONE.
YES.
DO I NEED TO REMIND YOU OF THE PROTOCOL?
NO, MAURICE, WE'RE PREPPED.
THEN PROVIDENCE IS READY FOR YOU BOTH.
NOW GO GET SOME SLEEP. YOU LEAVE IN TWO DAYS.
I BELIEVE IN YOU, MY SON.
THIS MISSION MEANS A GREAT DEAL TO THE HORDE.
AND, THE HORDE NEVER FORGETS ITS DEDICATED CHILDREN.

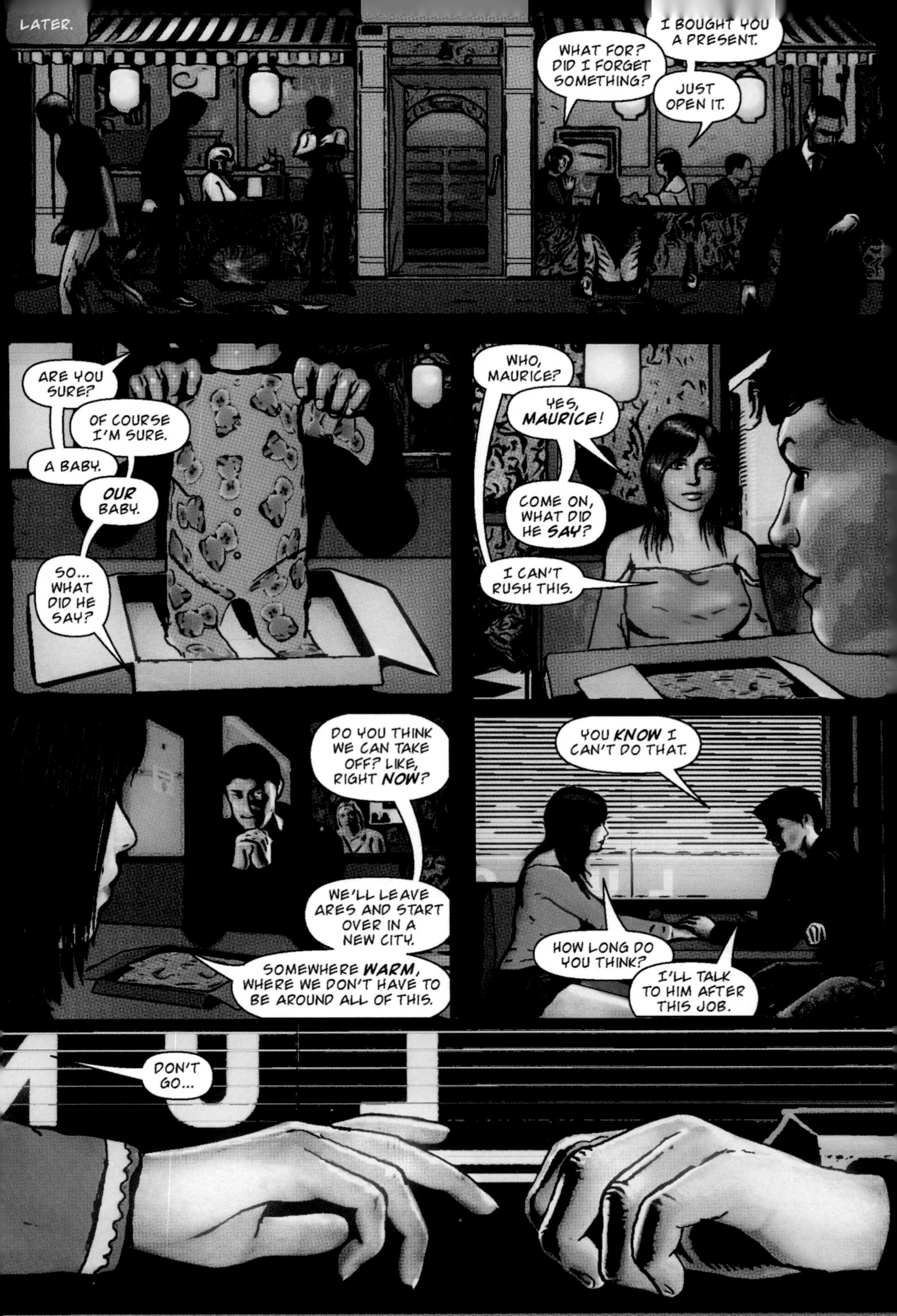
LATER.
WHAT FOR? DID I FORGET SOMETHING?
I BOUGHT YOU A PRESENT.
JUST OPEN IT.
ARE YOU SURE?
OF COURSE I'M SURE.
A BABY.
OUR BABY.
SO... WHAT DID HE SAY?
WHO, MAURICE?
YES, MAURICE!
COME ON, WHAT DID HE SAY?
I CAN'T RUSH THIS.
DO YOU THINK WE CAN TAKE OFF? LIKE, RIGHT NOW?
WE'LL LEAVE ARES AND START OVER IN A NEW CITY.
SOMEWHERE WARM, WHERE WE DON'T HAVE TO BE AROUND ALL OF THIS.
YOU KNOW I CAN'T DO THAT.
HOW LONG DO YOU THINK?
I'LL TALK TO HIM AFTER THIS JOB.
DON'T GO...

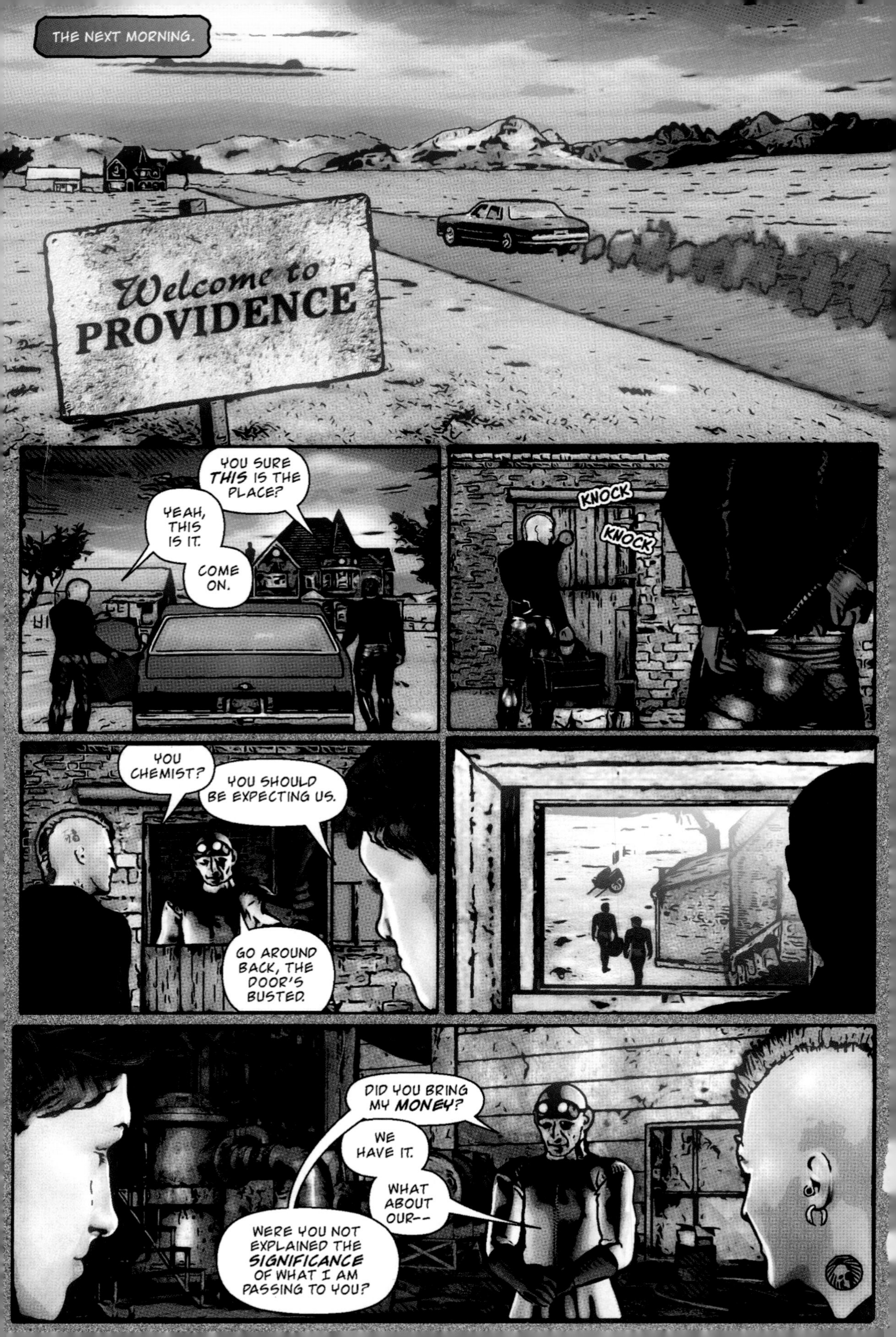
THE NEXT MORNING.
Welcome to PROVIDENCE
YOU SURE THIS IS THE PLACE?
YEAH, THIS IS IT.
COME ON.
KNOCK
KNOCK
YOU CHEMIST?
YOU SHOULD BE EXPECTING US.
GO AROUND BACK, THE DOOR'S BUSTED.
DID YOU BRING MY MONEY?
WE HAVE IT.
WHAT ABOUT OUR--
WERE YOU NOT EXPLAINED THE SIGNIFICANCE OF WHAT I AM PASSING TO YOU?

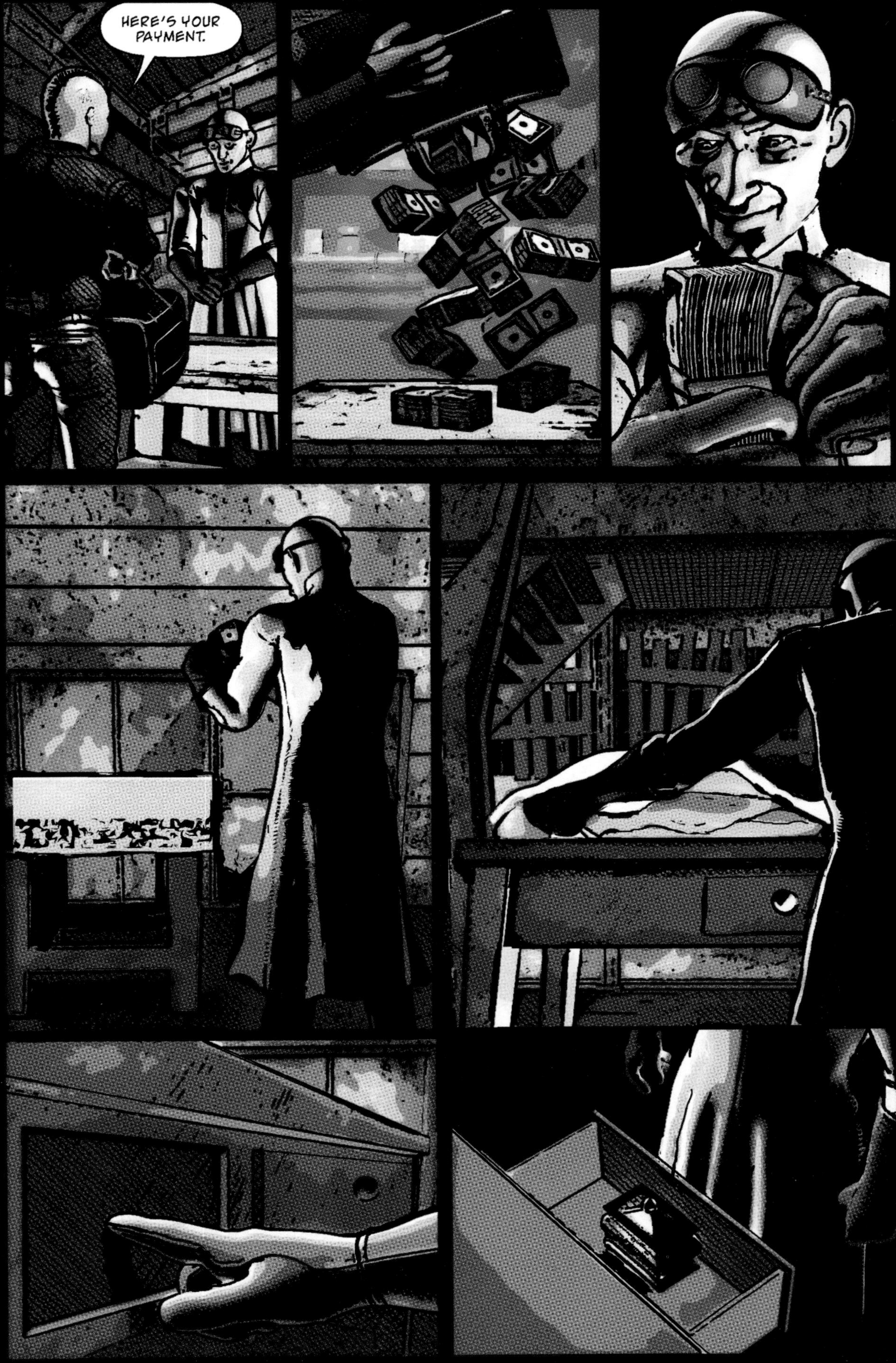
HERE'S YOUR PAYMENT.

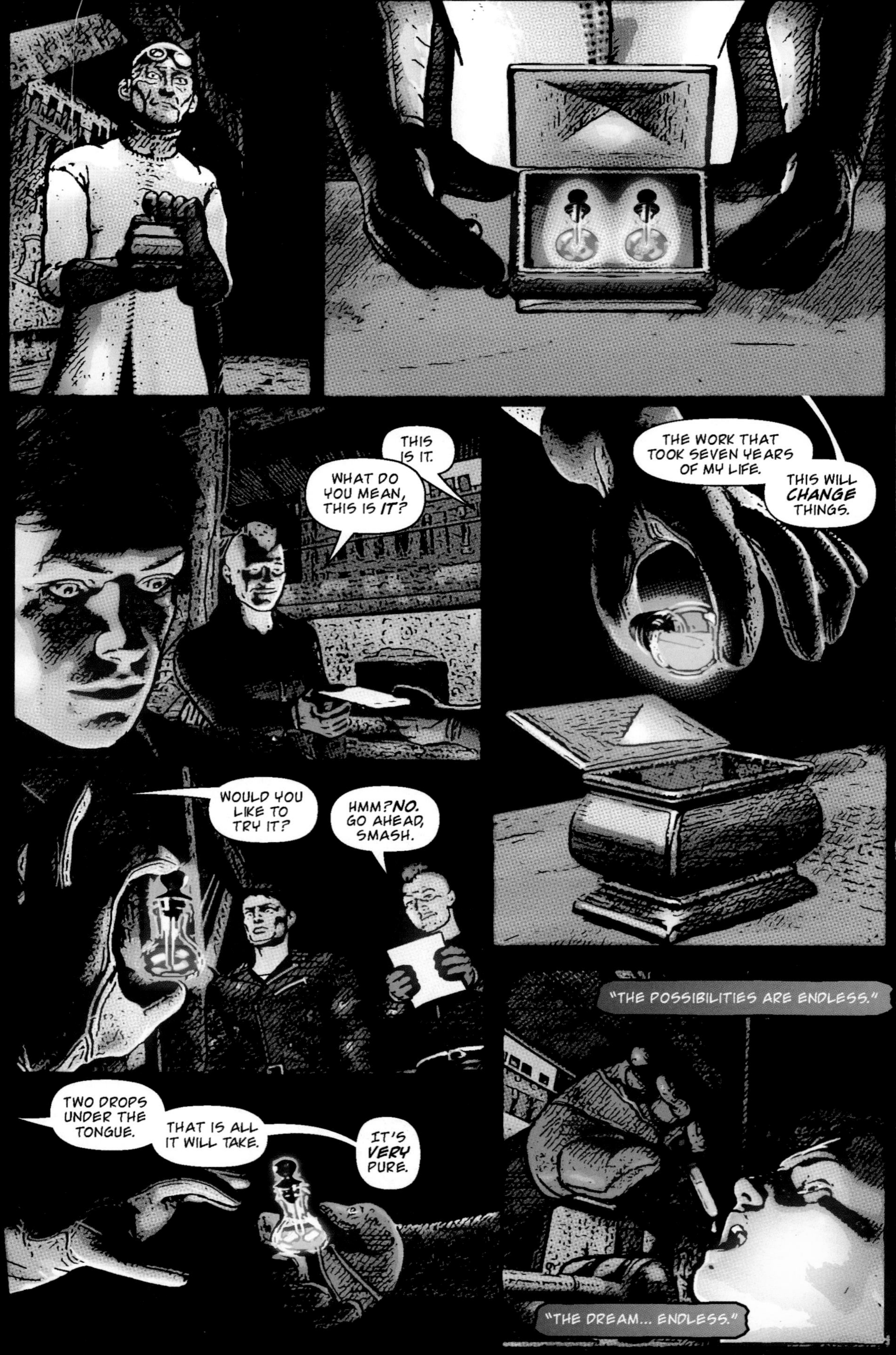
THIS IS IT.
WHAT DO YOU MEAN, THIS IS *IT*?
THE WORK THAT TOOK SEVEN YEARS OF MY LIFE.
THIS WILL ***CHANGE*** THINGS.
WOULD YOU LIKE TO TRY IT?
HMM? **NO.** GO AHEAD, SMASH.
TWO DROPS UNDER THE TONGUE.
THAT IS ALL IT WILL TAKE.
IT'S ***VERY*** PURE.
"THE POSSIBILITIES ARE ENDLESS."
"THE DREAM... ENDLESS."

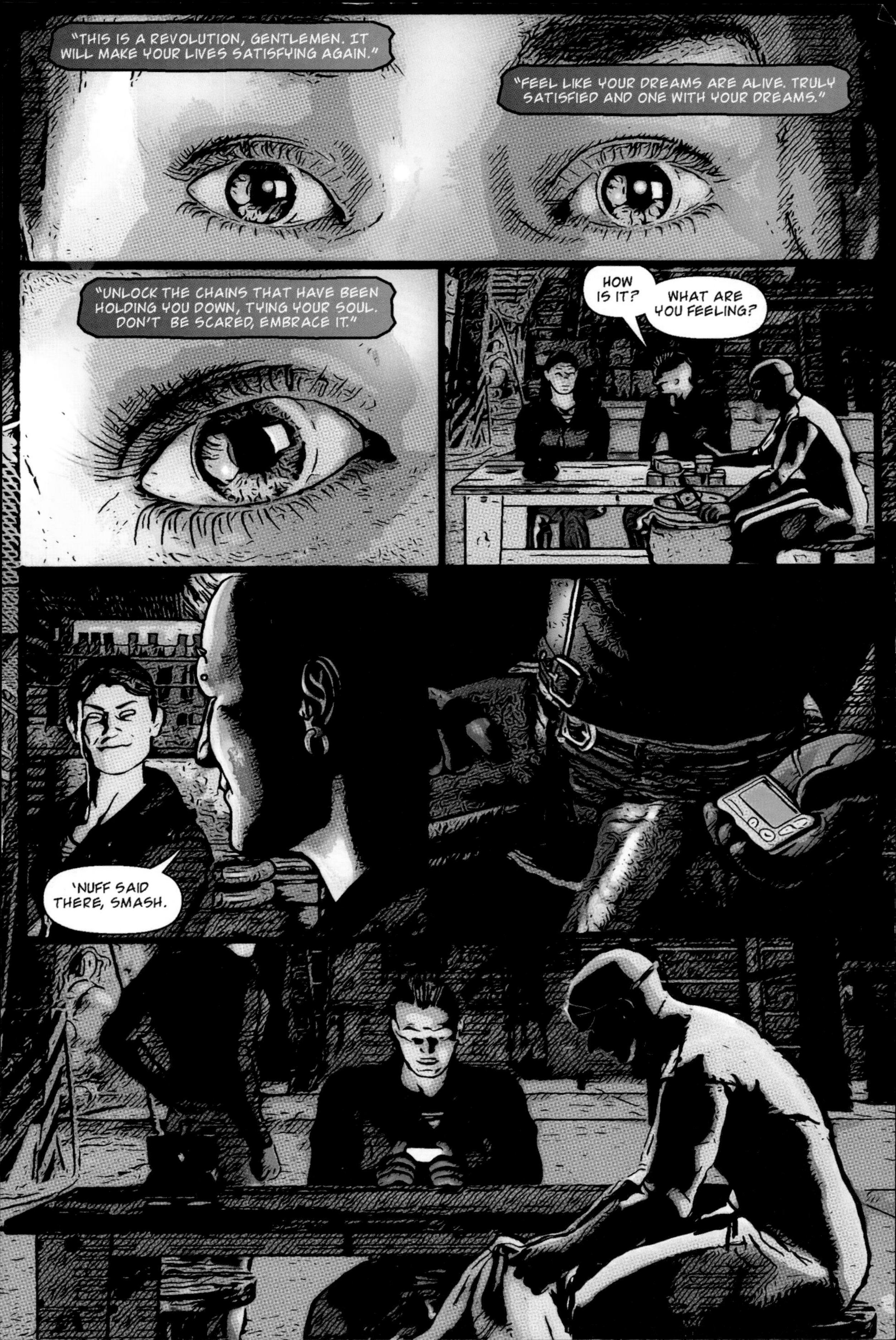
"THIS IS A REVOLUTION, GENTLEMEN. IT WILL MAKE YOUR LIVES SATISFYING AGAIN."
"FEEL LIKE YOUR DREAMS ARE ALIVE. TRULY SATISFIED AND ONE WITH YOUR DREAMS."
"UNLOCK THE CHAINS THAT HAVE BEEN HOLDING YOU DOWN, TYING YOUR SOUL. DON'T BE SCARED, EMBRACE IT."
HOW IS IT?
WHAT ARE YOU FEELING?
'NUFF SAID THERE, SMASH.

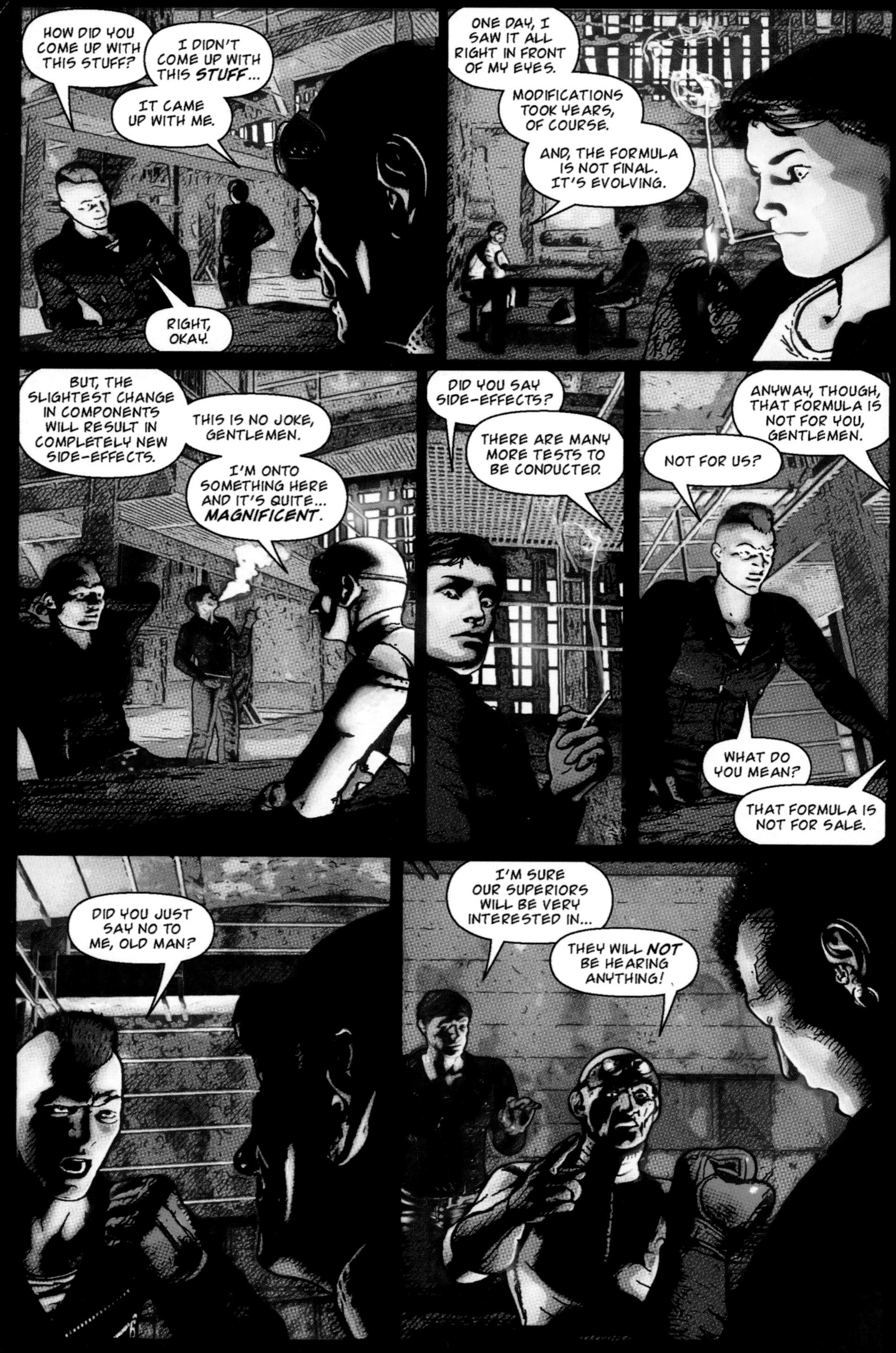
HOW DID YOU COME UP WITH THIS STUFF?
I DIDN'T COME UP WITH THIS STUFF...
IT CAME UP WITH ME.
RIGHT, OKAY.
ONE DAY, I SAW IT ALL RIGHT IN FRONT OF MY EYES.
MODIFICATIONS TOOK YEARS, OF COURSE.
AND, THE FORMULA IS NOT FINAL. IT'S EVOLVING.
BUT, THE SLIGHTEST CHANGE IN COMPONENTS WILL RESULT IN COMPLETELY NEW SIDE-EFFECTS.
THIS IS NO JOKE, GENTLEMEN.
I'M ONTO SOMETHING HERE AND IT'S QUITE... MAGNIFICENT.
DID YOU SAY SIDE-EFFECTS?
THERE ARE MANY MORE TESTS TO BE CONDUCTED.
ANYWAY, THOUGH, THAT FORMULA IS NOT FOR YOU, GENTLEMEN.
NOT FOR US?
WHAT DO YOU MEAN?
THAT FORMULA IS NOT FOR SALE.
DID YOU JUST SAY NO TO ME, OLD MAN?
I'M SURE OUR SUPERIORS WILL BE VERY INTERESTED IN...
THEY WILL NOT BE HEARING ANYTHING!

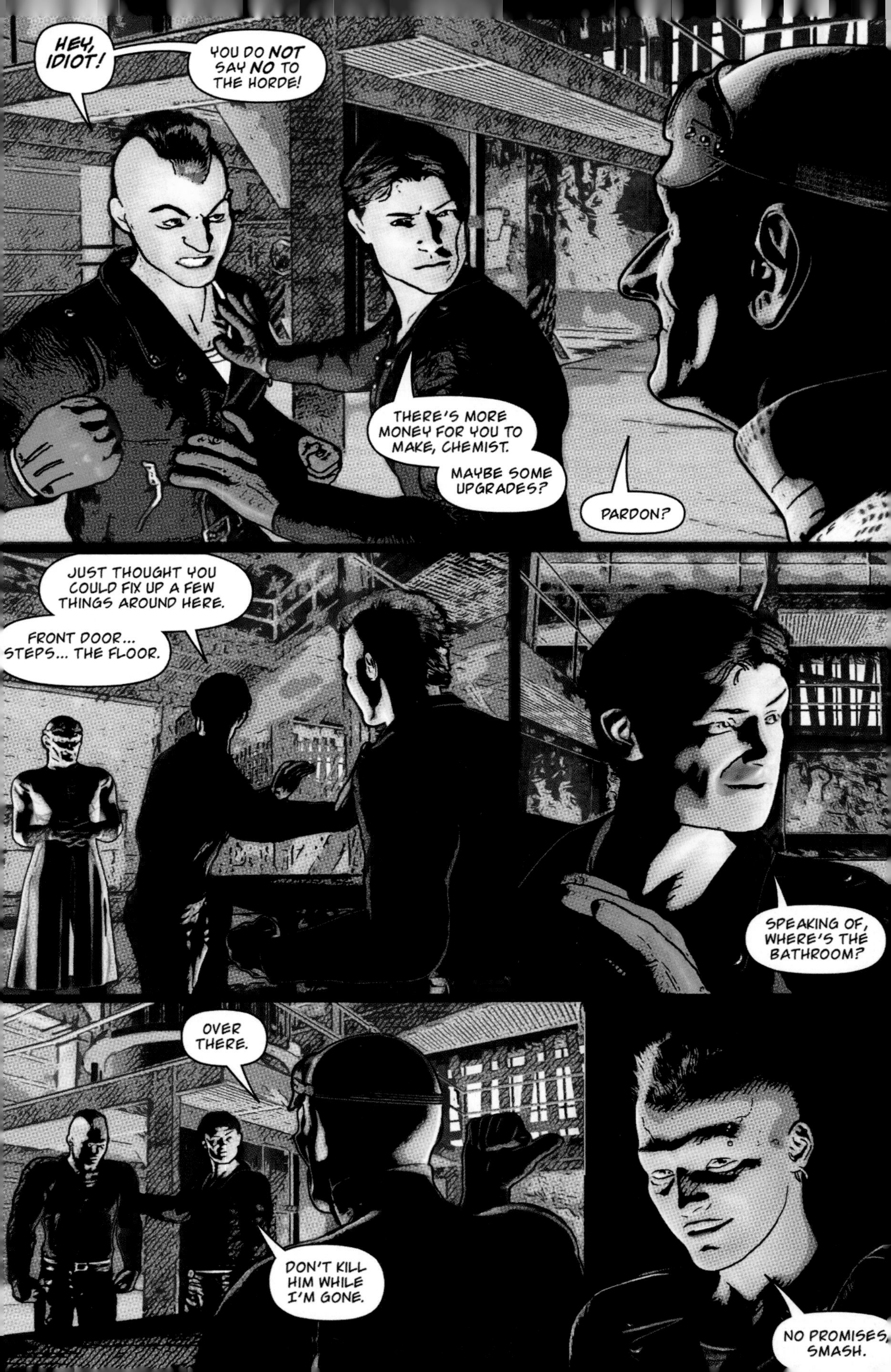
HEY, IDIOT!
YOU DO NOT SAY NO TO THE HORDE!
THERE'S MORE MONEY FOR YOU TO MAKE, CHEMIST.
MAYBE SOME UPGRADES?
PARDON?
JUST THOUGHT YOU COULD FIX UP A FEW THINGS AROUND HERE.
FRONT DOOR... STEPS... THE FLOOR.
SPEAKING OF, WHERE'S THE BATHROOM?
OVER THERE.
DON'T KILL HIM WHILE I'M GONE.
NO PROMISES, SMASH.

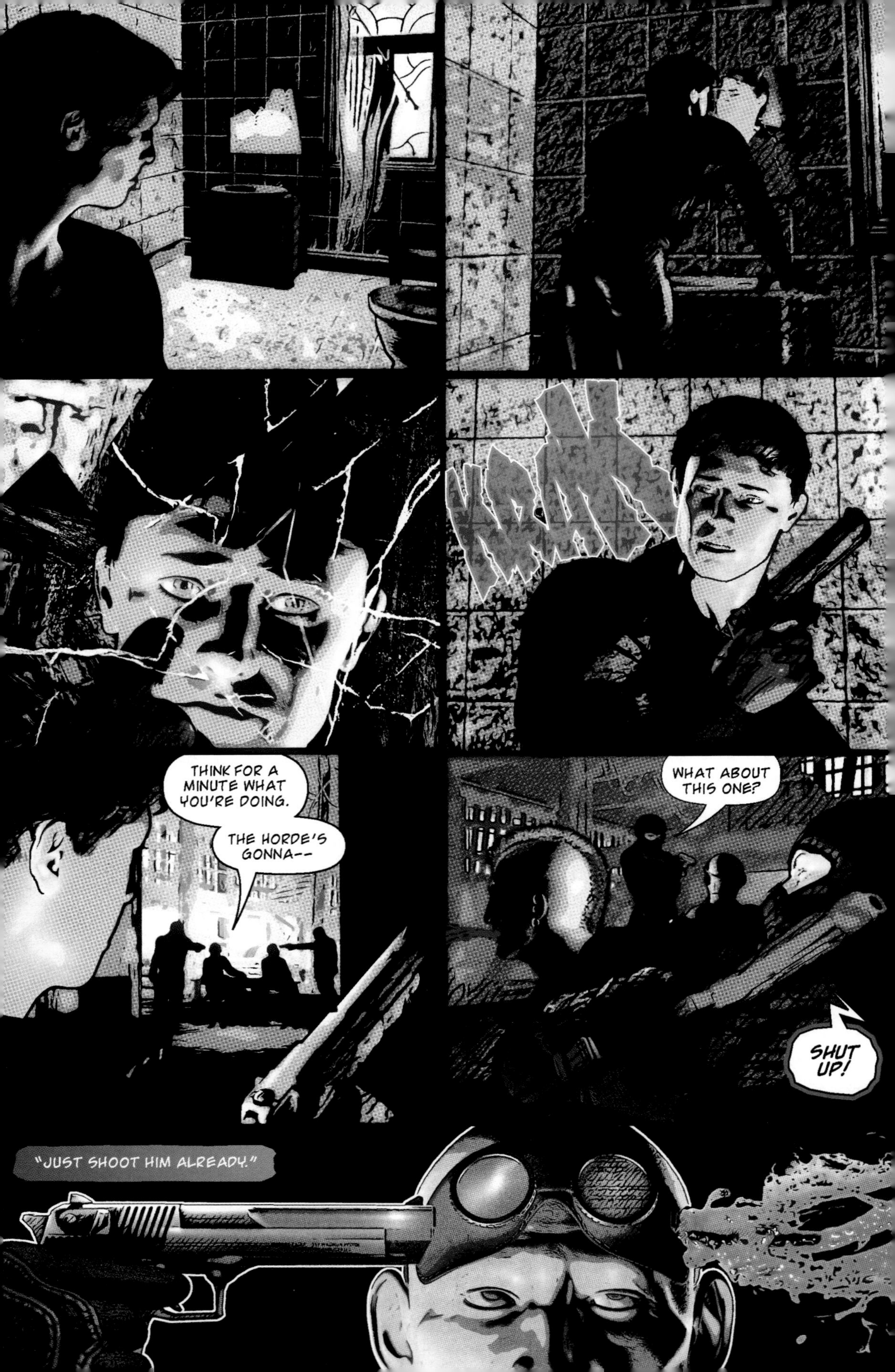
KRAM
THINK FOR A MINUTE WHAT YOU'RE DOING.
THE HORDE'S GONNA--
WHAT ABOUT THIS ONE?
SHUT UP!
"JUST SHOOT HIM ALREADY."

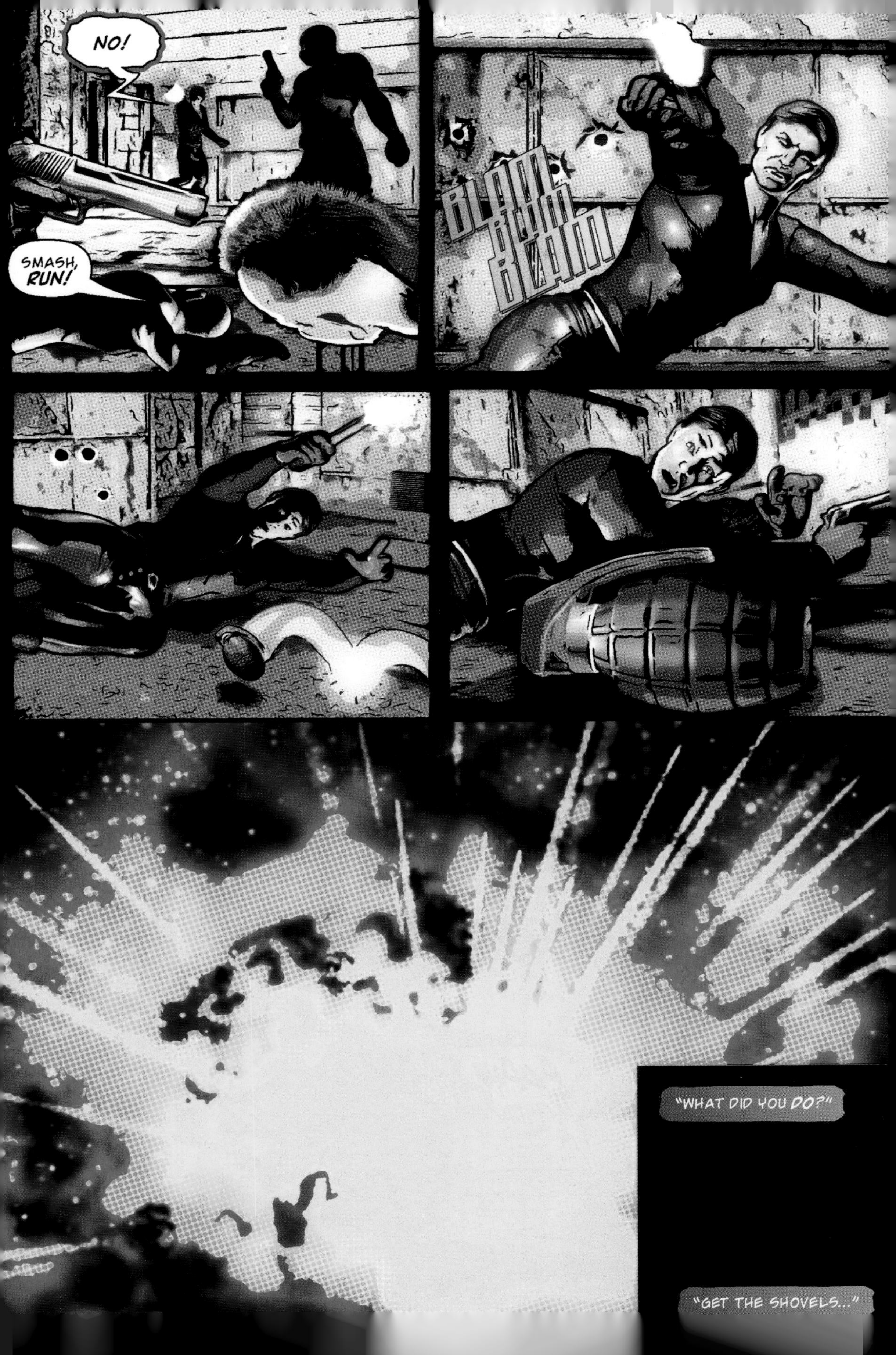
NO!
SMASH, RUN!
BLAM BLAM BLAM
"WHAT DID YOU DO?"
"GET THE SHOVELS..."

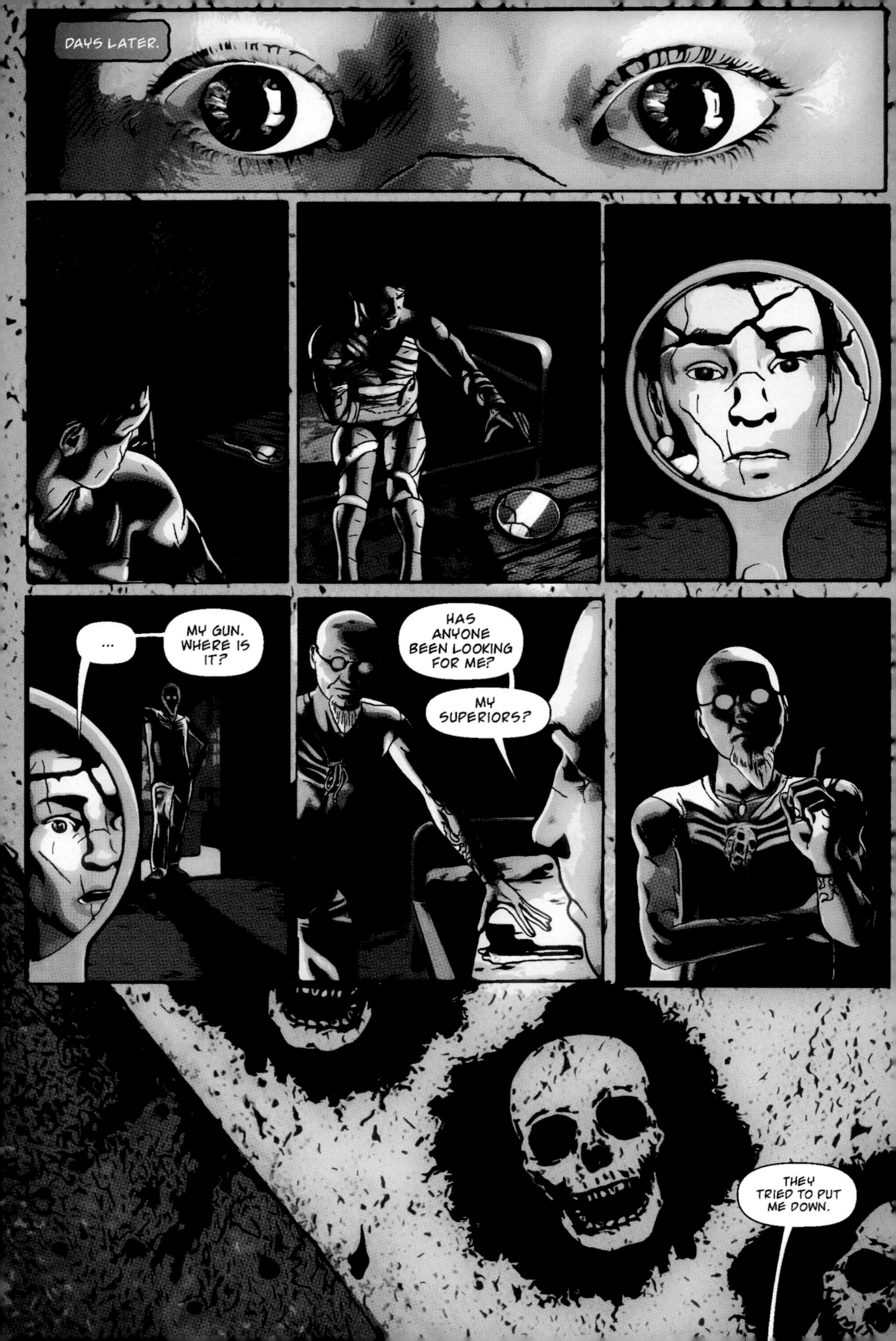
DAYS LATER.
...
MY GUN. WHERE IS IT?
HAS ANYONE BEEN LOOKING FOR ME?
MY SUPERIORS?
THEY TRIED TO PUT ME DOWN.

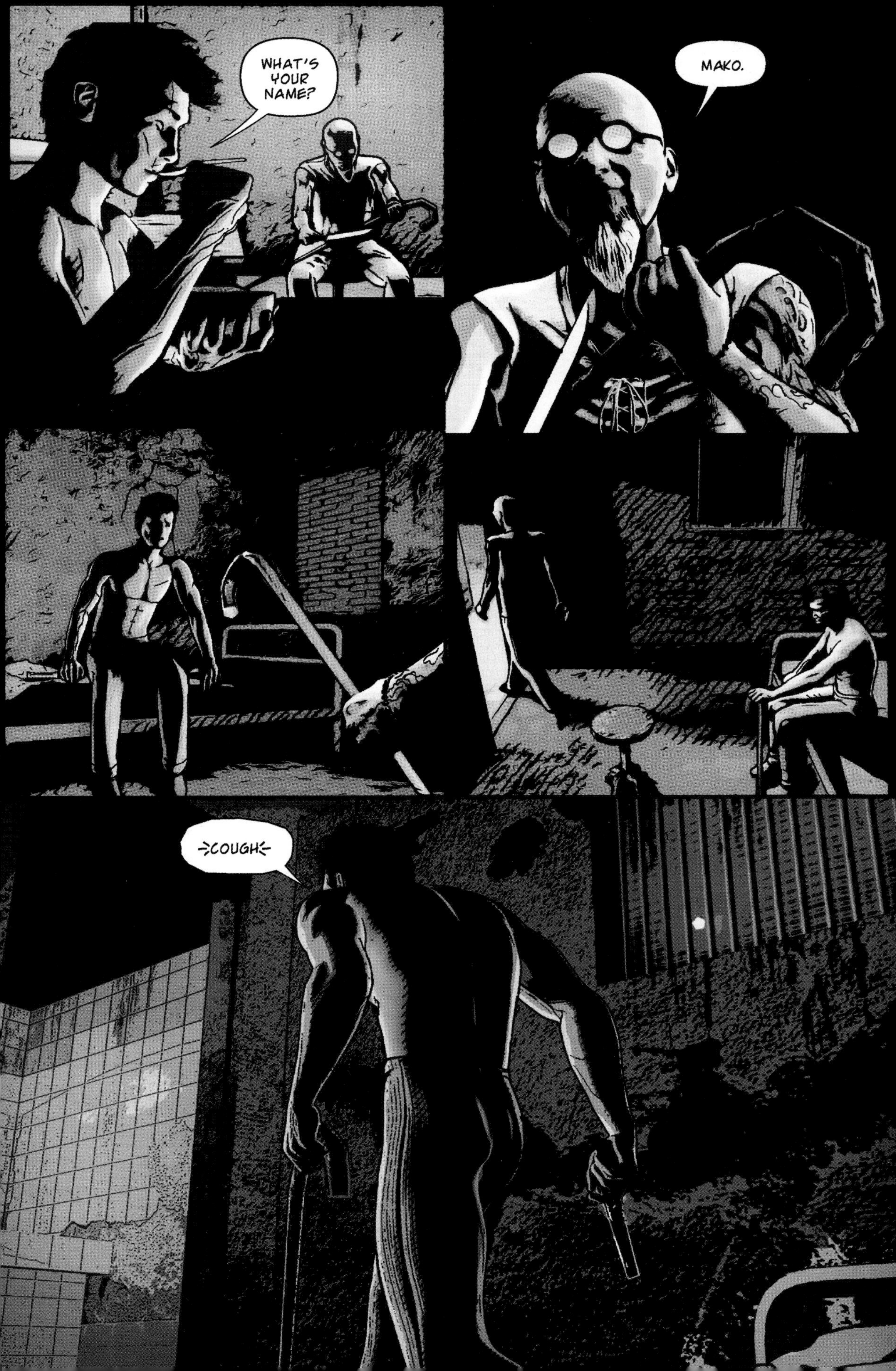
WHAT'S YOUR NAME?
MAKO.
COUGH

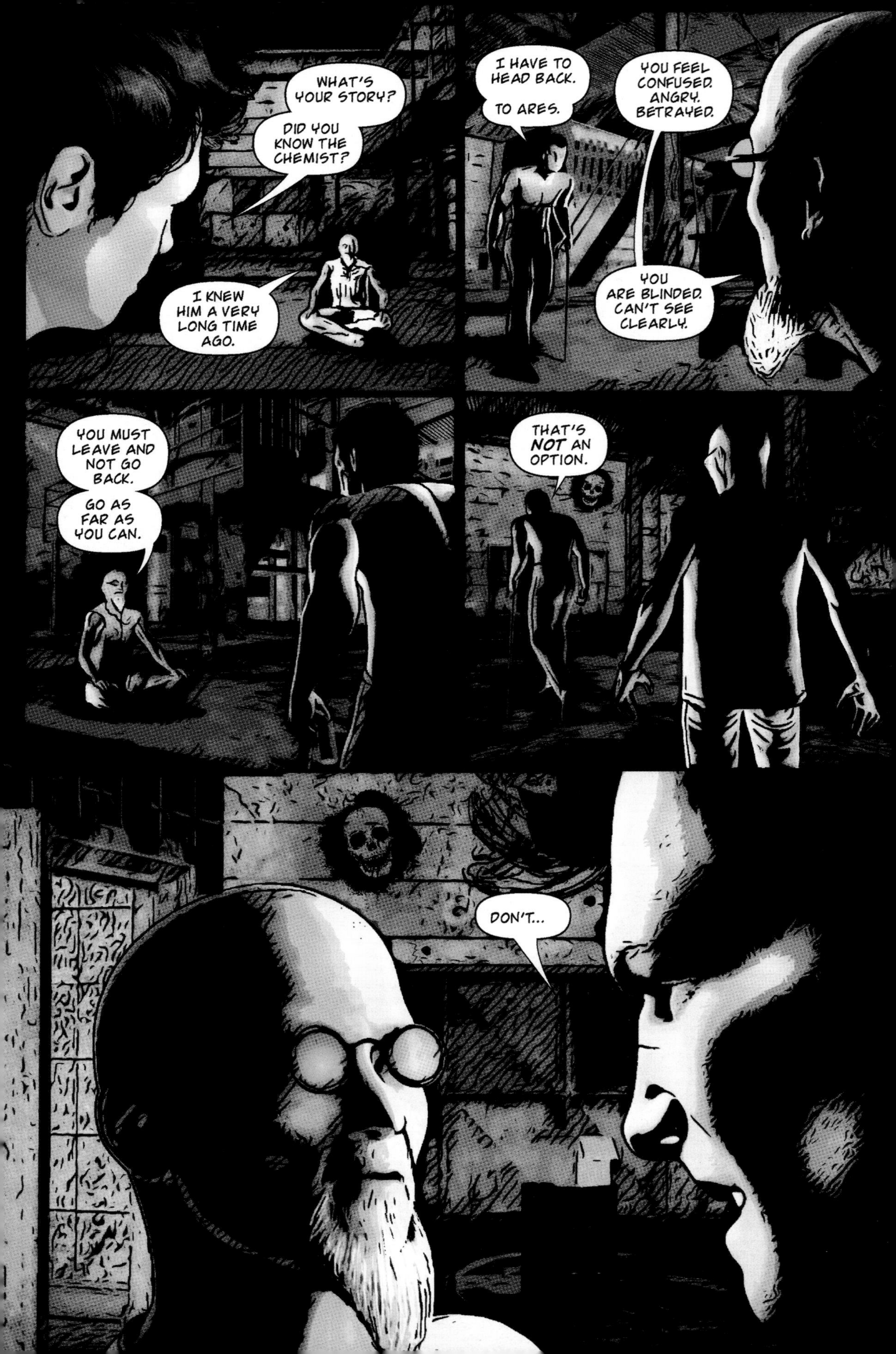
WHAT'S YOUR STORY?
DID YOU KNOW THE CHEMIST?
I KNEW HIM A VERY LONG TIME AGO.
I HAVE TO HEAD BACK.
TO ARES.
YOU FEEL CONFUSED. ANGRY. BETRAYED.
YOU ARE BLINDED. CAN'T SEE CLEARLY.
YOU MUST LEAVE AND NOT GO BACK.
GO AS FAR AS YOU CAN.
THAT'S NOT AN OPTION.
DON'T...

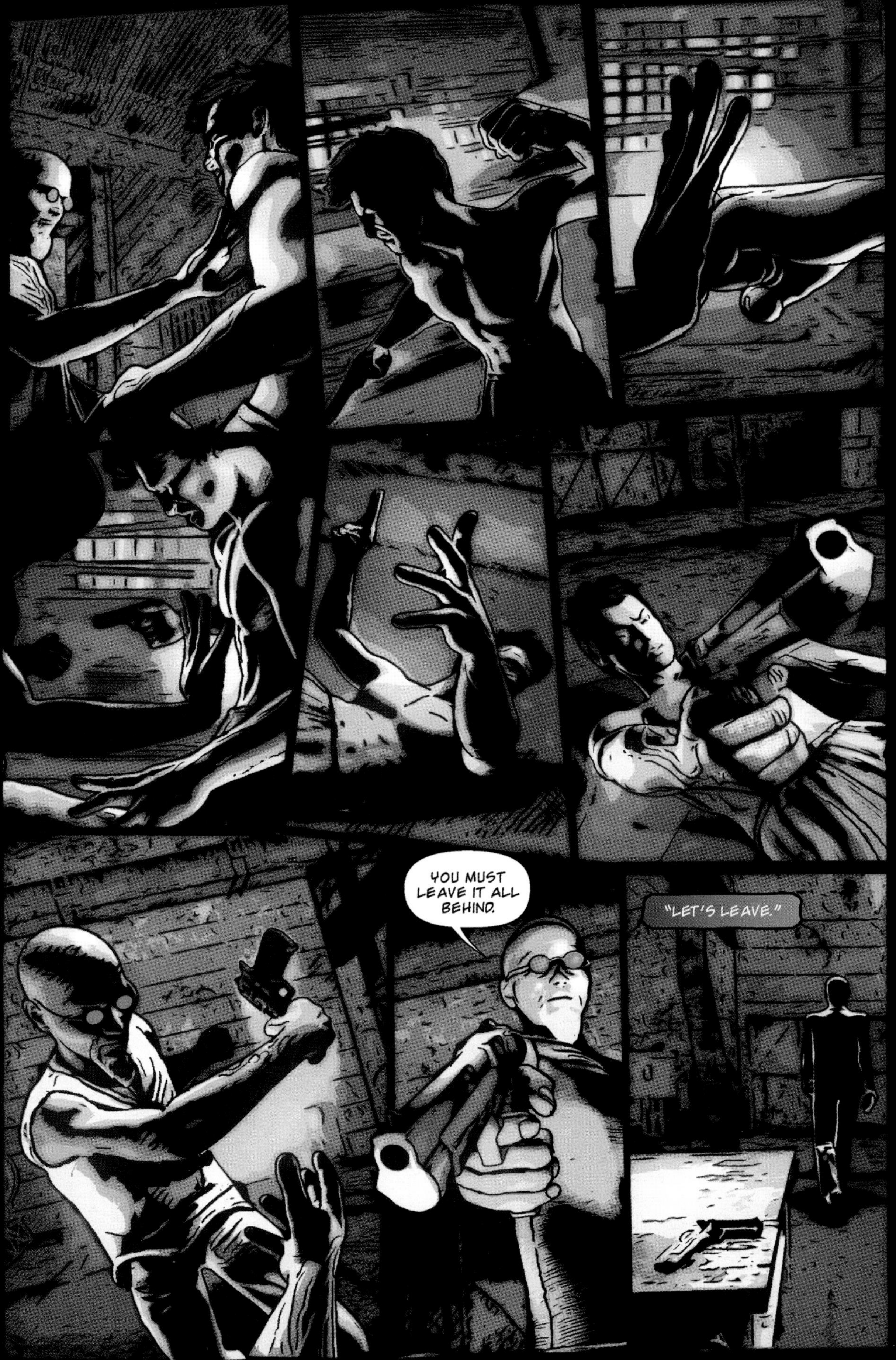
YOU MUST LEAVE IT ALL BEHIND.
"LET'S LEAVE."

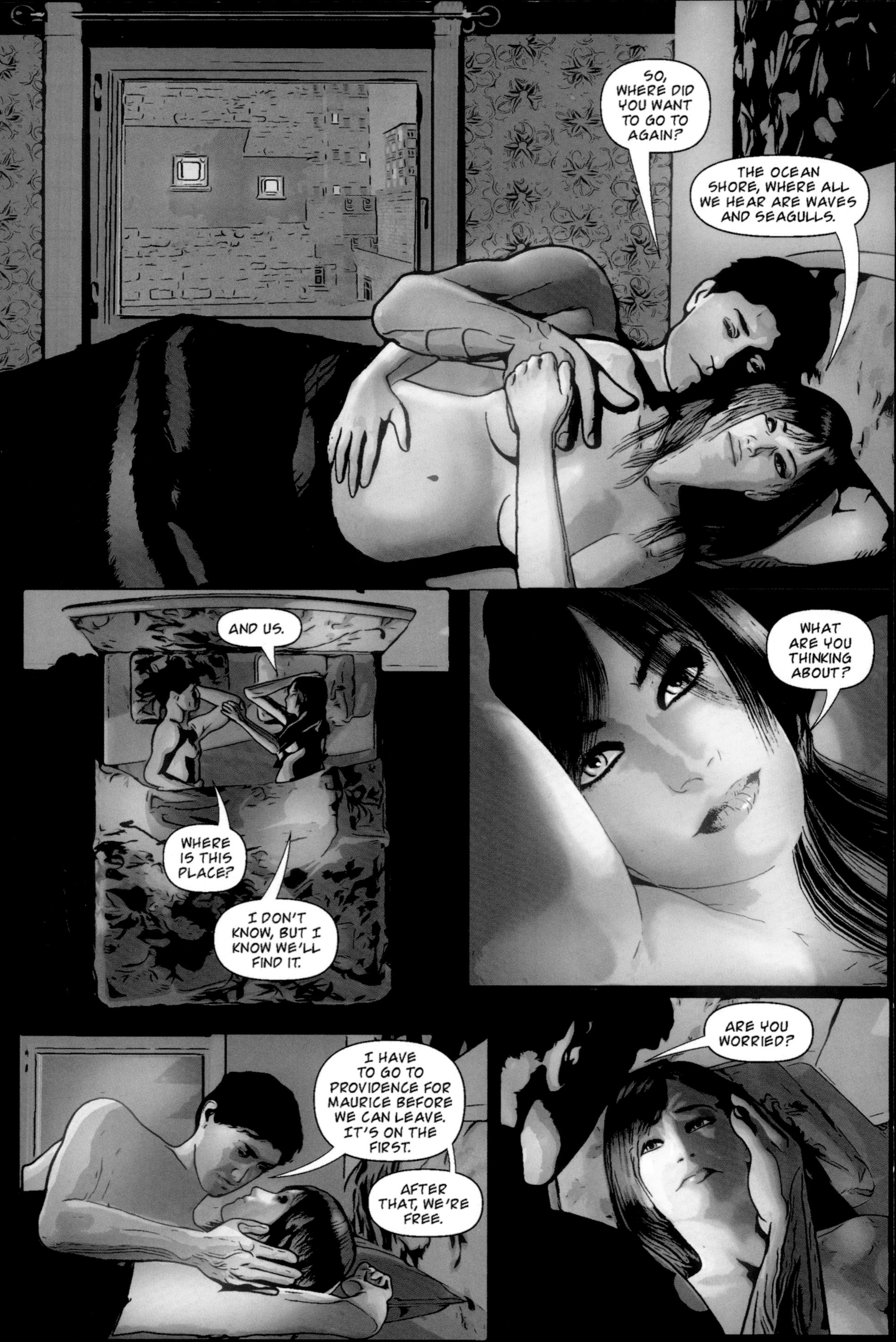
SO, WHERE DID YOU WANT TO GO TO AGAIN?
THE OCEAN SHORE, WHERE ALL WE HEAR ARE WAVES AND SEAGULLS.
AND US.
WHERE IS THIS PLACE?
I DON'T KNOW, BUT I KNOW WE'LL FIND IT.
WHAT ARE YOU THINKING ABOUT?
I HAVE TO GO TO PROVIDENCE FOR MAURICE BEFORE WE CAN LEAVE. IT'S ON THE FIRST.
AFTER THAT, WE'RE FREE.
ARE YOU WORRIED?

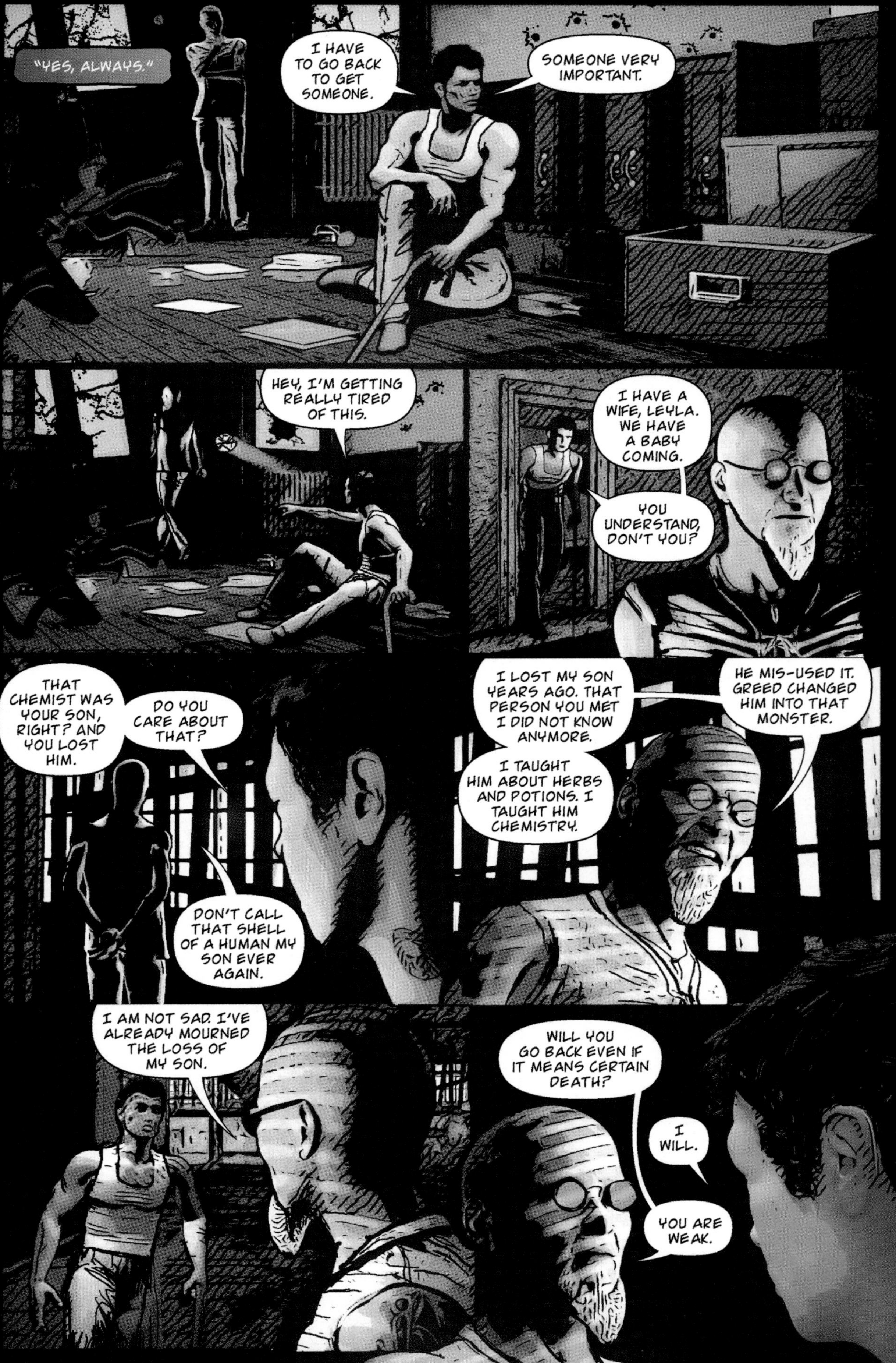
"YES, ALWAYS."
I HAVE TO GO BACK TO GET SOMEONE.
SOMEONE VERY IMPORTANT.
HEY, I'M GETTING REALLY TIRED OF THIS.
I HAVE A WIFE, LEYLA. WE HAVE A BABY COMING.
YOU UNDERSTAND, DON'T YOU?
THAT CHEMIST WAS YOUR SON, RIGHT? AND YOU LOST HIM.
DO YOU CARE ABOUT THAT?
DON'T CALL THAT SHELL OF A HUMAN MY SON EVER AGAIN.
I LOST MY SON YEARS AGO. THAT PERSON YOU MET I DID NOT KNOW ANYMORE.
I TAUGHT HIM ABOUT HERBS AND POTIONS. I TAUGHT HIM CHEMISTRY.
HE MIS-USED IT. GREED CHANGED HIM INTO THAT MONSTER.
I AM NOT SAD. I'VE ALREADY MOURNED THE LOSS OF MY SON.
WILL YOU GO BACK EVEN IF IT MEANS CERTAIN DEATH?
I WILL.
YOU ARE WEAK.

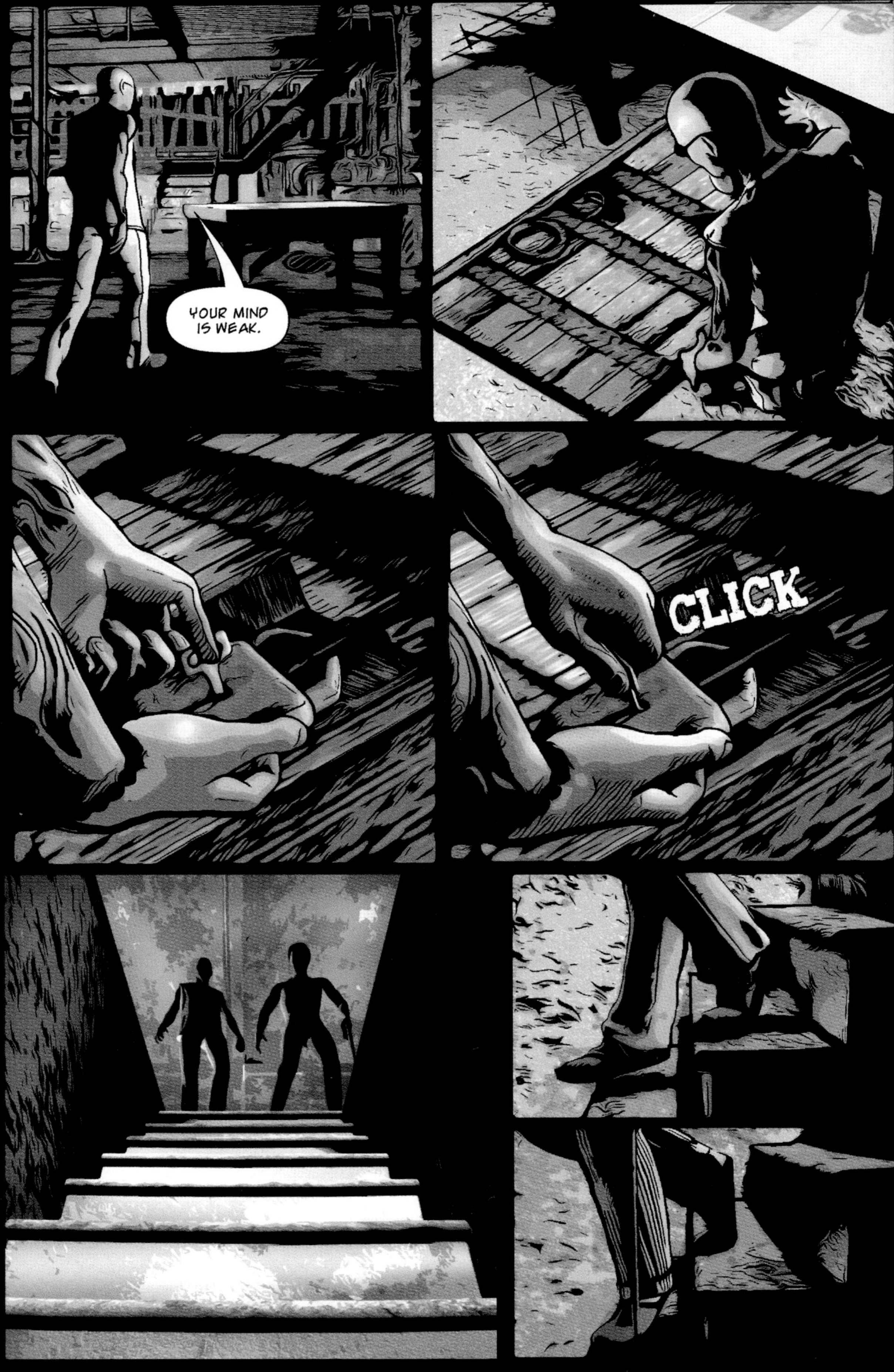
YOUR MIND IS WEAK.
CLICK

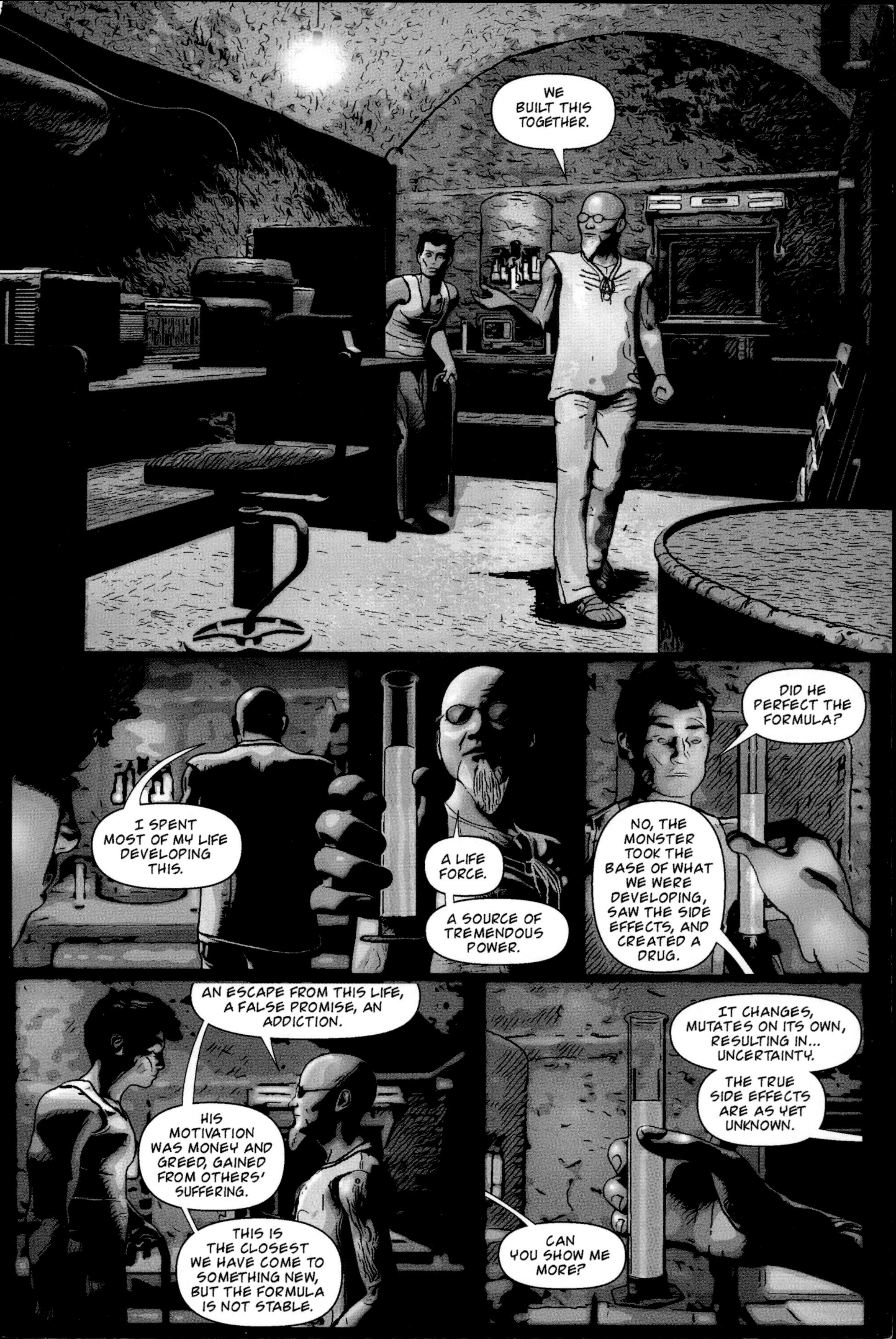

WE BUILT THIS TOGETHER.
I SPENT MOST OF MY LIFE DEVELOPING THIS.
A LIFE FORCE.
A SOURCE OF TREMENDOUS POWER.
DID HE PERFECT THE FORMULA?
NO, THE MONSTER TOOK THE BASE OF WHAT WE WERE DEVELOPING, SAW THE SIDE EFFECTS, AND CREATED A DRUG.
AN ESCAPE FROM THIS LIFE, A FALSE PROMISE, AN ADDICTION.
HIS MOTIVATION WAS MONEY AND GREED, GAINED FROM OTHERS' SUFFERING.
THIS IS THE CLOSEST WE HAVE COME TO SOMETHING NEW, BUT THE FORMULA IS NOT STABLE.
IT CHANGES, MUTATES ON ITS OWN, RESULTING IN... UNCERTAINTY.
THE TRUE SIDE EFFECTS ARE AS YET UNKNOWN.
CAN YOU SHOW ME MORE?

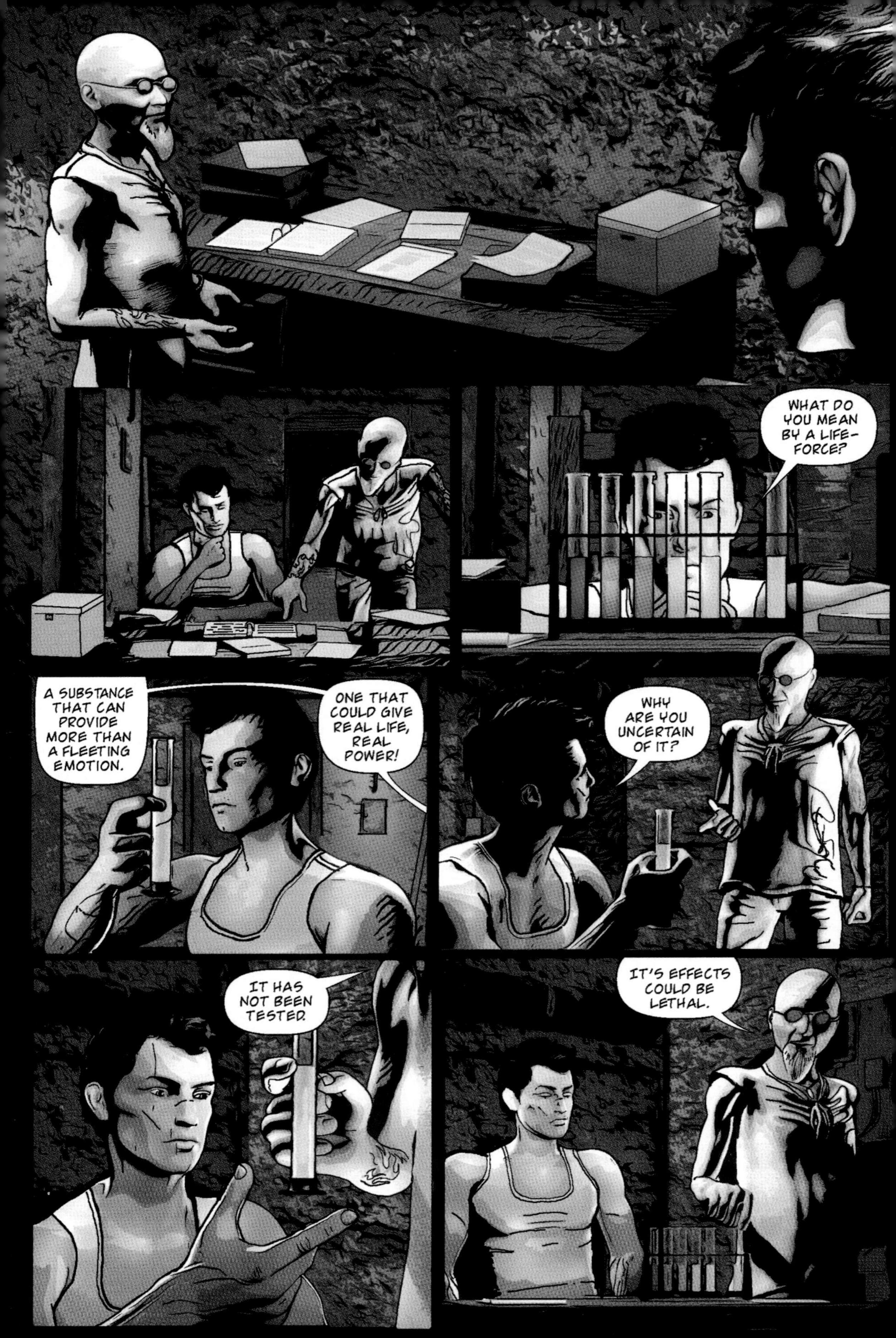
WHAT DO YOU MEAN BY A LIFE-FORCE?
A SUBSTANCE THAT CAN PROVIDE MORE THAN A FLEETING EMOTION.
ONE THAT COULD GIVE REAL LIFE, REAL POWER!
WHY ARE YOU UNCERTAIN OF IT?
IT HAS NOT BEEN TESTED.
IT'S EFFECTS COULD BE LETHAL.

THAT NIGHT...
"..THE FORMULA IS NOT FINAL."
"THE SLIGHTEST MARGIN OFF WILL RESULT IN A NEW SIDE-EFFECT."
"IT IS A LIFE FORCE."
"IT COULD BE LETHAL."
RRRRAAAAHHHH!!

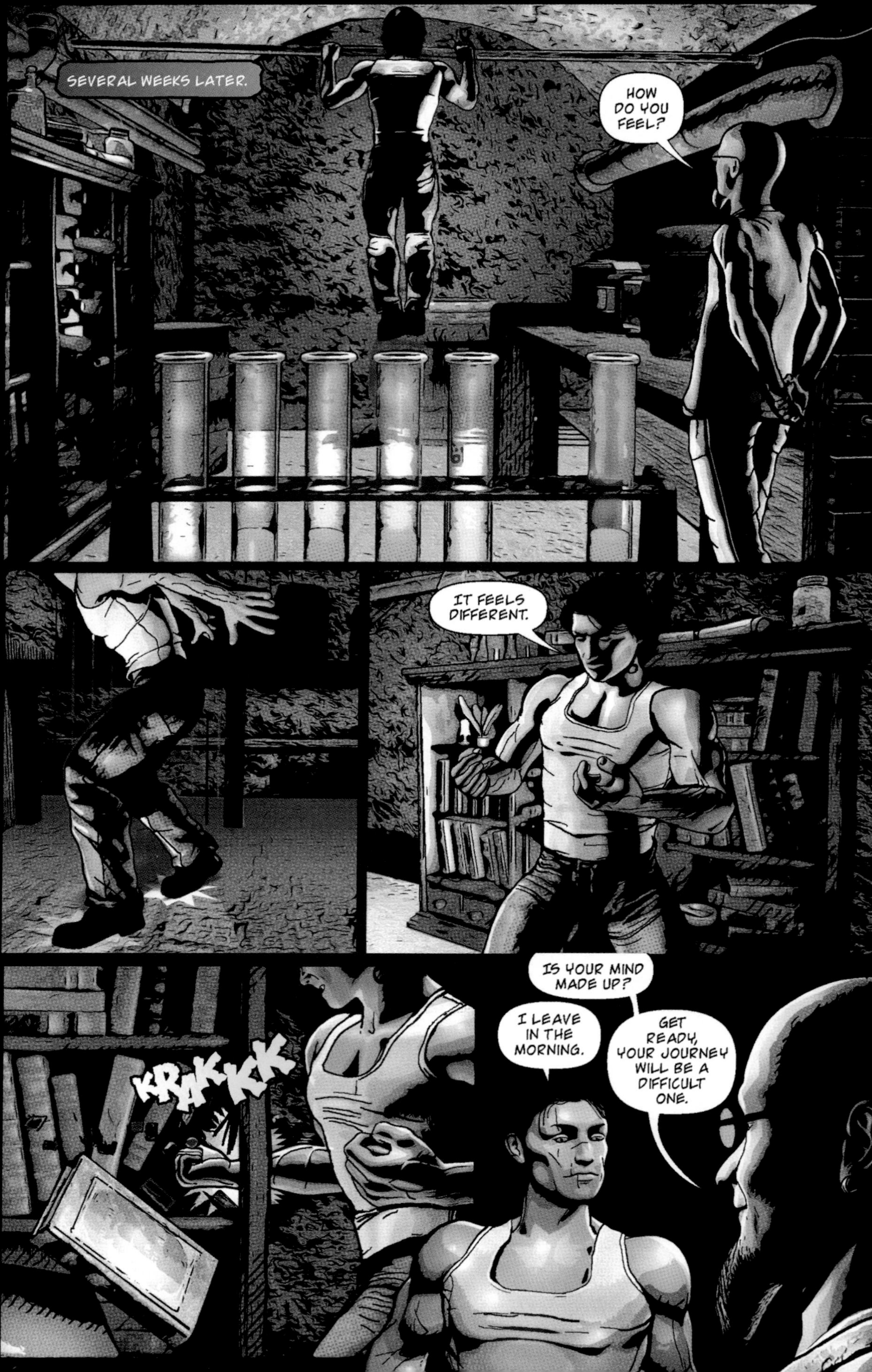
SEVERAL WEEKS LATER.
HOW DO YOU FEEL?
IT FEELS DIFFERENT.
KRAKKK
IS YOUR MIND MADE UP?
I LEAVE IN THE MORNING.
GET READY, YOUR JOURNEY WILL BE A DIFFICULT ONE.

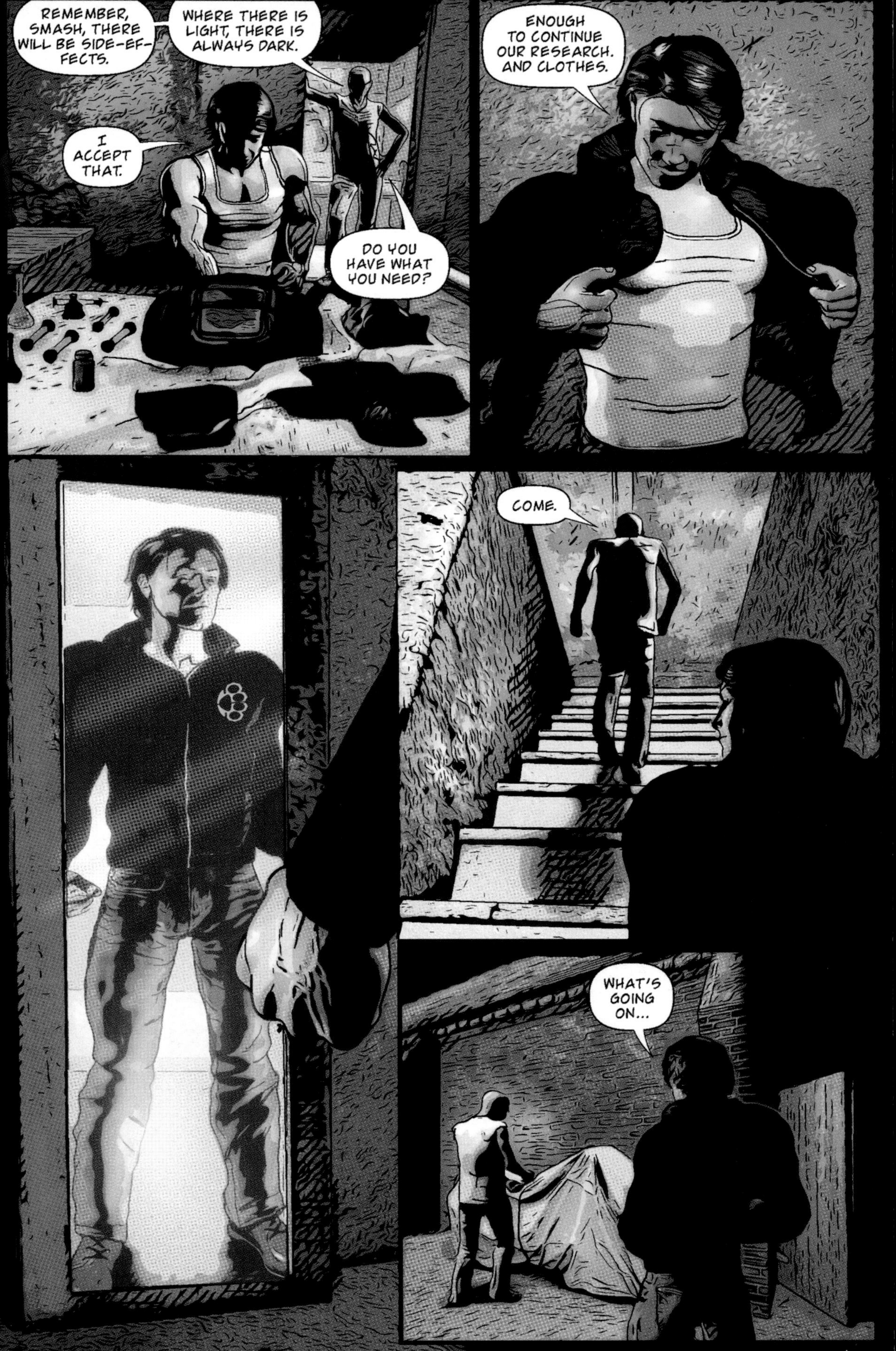
REMEMBER, SMASH, THERE WILL BE SIDE-EFFECTS.
WHERE THERE IS LIGHT, THERE IS ALWAYS DARK.
I ACCEPT THAT.
DO YOU HAVE WHAT YOU NEED?
ENOUGH TO CONTINUE OUR RESEARCH. AND CLOTHES.
COME.
WHAT'S GOING ON...

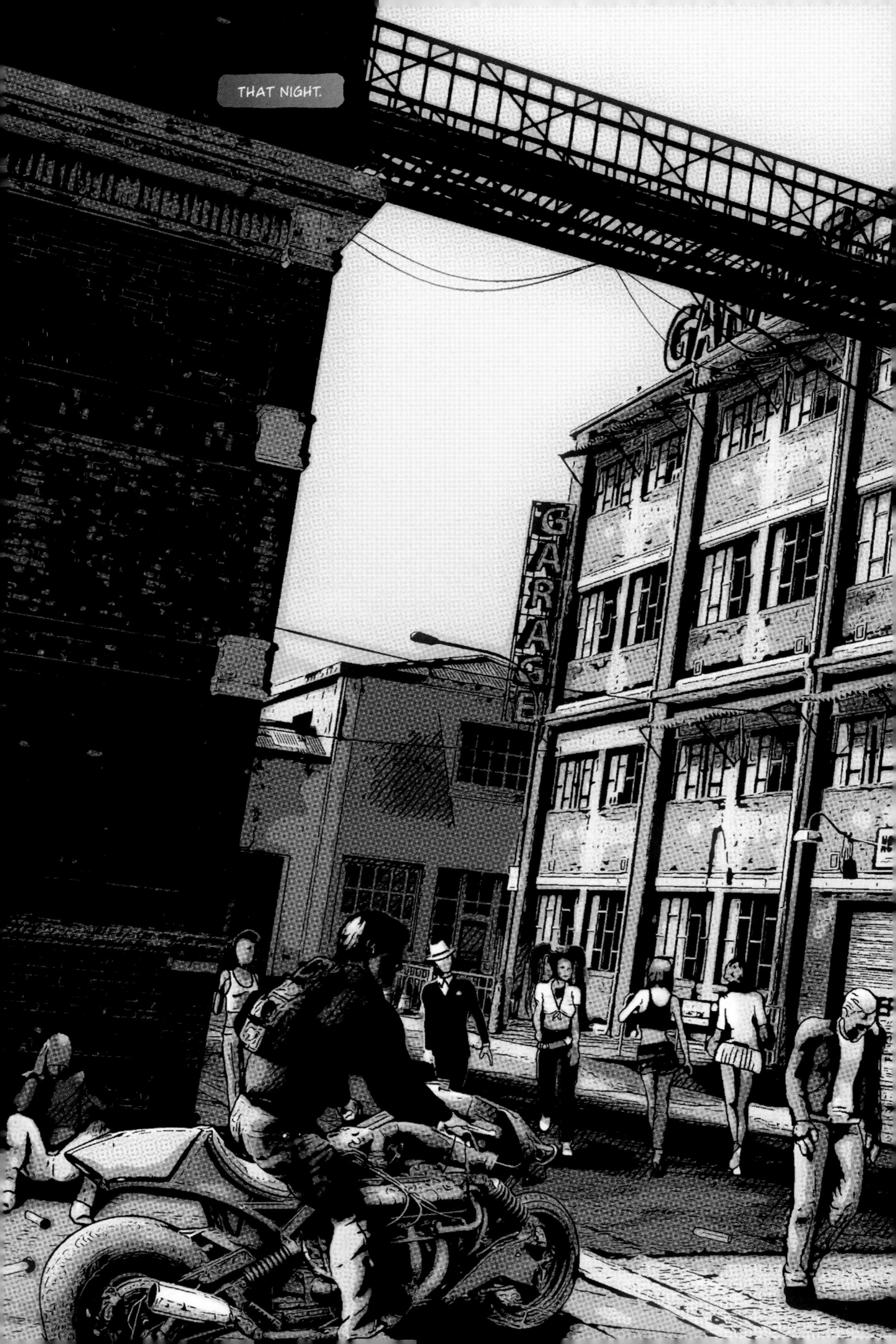
THAT NIGHT.

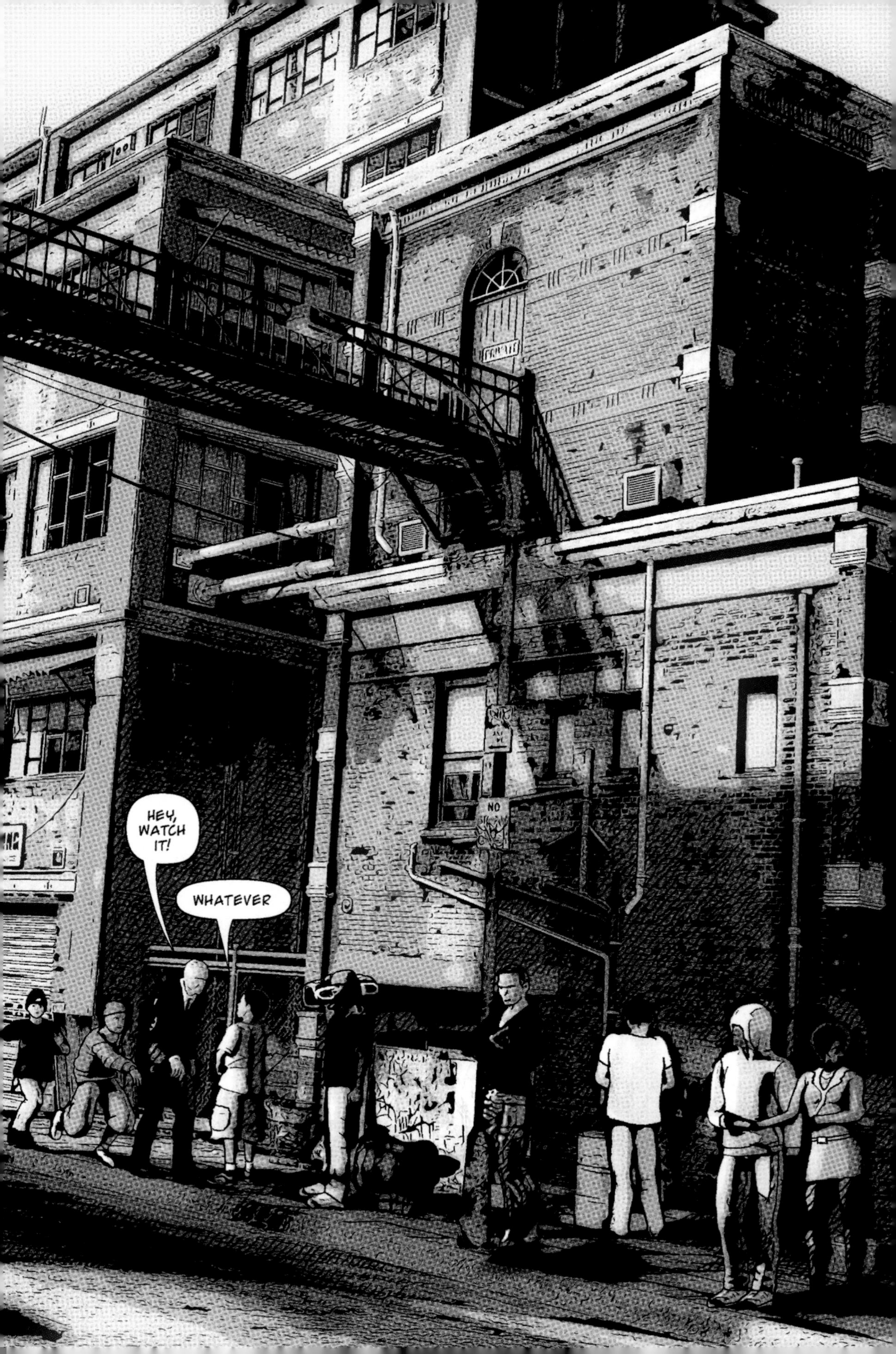
HEY, WATCH IT!
WHATEVER
NO

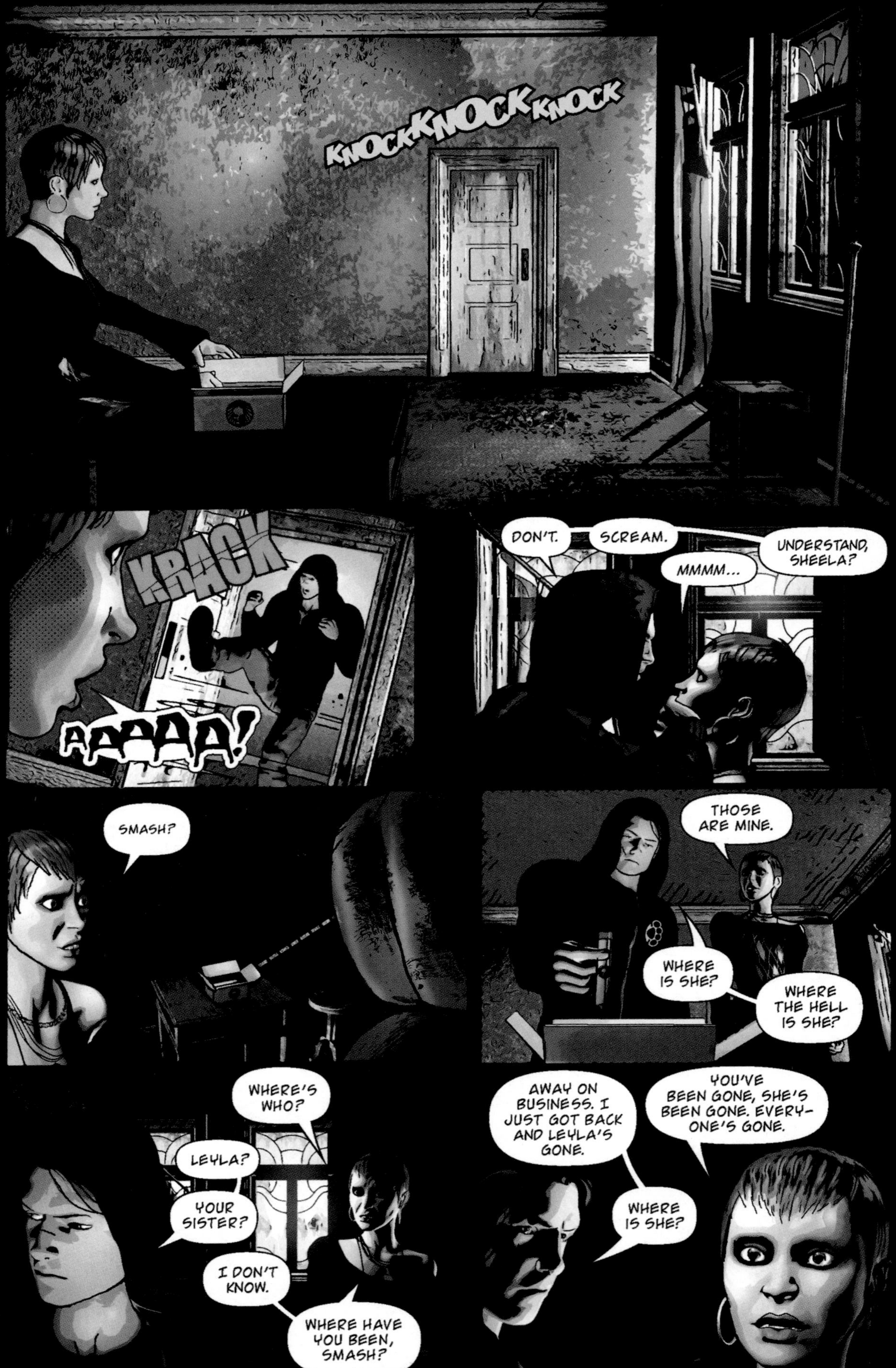
KNOCK KNOCK KNOCK
KRACK
AAAAA!
DON'T.
SCREAM.
UNDERSTAND, SHEELA?
MMMM...
SMASH?
THOSE ARE MINE.
WHERE IS SHE?
WHERE THE HELL IS SHE?
WHERE'S WHO?
LEYLA?
YOUR SISTER?
I DON'T KNOW.
WHERE HAVE YOU BEEN, SMASH?
AWAY ON BUSINESS. I JUST GOT BACK AND LEYLA'S GONE.
WHERE IS SHE?
YOU'VE BEEN GONE, SHE'S BEEN GONE. EVERY-ONE'S GONE.

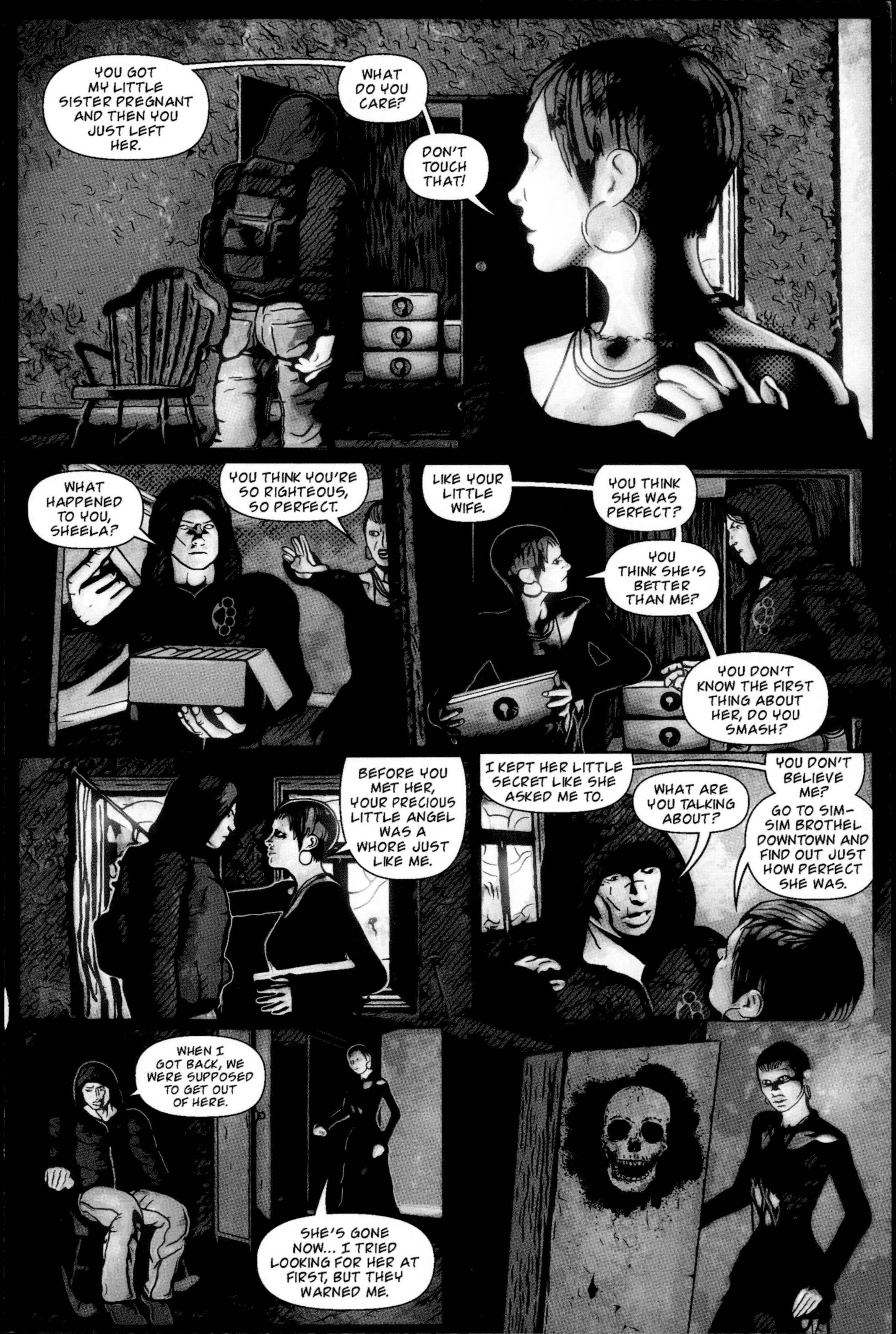

YOU GOT MY LITTLE SISTER PREGNANT AND THEN YOU JUST LEFT HER.
WHAT DO YOU CARE?
DON'T TOUCH THAT!
WHAT HAPPENED TO YOU, SHEELA?
YOU THINK YOU'RE SO RIGHTEOUS, SO PERFECT.
LIKE YOUR LITTLE WIFE.
YOU THINK SHE WAS PERFECT?
YOU THINK SHE'S BETTER THAN ME?
YOU DON'T KNOW THE FIRST THING ABOUT HER, DO YOU SMASH?
BEFORE YOU MET HER, YOUR PRECIOUS LITTLE ANGEL WAS A WHORE JUST LIKE ME.
I KEPT HER LITTLE SECRET LIKE SHE ASKED ME TO.
WHAT ARE YOU TALKING ABOUT?
YOU DON'T BELIEVE ME?
GO TO SIM-SIM BROTHEL DOWNTOWN AND FIND OUT JUST HOW PERFECT SHE WAS.
WHEN I GOT BACK, WE WERE SUPPOSED TO GET OUT OF HERE.
SHE'S GONE NOW... I TRIED LOOKING FOR HER AT FIRST, BUT THEY WARNED ME.

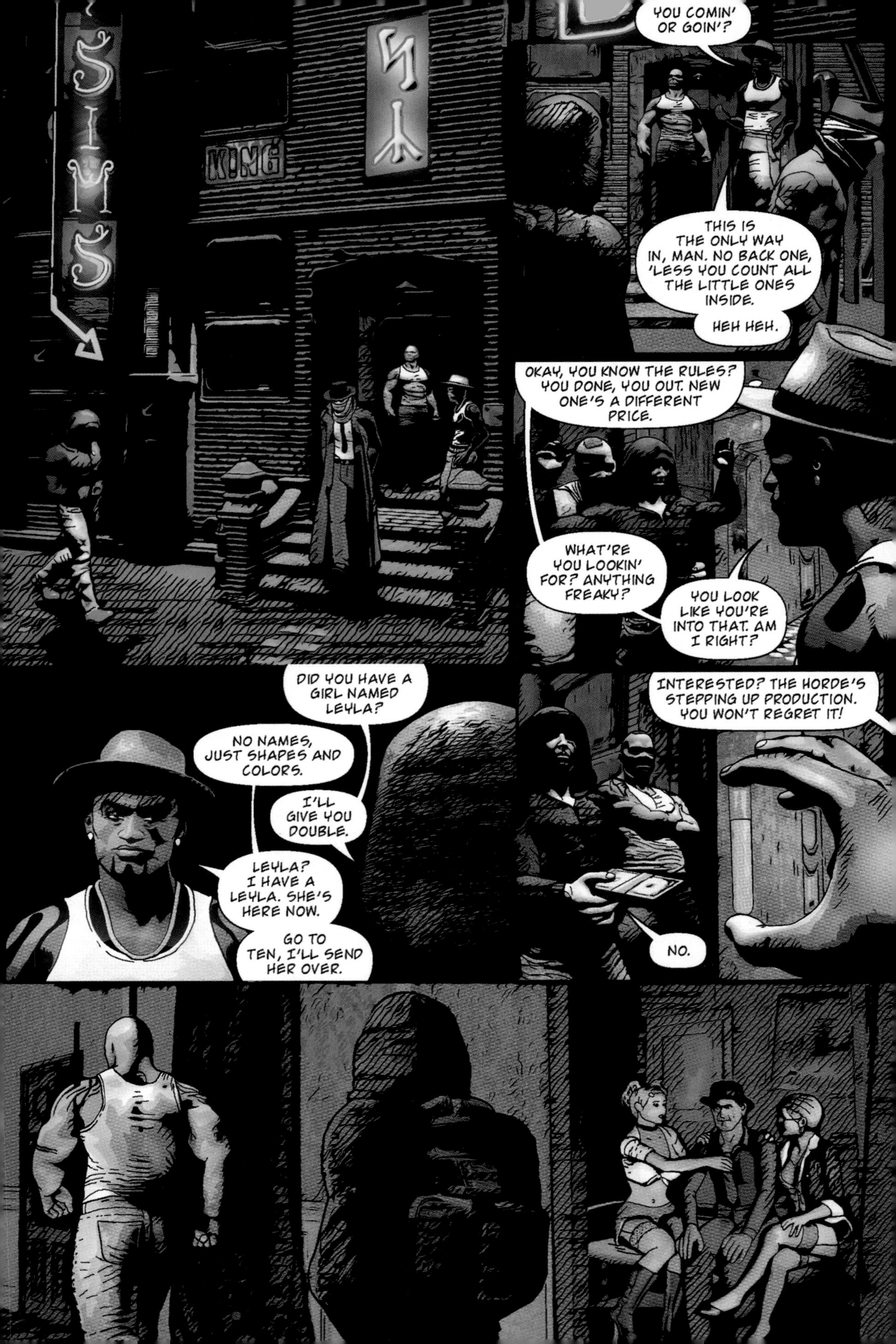
SINS
KING
YOU COMIN' OR GOIN'?
THIS IS THE ONLY WAY IN, MAN. NO BACK ONE, 'LESS YOU COUNT ALL THE LITTLE ONES INSIDE.
HEH HEH.
OKAY, YOU KNOW THE RULES? YOU DONE, YOU OUT. NEW ONE'S A DIFFERENT PRICE.
WHAT'RE YOU LOOKIN' FOR? ANYTHING FREAKY?
YOU LOOK LIKE YOU'RE INTO THAT. AM I RIGHT?
DID YOU HAVE A GIRL NAMED LEYLA?
NO NAMES, JUST SHAPES AND COLORS.
I'LL GIVE YOU DOUBLE.
LEYLA? I HAVE A LEYLA. SHE'S HERE NOW.
GO TO TEN, I'LL SEND HER OVER.
INTERESTED? THE HORDE'S STEPPING UP PRODUCTION. YOU WON'T REGRET IT!
NO.

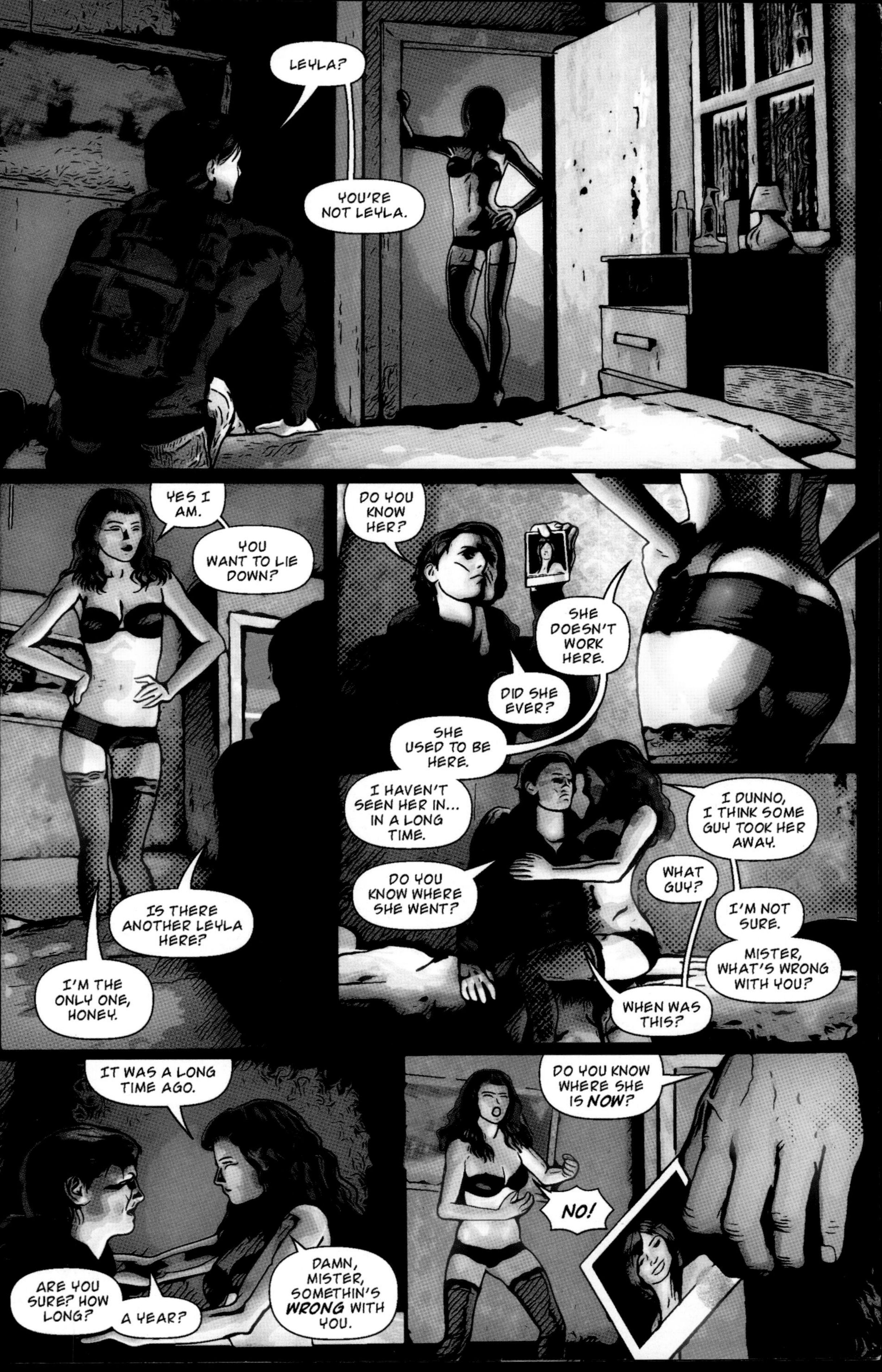
LEYLA?
YOU'RE NOT LEYLA.
YES I AM.
YOU WANT TO LIE DOWN?
IS THERE ANOTHER LEYLA HERE?
I'M THE ONLY ONE, HONEY.
DO YOU KNOW HER?
SHE DOESN'T WORK HERE.
DID SHE EVER?
SHE USED TO BE HERE.
I HAVEN'T SEEN HER IN... IN A LONG TIME.
DO YOU KNOW WHERE SHE WENT?
I DUNNO, I THINK SOME GUY TOOK HER AWAY.
WHAT GUY?
I'M NOT SURE.
MISTER, WHAT'S WRONG WITH YOU?
WHEN WAS THIS?
IT WAS A LONG TIME AGO.
ARE YOU SURE? HOW LONG?
A YEAR?
DAMN, MISTER, SOMETHIN'S WRONG WITH YOU.
DO YOU KNOW WHERE SHE IS NOW?
NO!

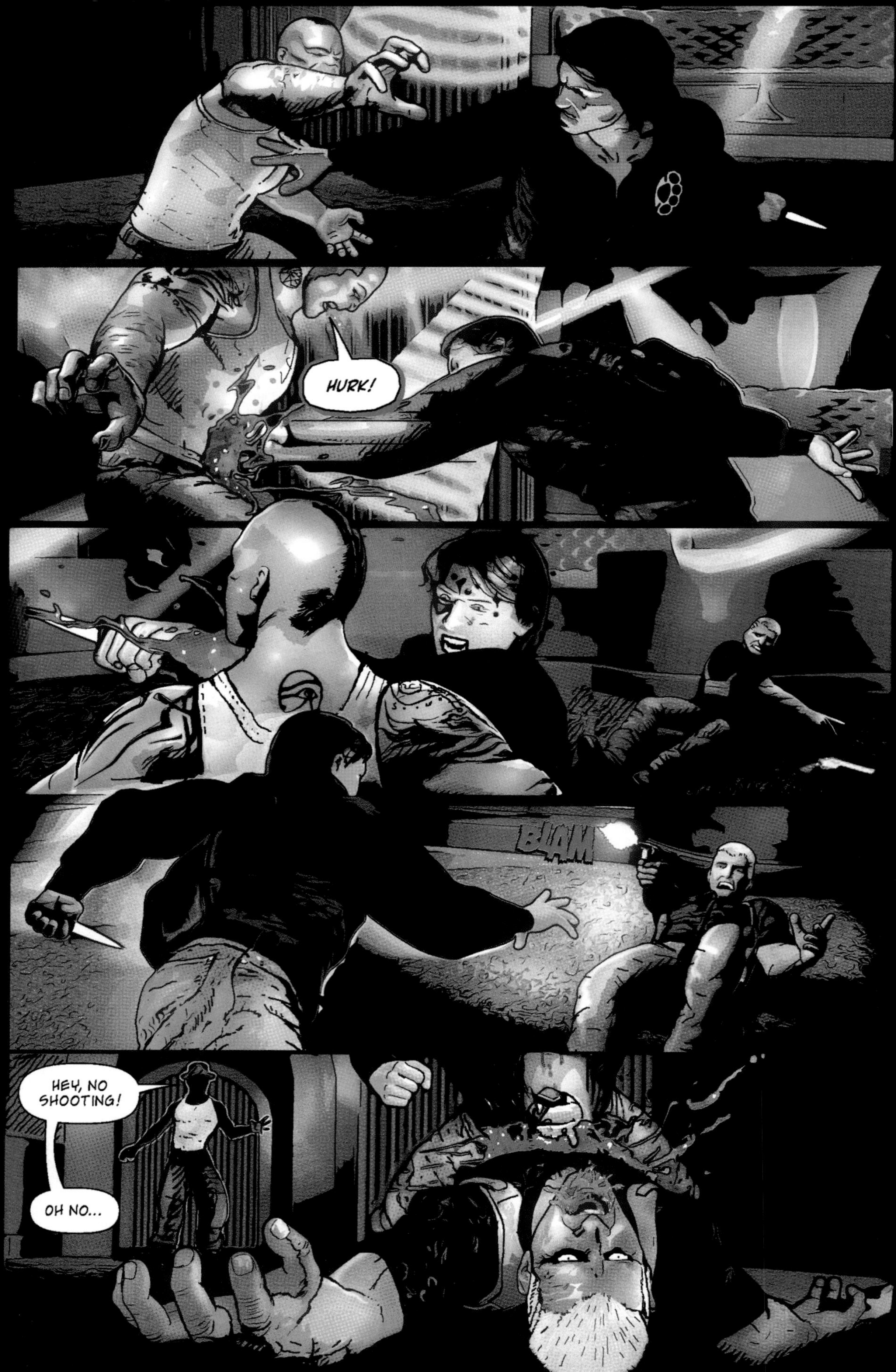
HURK!
BLAM
HEY, NO SHOOTING!
OH NO...

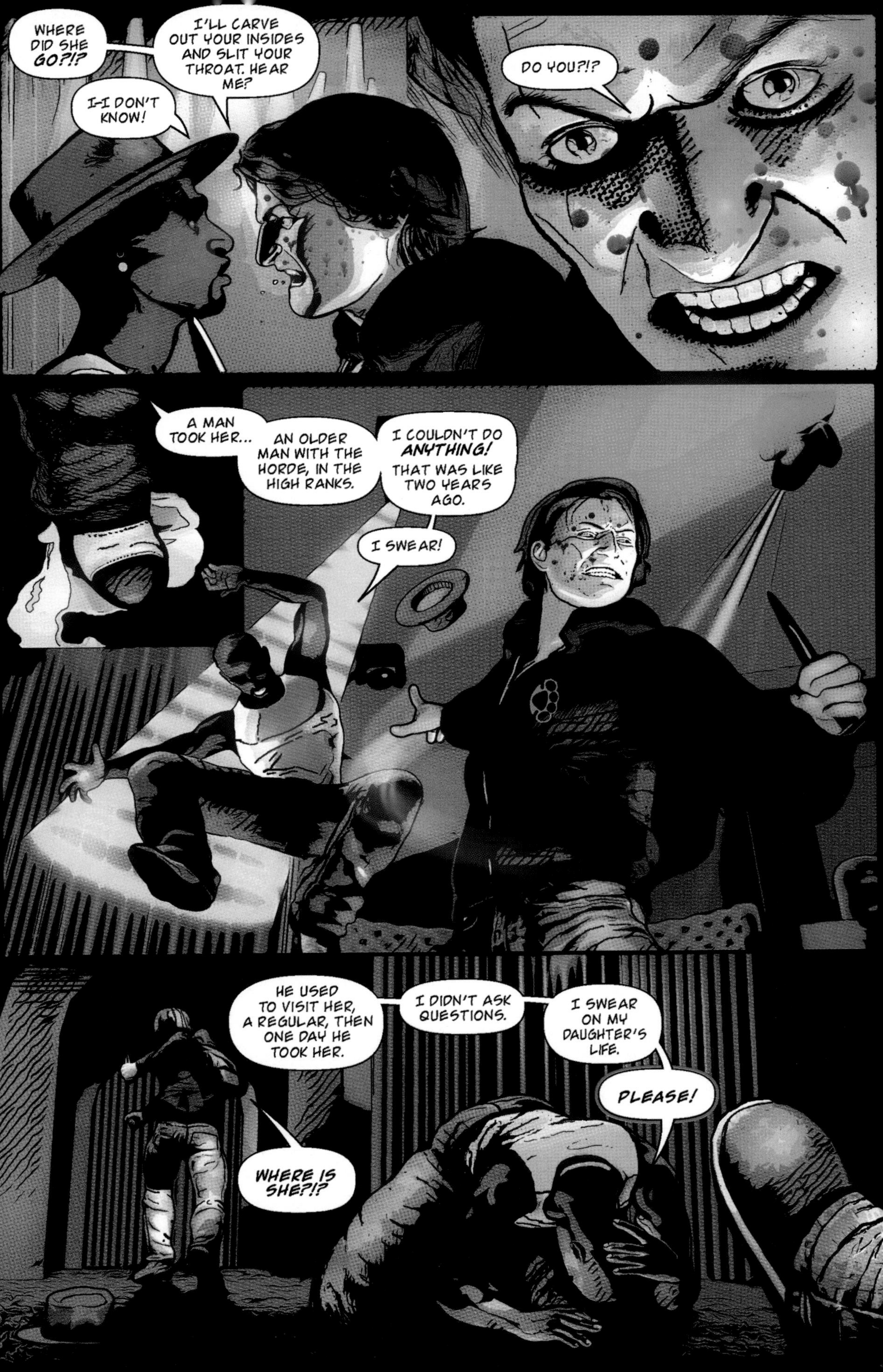
WHERE DID SHE GO?!?
I'LL CARVE OUT YOUR INSIDES AND SLIT YOUR THROAT. HEAR ME?
I-I DON'T KNOW!
DO YOU?!?
A MAN TOOK HER...
AN OLDER MAN WITH THE HORDE, IN THE HIGH RANKS.
I COULDN'T DO ANYTHING!
THAT WAS LIKE TWO YEARS AGO.
I SWEAR!
HE USED TO VISIT HER, A REGULAR, THEN ONE DAY HE TOOK HER.
I DIDN'T ASK QUESTIONS.
I SWEAR ON MY DAUGHTER'S LIFE.
PLEASE!
WHERE IS SHE?!?

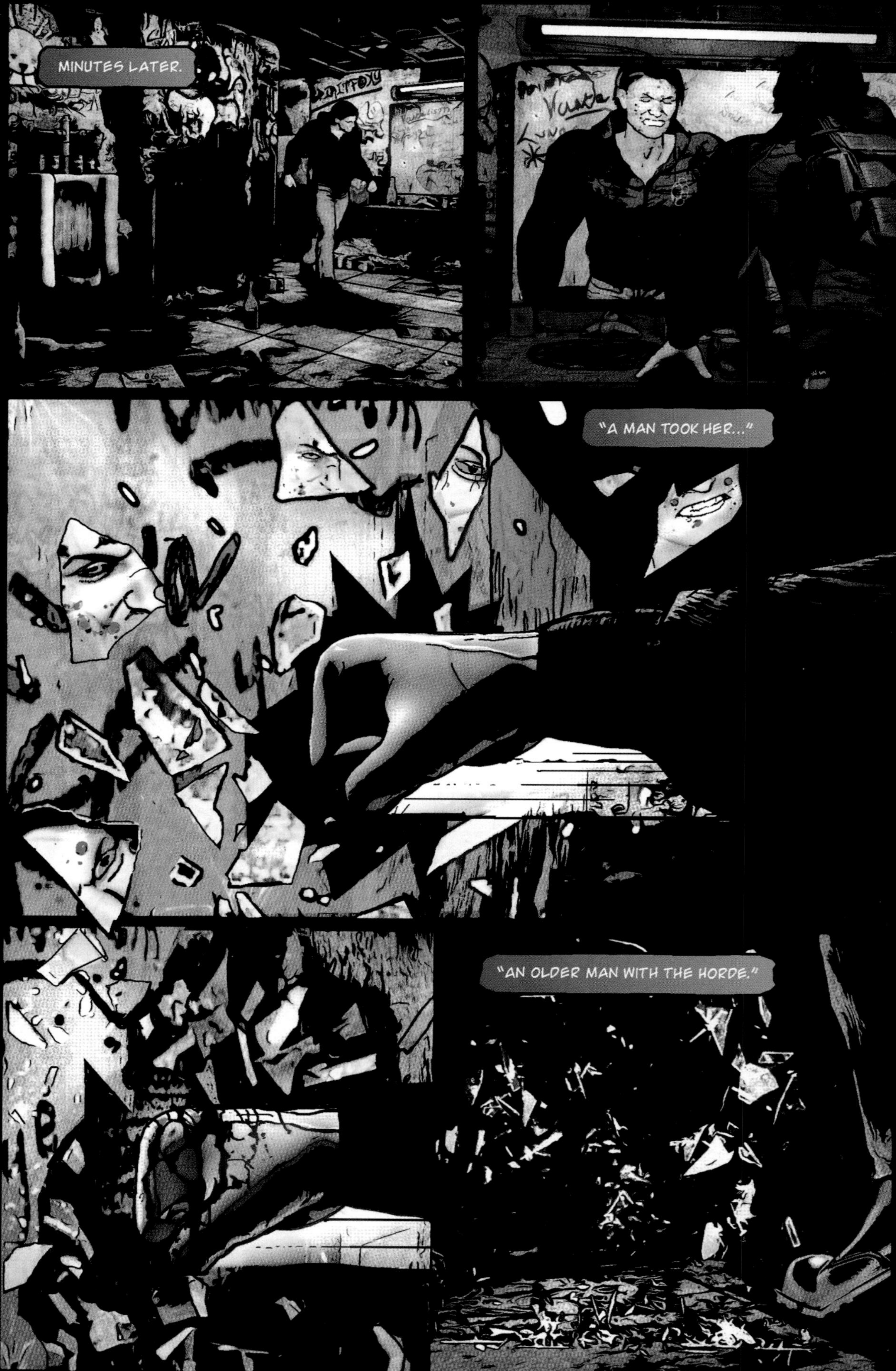
MINUTES LATER.
"A MAN TOOK HER..."
"AN OLDER MAN WITH THE HORDE."

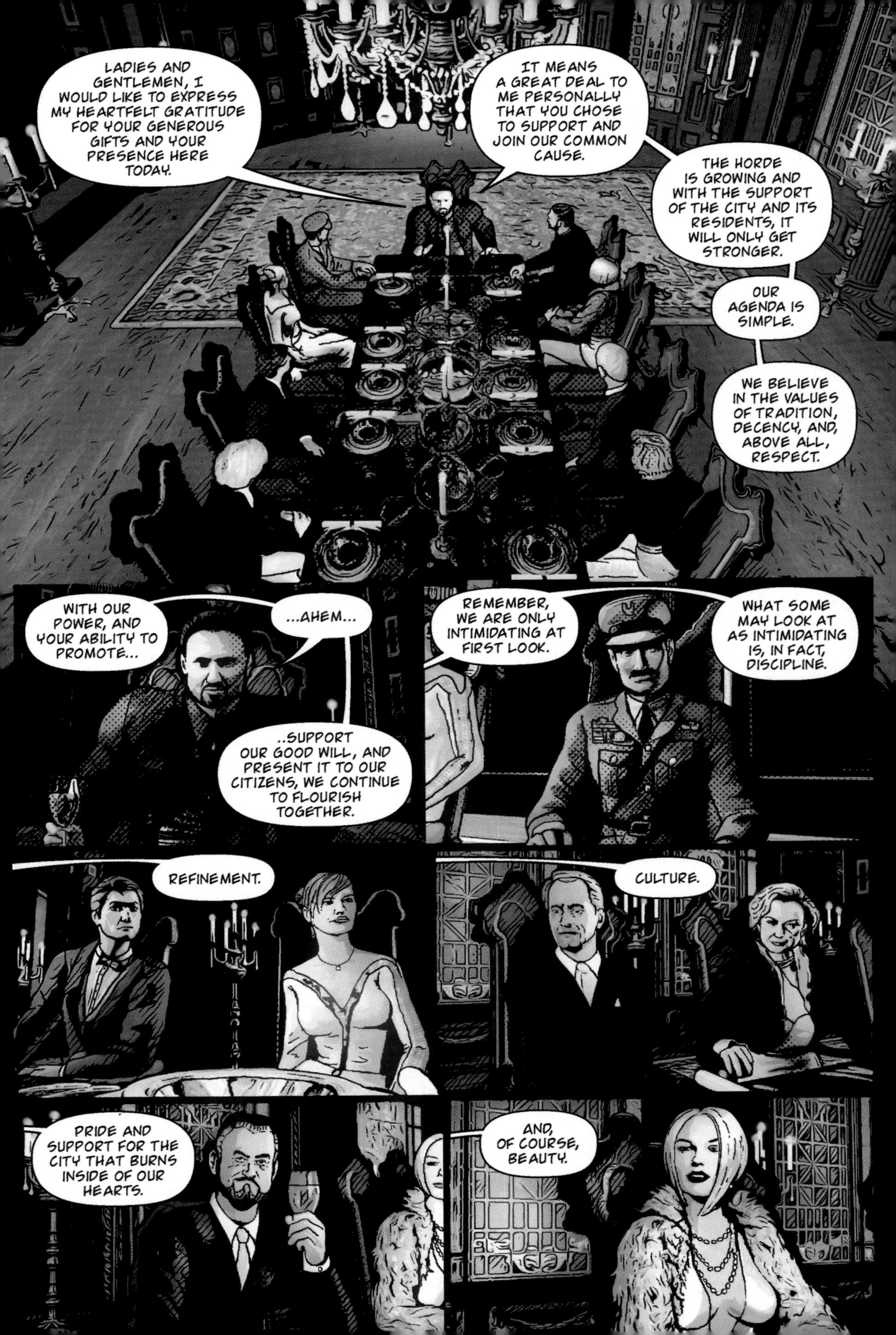
LADIES AND GENTLEMEN, I WOULD LIKE TO EXPRESS MY HEARTFELT GRATITUDE FOR YOUR GENEROUS GIFTS AND YOUR PRESENCE HERE TODAY.
IT MEANS A GREAT DEAL TO ME PERSONALLY THAT YOU CHOSE TO SUPPORT AND JOIN OUR COMMON CAUSE.
THE HORDE IS GROWING AND WITH THE SUPPORT OF THE CITY AND ITS RESIDENTS, IT WILL ONLY GET STRONGER.
OUR AGENDA IS SIMPLE.
WE BELIEVE IN THE VALUES OF TRADITION, DECENCY, AND, ABOVE ALL, RESPECT.
WITH OUR POWER, AND YOUR ABILITY TO PROMOTE...
...AHEM...
..SUPPORT OUR GOOD WILL, AND PRESENT IT TO OUR CITIZENS, WE CONTINUE TO FLOURISH TOGETHER.
REMEMBER, WE ARE ONLY INTIMIDATING AT FIRST LOOK.
WHAT SOME MAY LOOK AT AS INTIMIDATING IS, IN FACT, DISCIPLINE.
REFINEMENT.
CULTURE.
PRIDE AND SUPPORT FOR THE CITY THAT BURNS INSIDE OF OUR HEARTS.
AND, OF COURSE, BEAUTY.

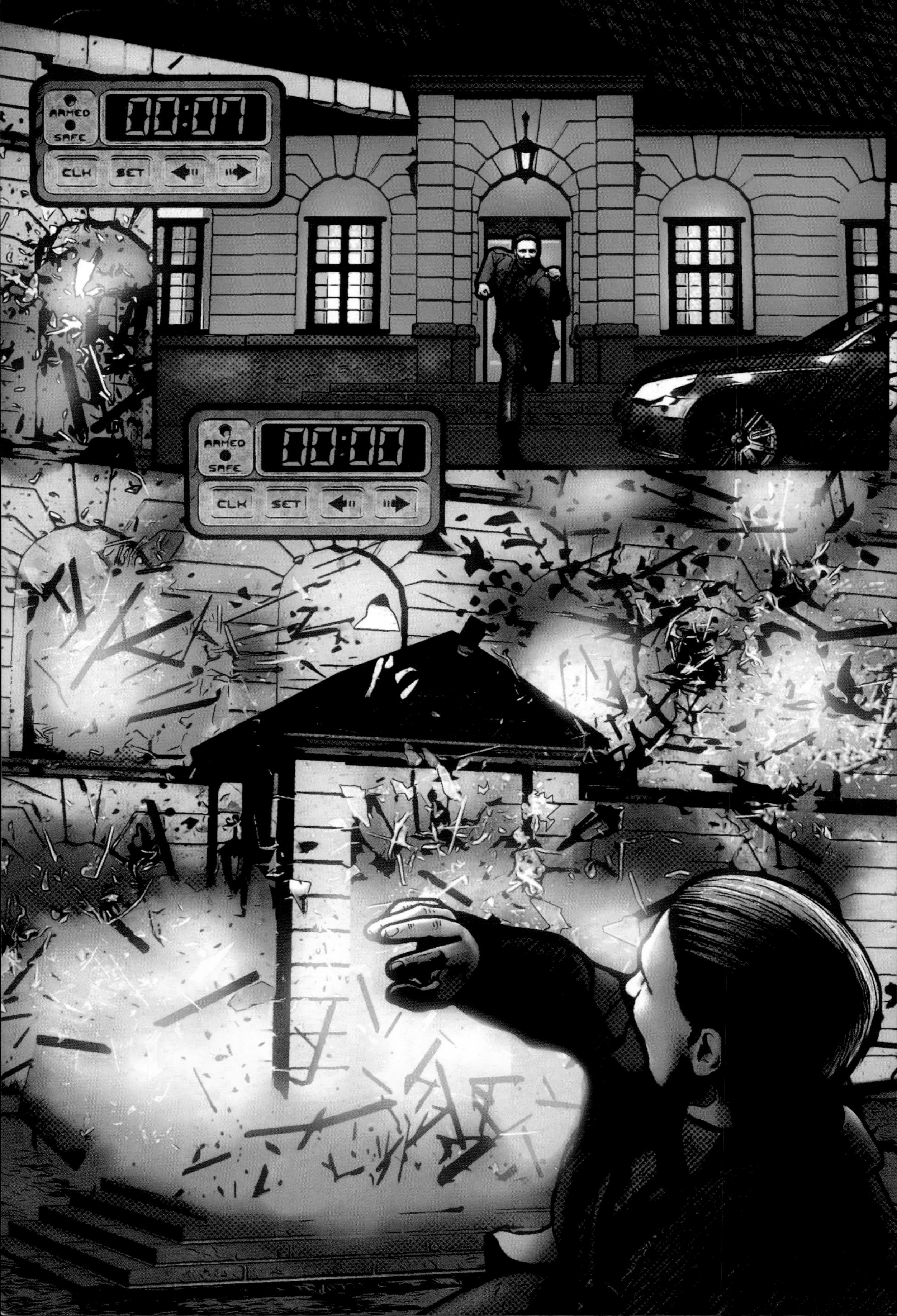
ARMED
SAFE
00:07
CLK
SET
ARMED
SAFE
00:00
CLK
SET

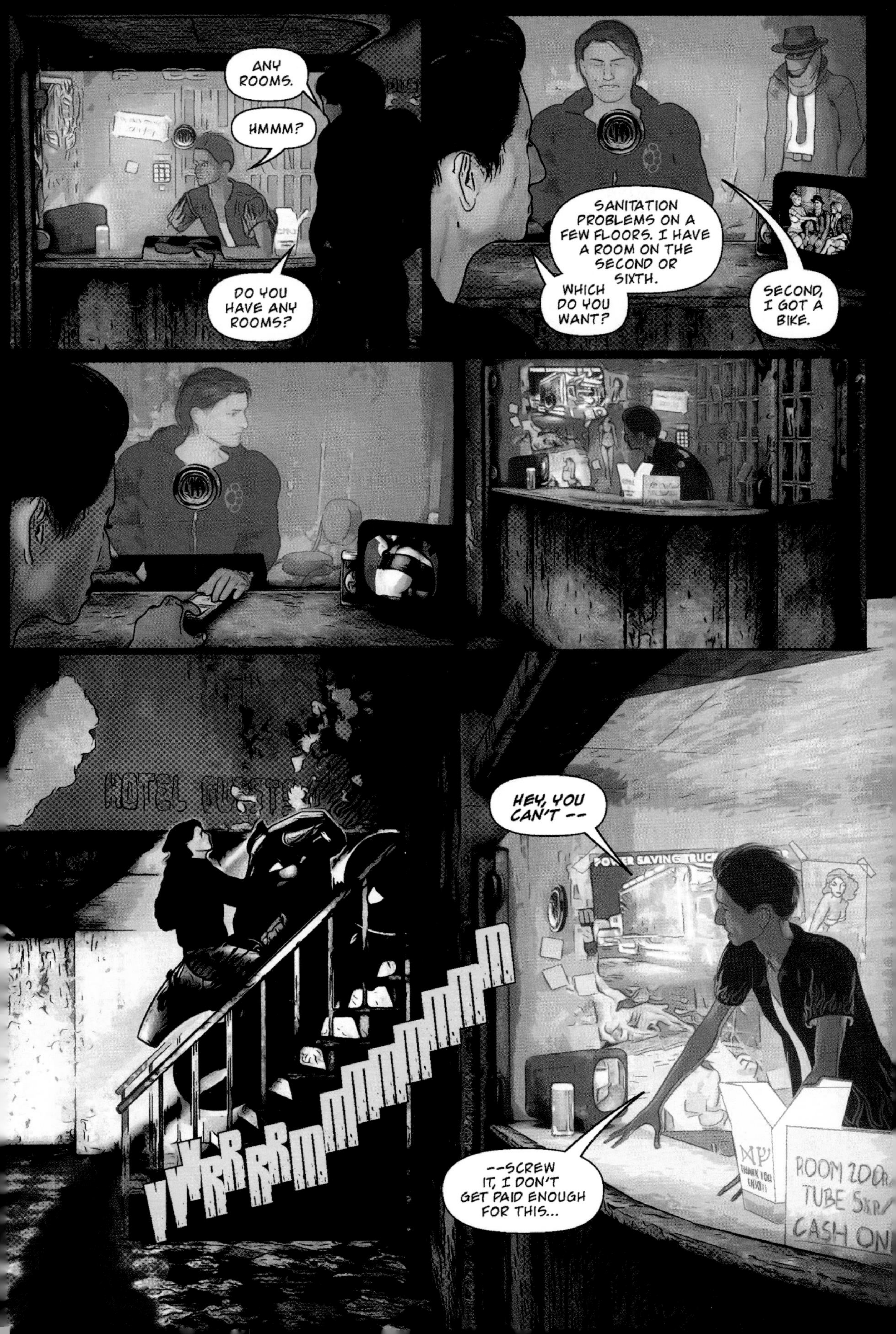
ANY ROOMS.
HMMM?
DO YOU HAVE ANY ROOMS?
SANITATION PROBLEMS ON A FEW FLOORS. I HAVE A ROOM ON THE SECOND OR SIXTH.
WHICH DO YOU WANT?
SECOND, I GOT A BIKE.
HEY, YOU CAN'T --
--SCREW IT, I DON'T GET PAID ENOUGH FOR THIS...

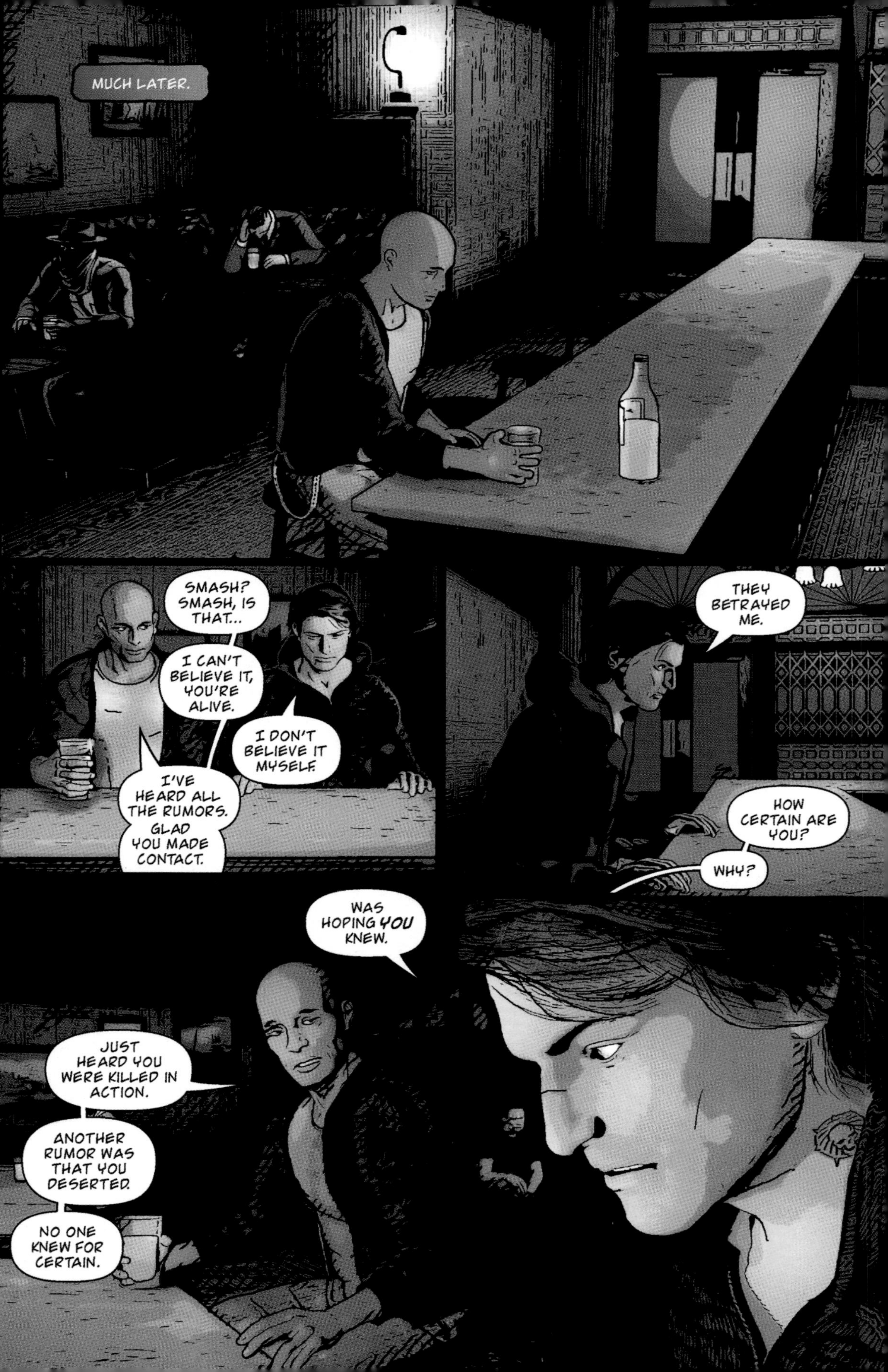
MUCH LATER.
SMASH? SMASH, IS THAT...
I CAN'T BELIEVE IT, YOU'RE ALIVE.
I DON'T BELIEVE IT MYSELF.
I'VE HEARD ALL THE RUMORS.
GLAD YOU MADE CONTACT.
THEY BETRAYED ME.
HOW CERTAIN ARE YOU?
WHY?
WAS HOPING YOU KNEW.
JUST HEARD YOU WERE KILLED IN ACTION.
ANOTHER RUMOR WAS THAT YOU DESERTED.
NO ONE KNEW FOR CERTAIN.

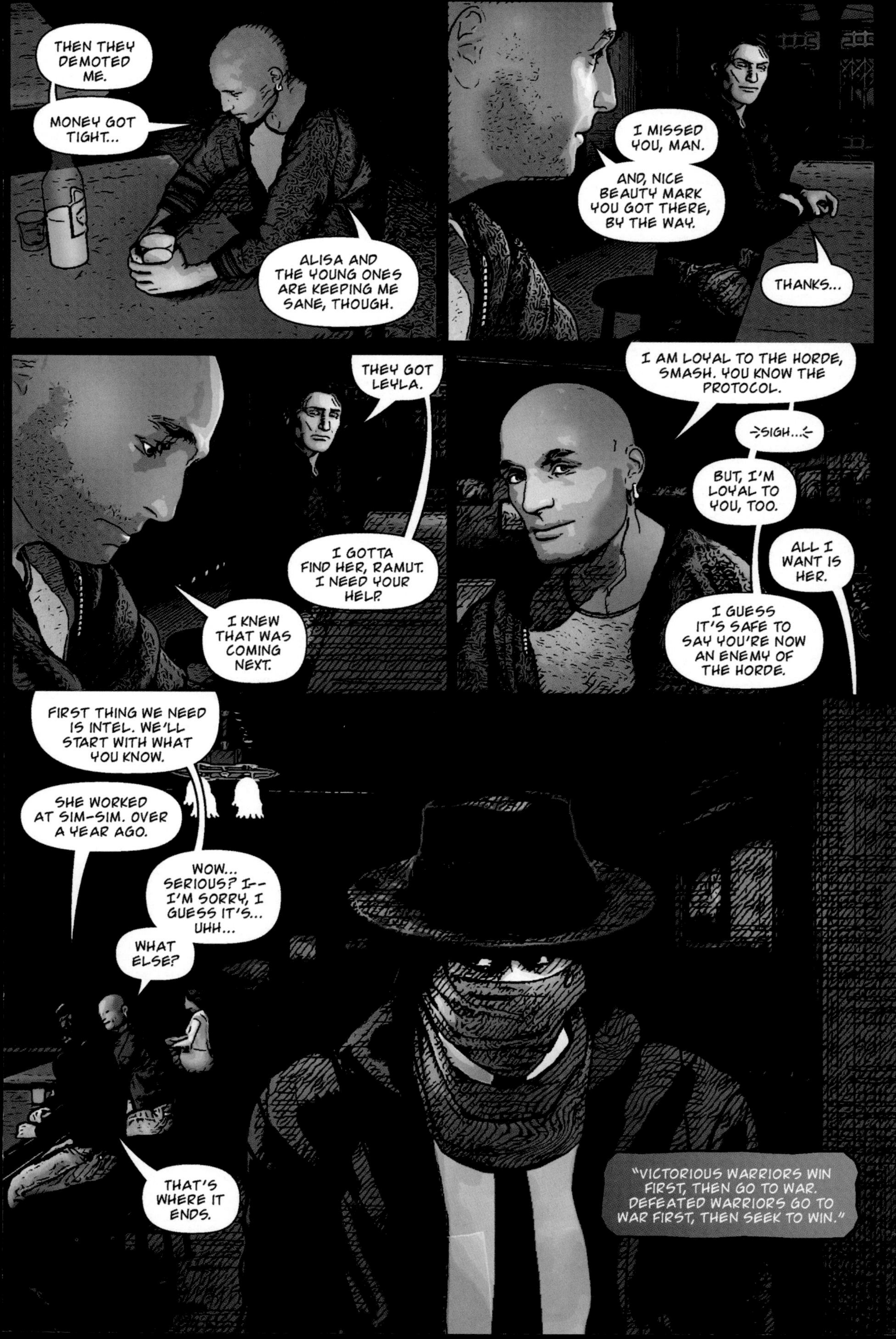
THEN THEY DEMOTED ME.
MONEY GOT TIGHT...
ALISA AND THE YOUNG ONES ARE KEEPING ME SANE, THOUGH.
I MISSED YOU, MAN.
AND, NICE BEAUTY MARK YOU GOT THERE, BY THE WAY.
THANKS...
THEY GOT LEYLA.
I GOTTA FIND HER, RAMUT. I NEED YOUR HELP.
I KNEW THAT WAS COMING NEXT.
I AM LOYAL TO THE HORDE, SMASH. YOU KNOW THE PROTOCOL.
SIGH...
BUT, I'M LOYAL TO YOU, TOO.
ALL I WANT IS HER.
I GUESS IT'S SAFE TO SAY YOU'RE NOW AN ENEMY OF THE HORDE.
FIRST THING WE NEED IS INTEL. WE'LL START WITH WHAT YOU KNOW.
SHE WORKED AT SIM-SIM. OVER A YEAR AGO.
WOW... SERIOUS? I-- I'M SORRY, I GUESS IT'S... UHH...
WHAT ELSE?
THAT'S WHERE IT ENDS.
"VICTORIOUS WARRIORS WIN FIRST, THEN GO TO WAR. DEFEATED WARRIORS GO TO WAR FIRST, THEN SEEK TO WIN."

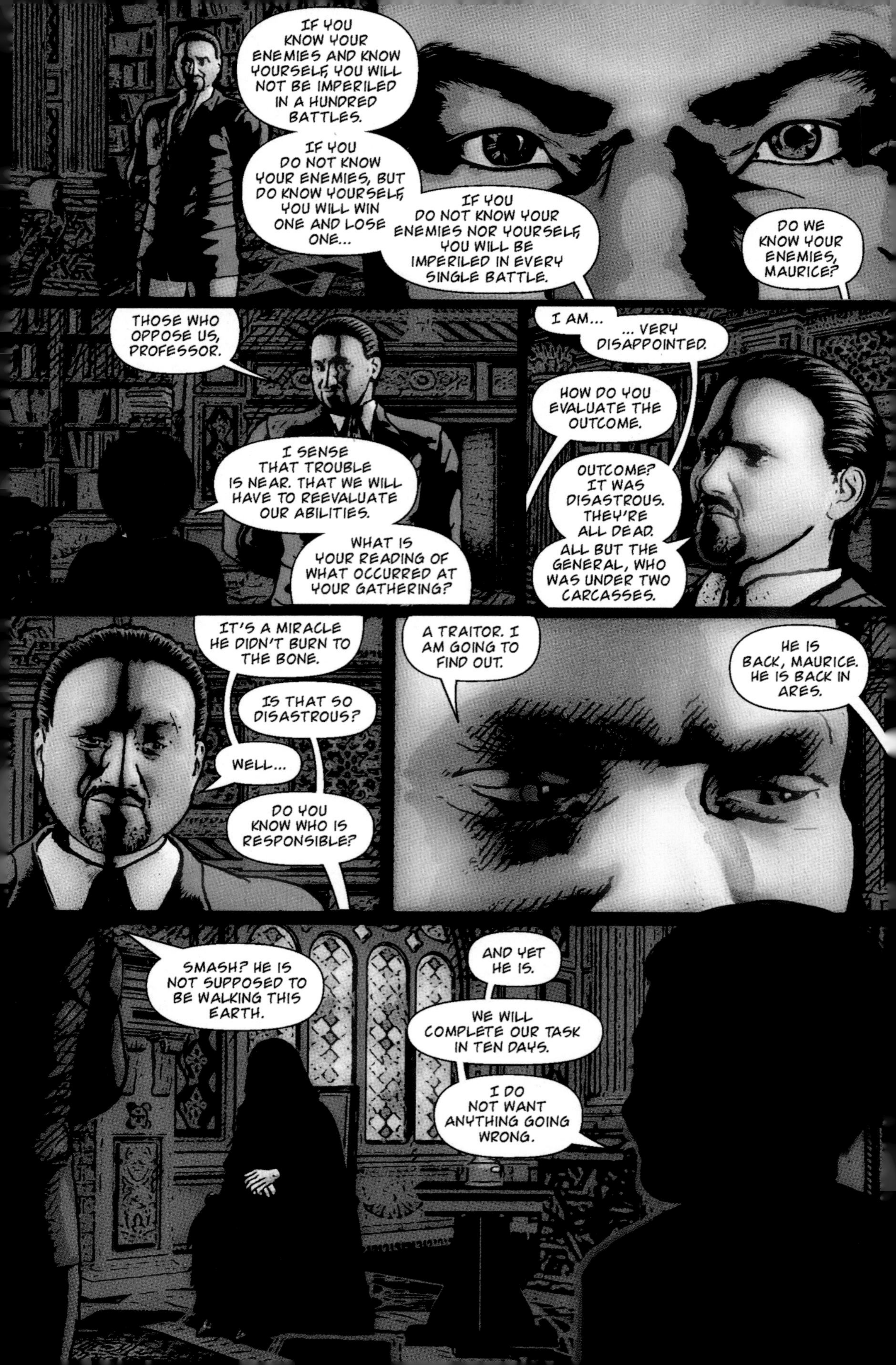
IF YOU KNOW YOUR ENEMIES AND KNOW YOURSELF, YOU WILL NOT BE IMPERILED IN A HUNDRED BATTLES.
IF YOU DO NOT KNOW YOUR ENEMIES, BUT DO KNOW YOURSELF, YOU WILL WIN ONE AND LOSE ONE...
IF YOU DO NOT KNOW YOUR ENEMIES NOR YOURSELF, YOU WILL BE IMPERILED IN EVERY SINGLE BATTLE.
DO WE KNOW YOUR ENEMIES, MAURICE?
THOSE WHO OPPOSE US, PROFESSOR.
I SENSE THAT TROUBLE IS NEAR. THAT WE WILL HAVE TO REEVALUATE OUR ABILITIES.
WHAT IS YOUR READING OF WHAT OCCURRED AT YOUR GATHERING?
I AM...
... VERY DISAPPOINTED.
HOW DO YOU EVALUATE THE OUTCOME.
OUTCOME? IT WAS DISASTROUS. THEY'RE ALL DEAD.
ALL BUT THE GENERAL, WHO WAS UNDER TWO CARCASSES.
IT'S A MIRACLE HE DIDN'T BURN TO THE BONE.
IS THAT SO DISASTROUS?
WELL...
DO YOU KNOW WHO IS RESPONSIBLE?
A TRAITOR. I AM GOING TO FIND OUT.
HE IS BACK, MAURICE. HE IS BACK IN ARES.
SMASH? HE IS NOT SUPPOSED TO BE WALKING THIS EARTH.
AND YET HE IS.
WE WILL COMPLETE OUR TASK IN TEN DAYS.
I DO NOT WANT ANYTHING GOING WRONG.

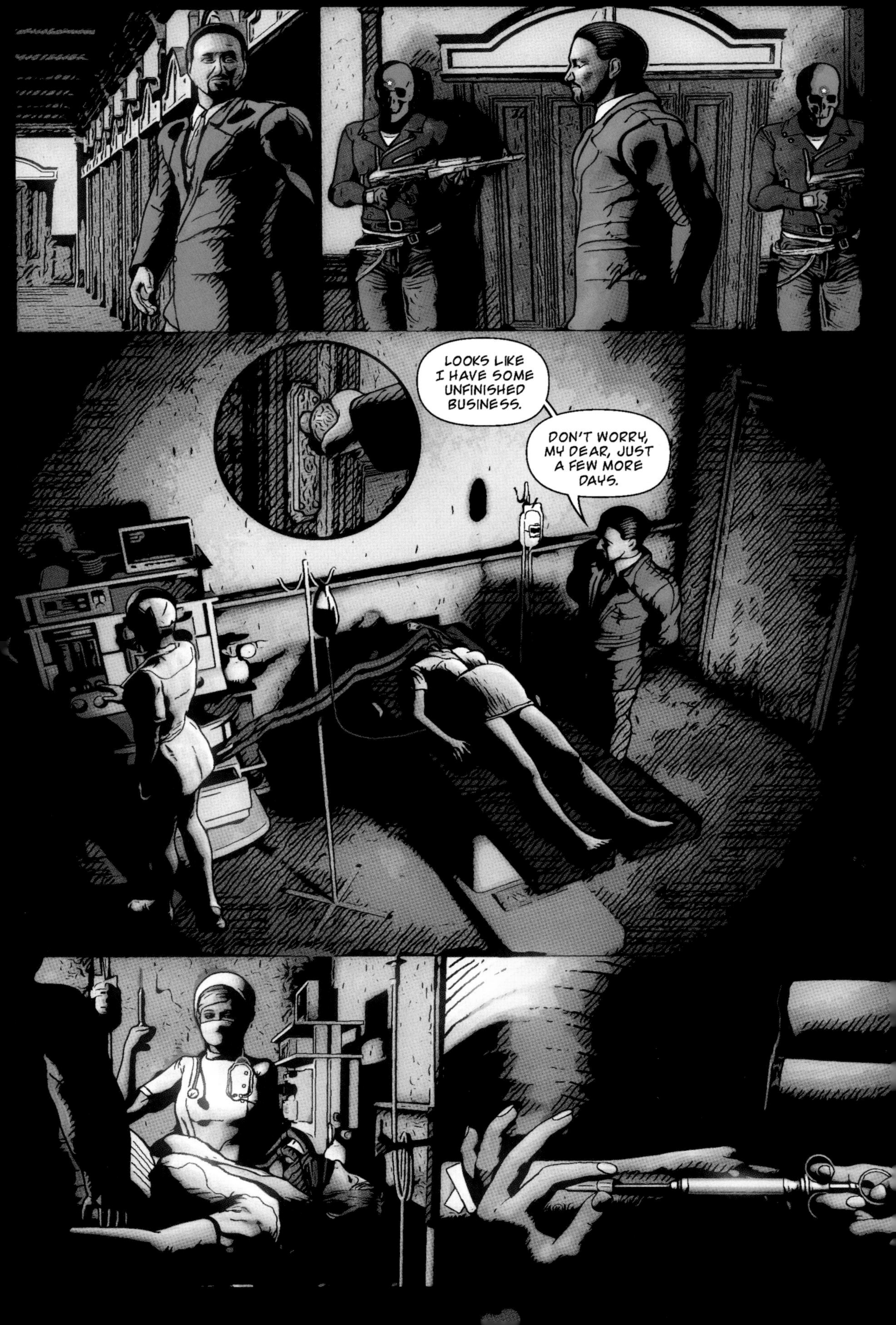
LOOKS LIKE I HAVE SOME UNFINISHED BUSINESS.
DON'T WORRY, MY DEAR, JUST A FEW MORE DAYS.

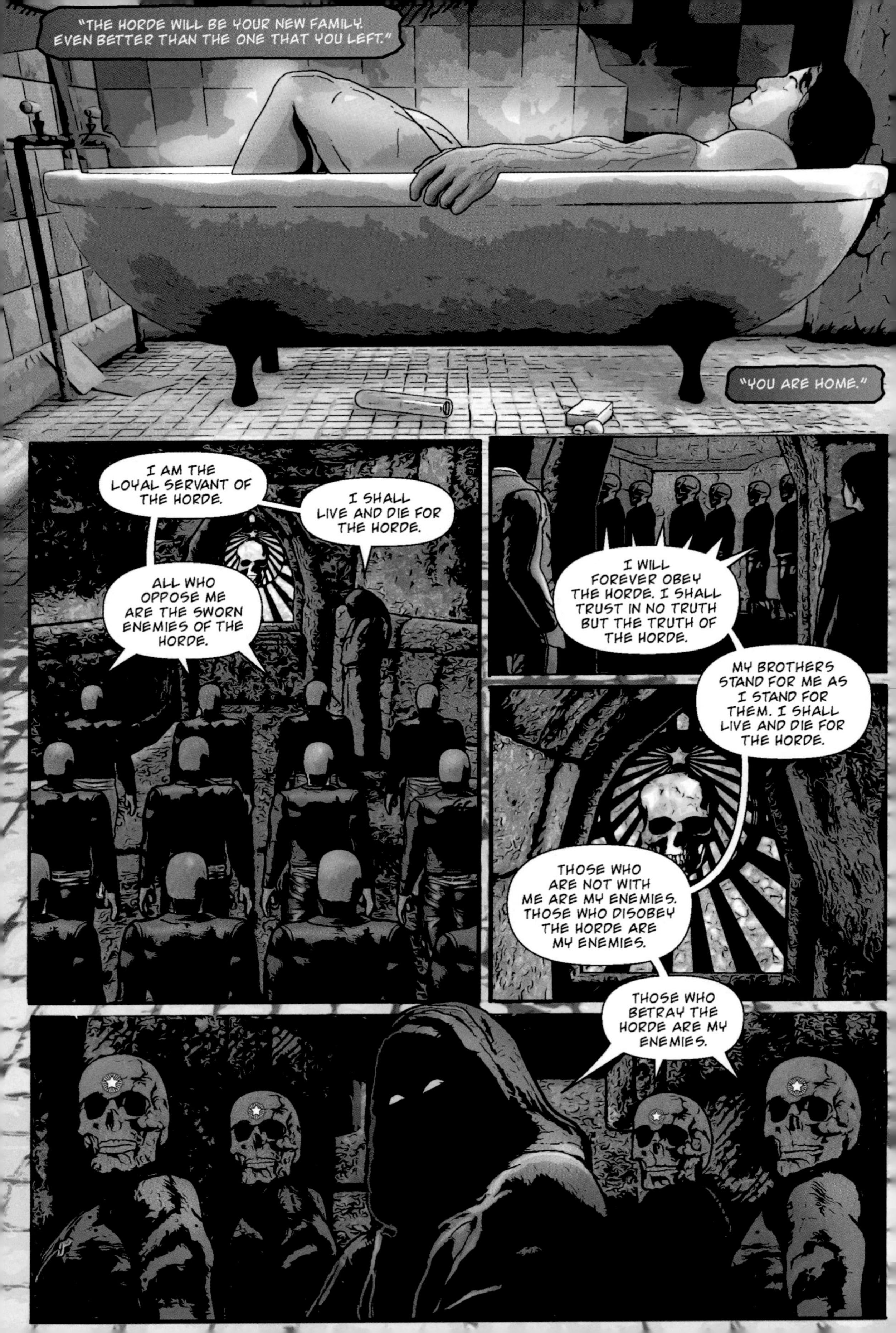
"THE HORDE WILL BE YOUR NEW FAMILY. EVEN BETTER THAN THE ONE THAT YOU LEFT."
"YOU ARE HOME."
I AM THE LOYAL SERVANT OF THE HORDE.
I SHALL LIVE AND DIE FOR THE HORDE.
ALL WHO OPPOSE ME ARE THE SWORN ENEMIES OF THE HORDE.
I WILL FOREVER OBEY THE HORDE. I SHALL TRUST IN NO TRUTH BUT THE TRUTH OF THE HORDE.
MY BROTHERS STAND FOR ME AS I STAND FOR THEM. I SHALL LIVE AND DIE FOR THE HORDE.
THOSE WHO ARE NOT WITH ME ARE MY ENEMIES. THOSE WHO DISOBEY THE HORDE ARE MY ENEMIES.
THOSE WHO BETRAY THE HORDE ARE MY ENEMIES.

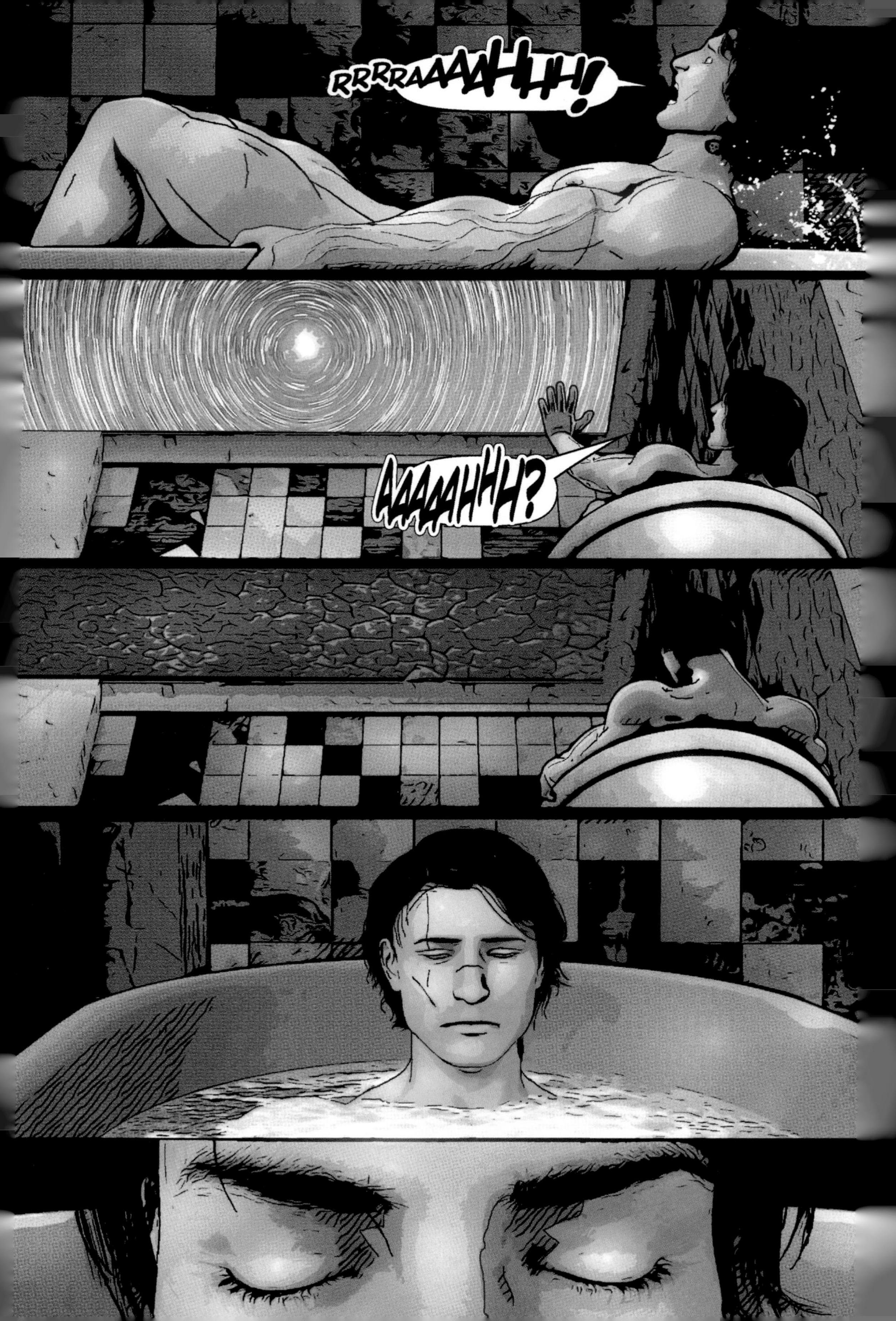
RRRRAAAAHHH!
AAAAAHHH?

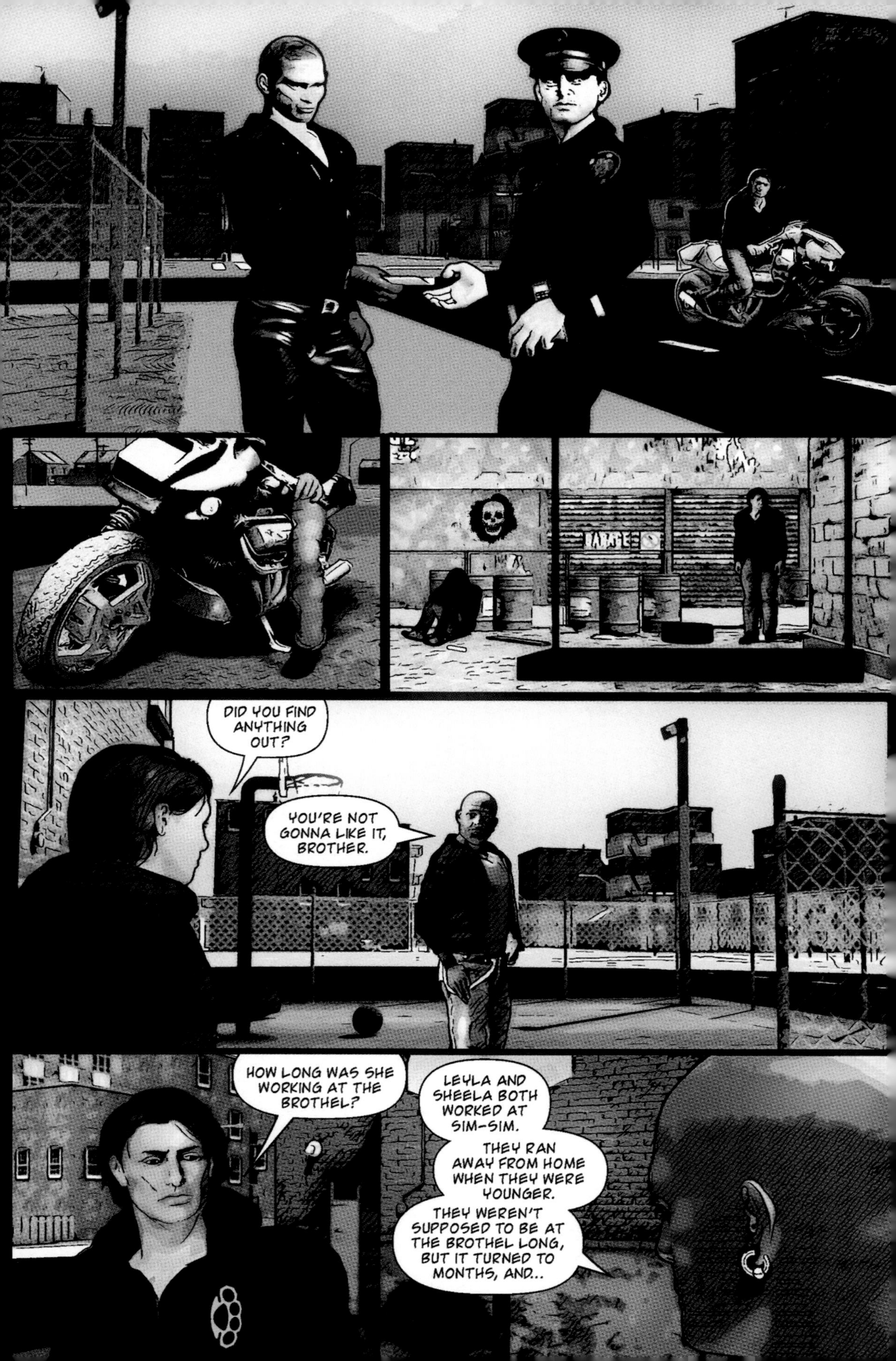

GARAGE
DID YOU FIND ANYTHING OUT?
YOU'RE NOT GONNA LIKE IT, BROTHER.
HOW LONG WAS SHE WORKING AT THE BROTHEL?
LEYLA AND SHEELA BOTH WORKED AT SIM-SIM.
THEY RAN AWAY FROM HOME WHEN THEY WERE YOUNGER.
THEY WEREN'T SUPPOSED TO BE AT THE BROTHEL LONG, BUT IT TURNED TO MONTHS, AND...

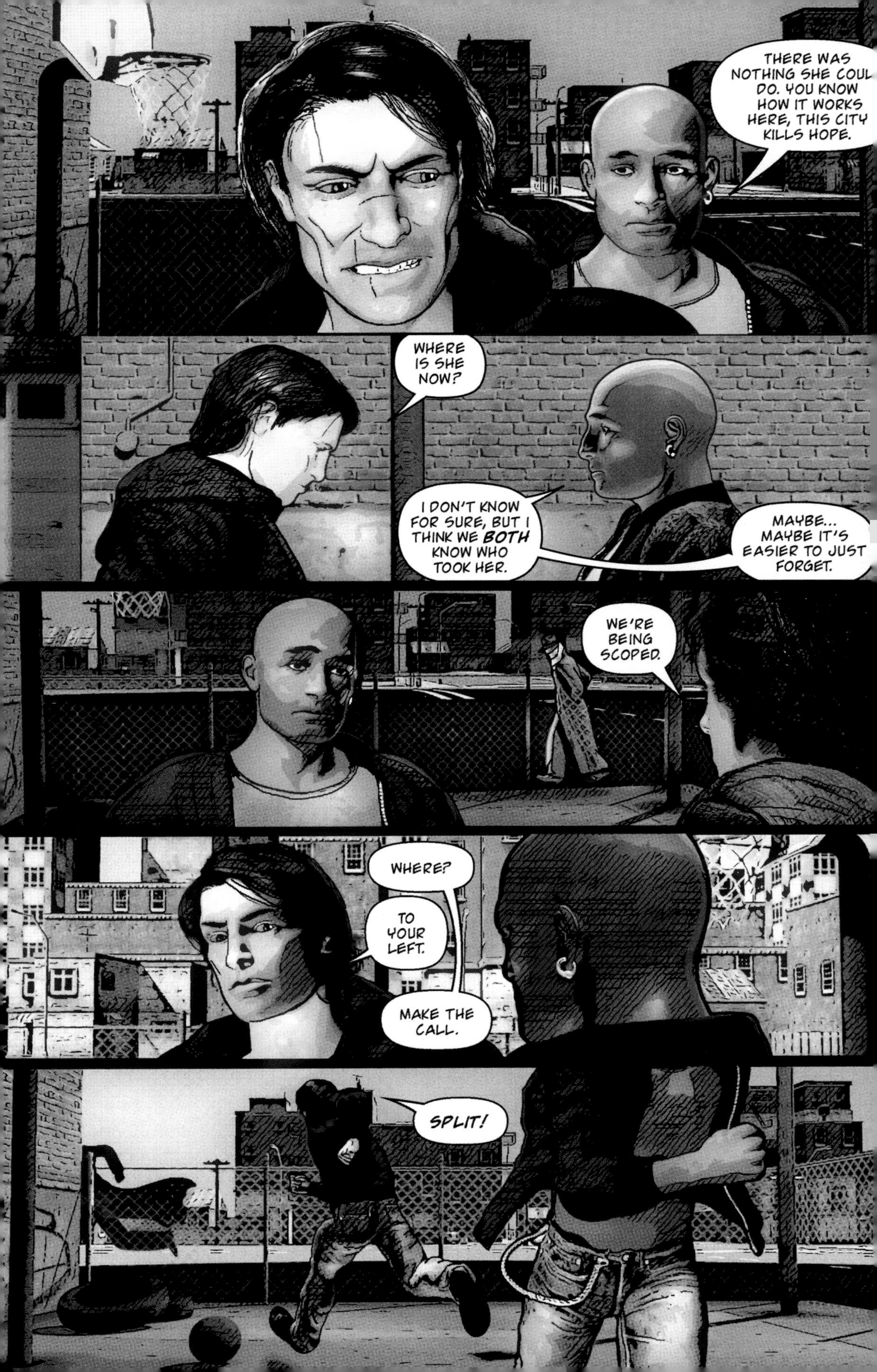
THERE WAS NOTHING SHE COUL DO. YOU KNOW HOW IT WORKS HERE, THIS CITY KILLS HOPE.
WHERE IS SHE NOW?
I DON'T KNOW FOR SURE, BUT I THINK WE BOTH KNOW WHO TOOK HER.
MAYBE... MAYBE IT'S EASIER TO JUST FORGET.
WE'RE BEING SCOPED.
WHERE?
TO YOUR LEFT.
MAKE THE CALL.
SPLIT!

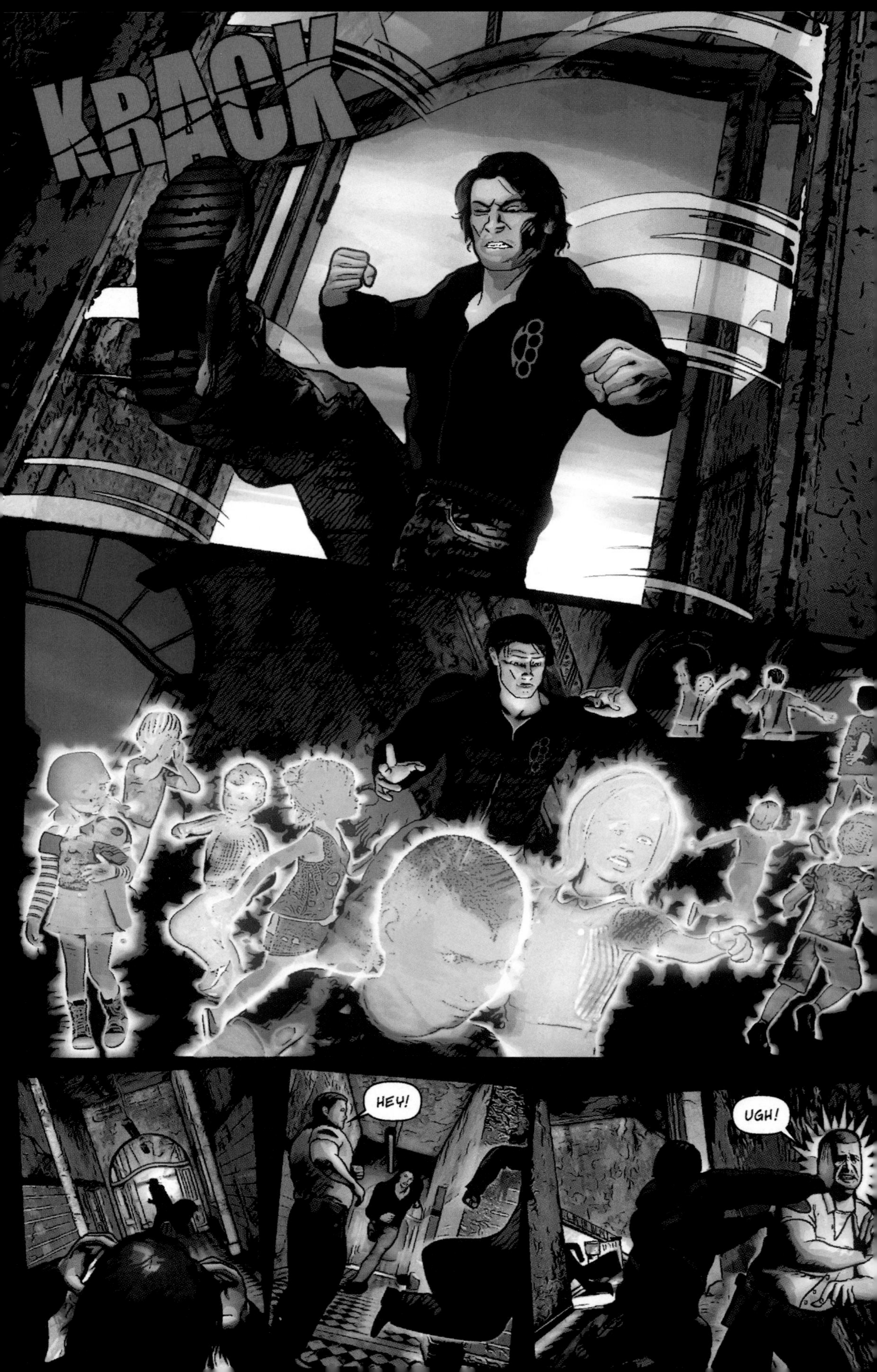
KRACK
HEY!
UGH!

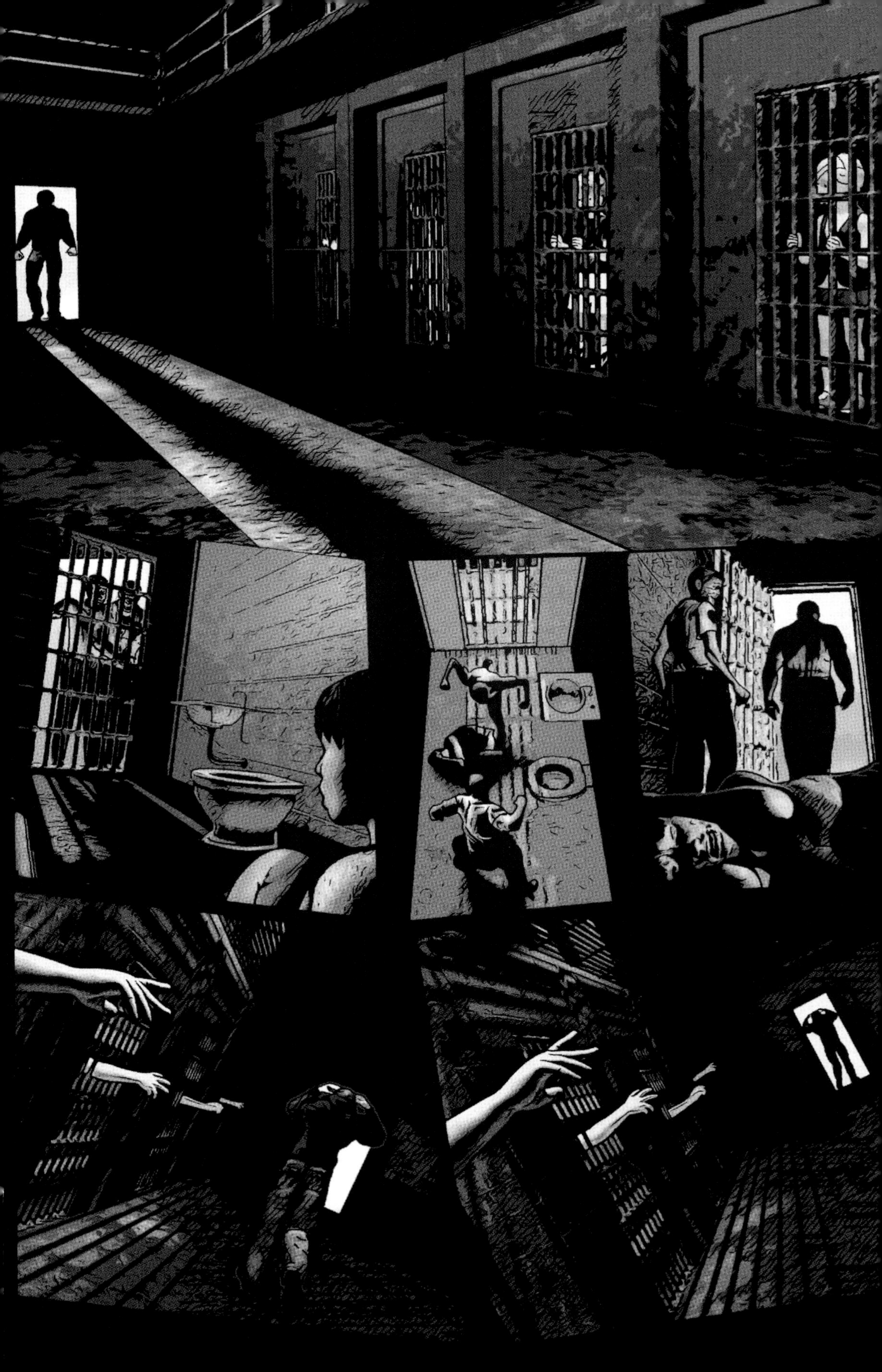

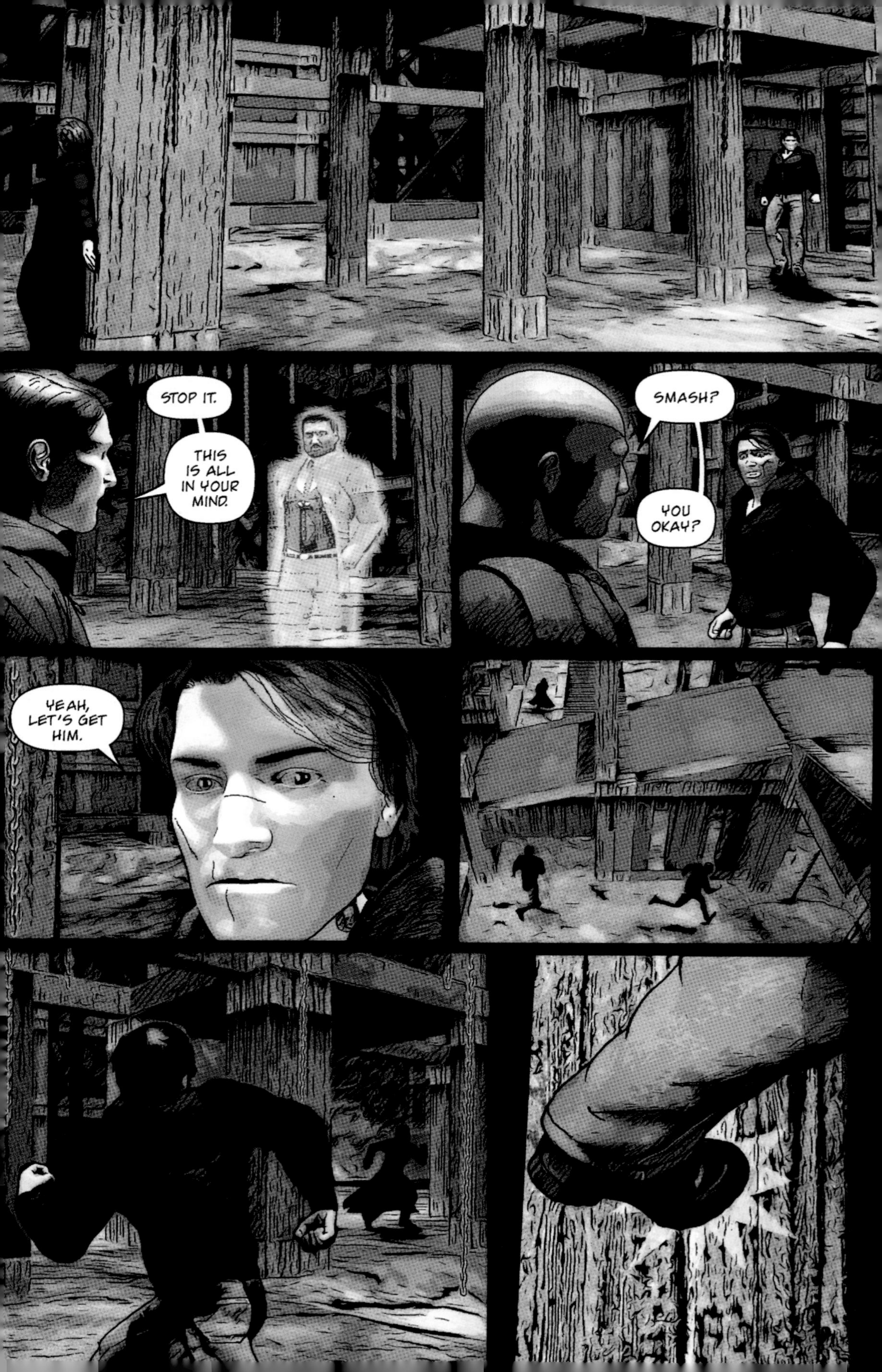
STOP IT.
THIS IS ALL IN YOUR MIND.
SMASH?
YOU OKAY?
YEAH, LET'S GET HIM.

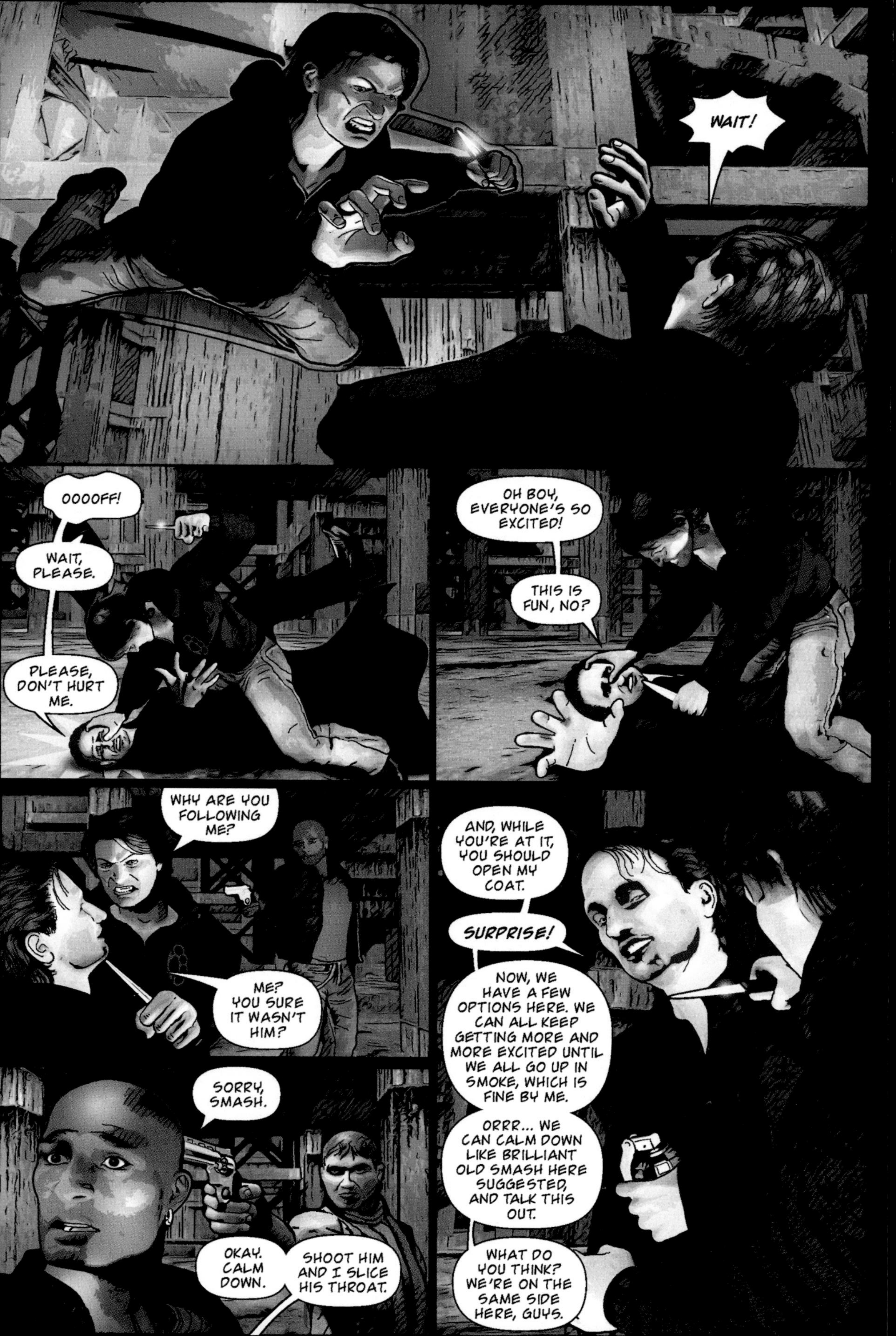
WAIT!
OOOOFF!
WAIT, PLEASE.
PLEASE, DON'T HURT ME.
OH BOY, EVERYONE'S SO EXCITED!
THIS IS FUN, NO?
WHY ARE YOU FOLLOWING ME?
ME? YOU SURE IT WASN'T HIM?
AND, WHILE YOU'RE AT IT, YOU SHOULD OPEN MY COAT.
SURPRISE!
NOW, WE HAVE A FEW OPTIONS HERE. WE CAN ALL KEEP GETTING MORE AND MORE EXCITED UNTIL WE ALL GO UP IN SMOKE, WHICH IS FINE BY ME.
ORRR... WE CAN CALM DOWN LIKE BRILLIANT OLD SMASH HERE SUGGESTED, AND TALK THIS OUT.
WHAT DO YOU THINK? WE'RE ON THE SAME SIDE HERE, GUYS.
SORRY, SMASH.
OKAY. CALM DOWN.
SHOOT HIM AND I SLICE HIS THROAT.

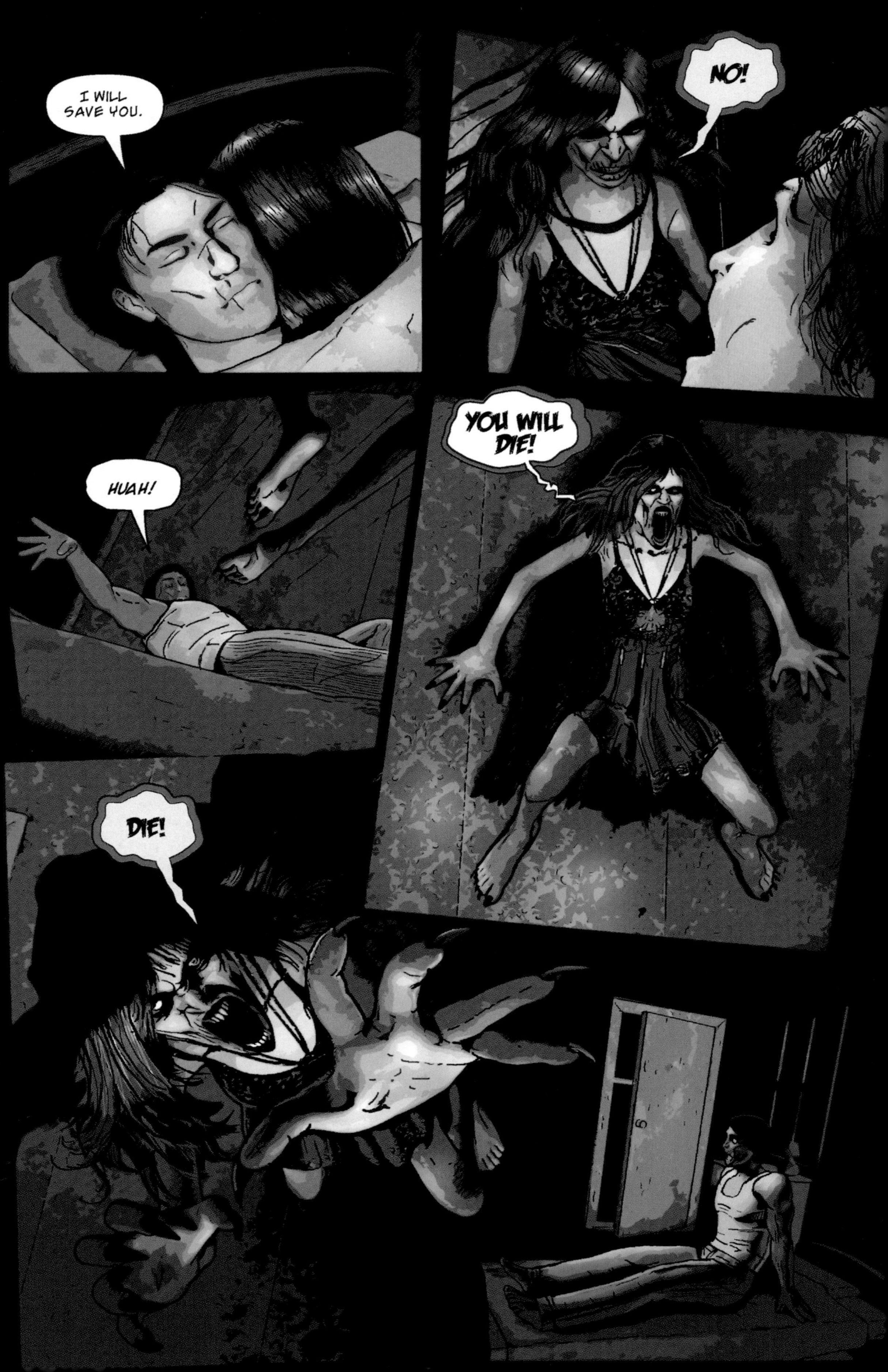
I WILL SAVE YOU.
NO!
HUAH!
YOU WILL DIE!
DIE!

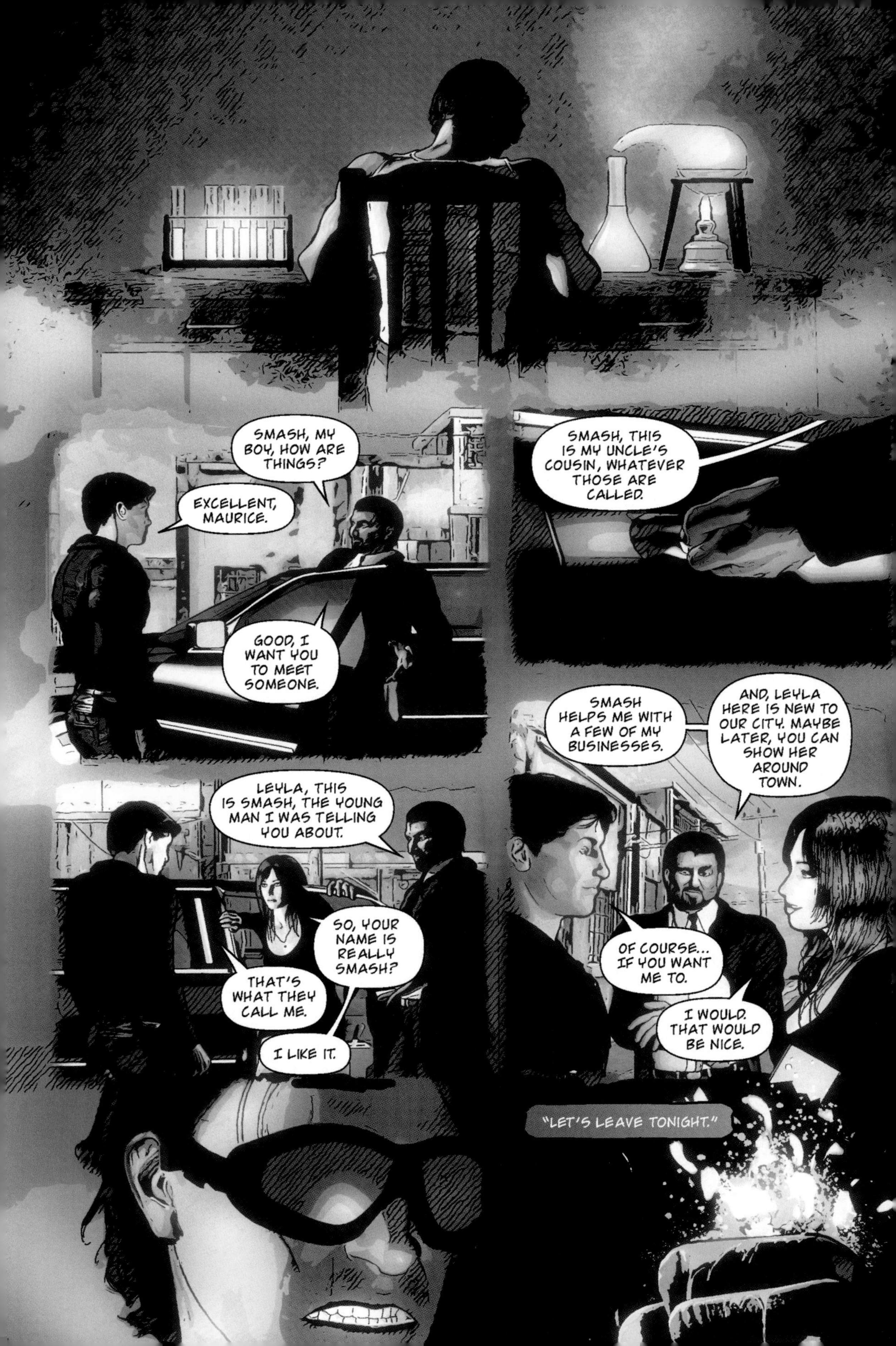
SMASH, MY BOY, HOW ARE THINGS?
EXCELLENT, MAURICE.
GOOD, I WANT YOU TO MEET SOMEONE.
SMASH, THIS IS MY UNCLE'S COUSIN, WHATEVER THOSE ARE CALLED.
LEYLA, THIS IS SMASH, THE YOUNG MAN I WAS TELLING YOU ABOUT.
SO, YOUR NAME IS REALLY SMASH?
THAT'S WHAT THEY CALL ME.
I LIKE IT.
SMASH HELPS ME WITH A FEW OF MY BUSINESSES.
AND, LEYLA HERE IS NEW TO OUR CITY. MAYBE LATER, YOU CAN SHOW HER AROUND TOWN.
OF COURSE... IF YOU WANT ME TO.
I WOULD. THAT WOULD BE NICE.
"LET'S LEAVE TONIGHT."

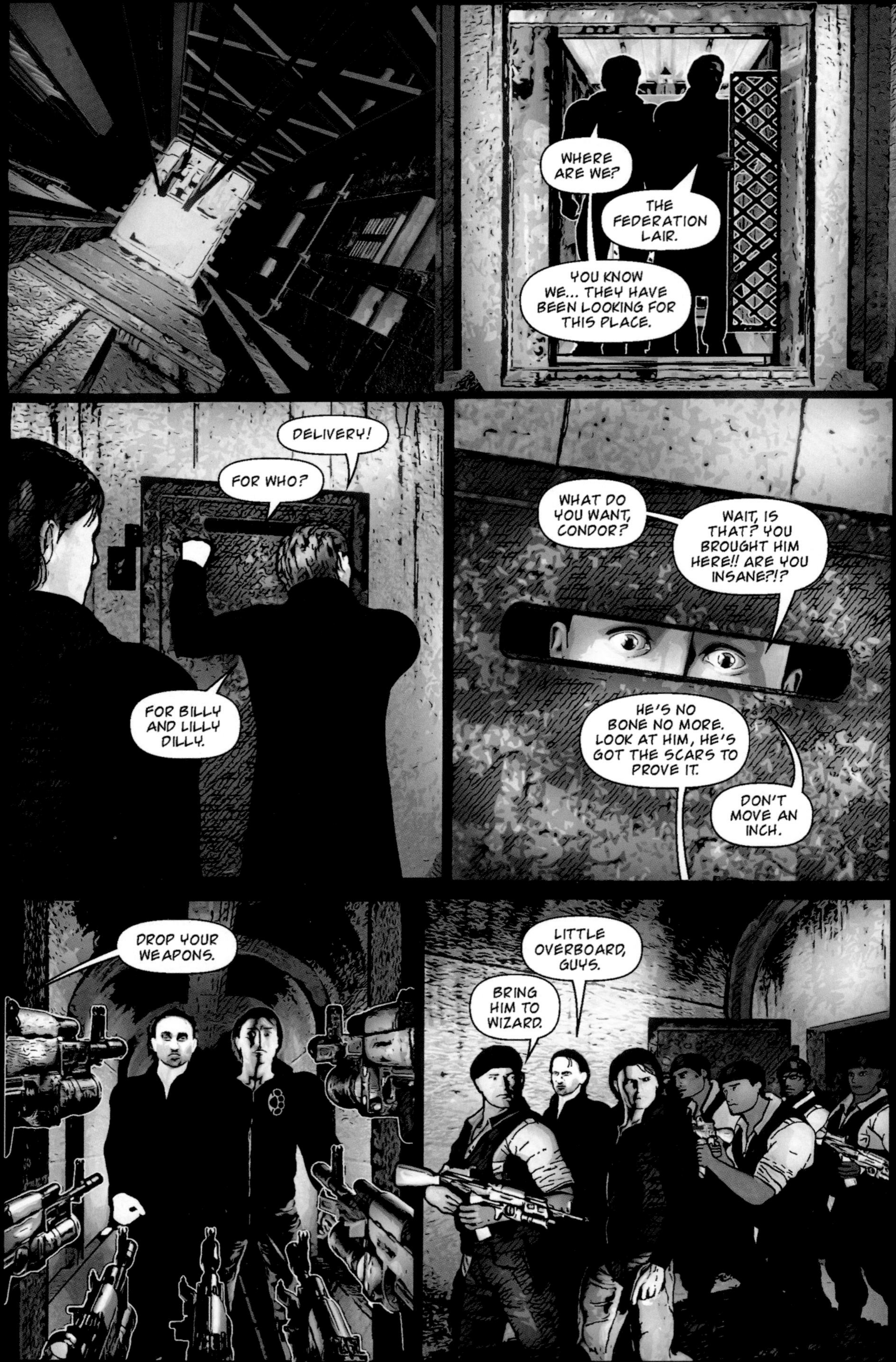
WHERE ARE WE?
THE FEDERATION LAIR.
YOU KNOW WE... THEY HAVE BEEN LOOKING FOR THIS PLACE.
DELIVERY!
FOR WHO?
FOR BILLY AND LILLY DILLY.
WHAT DO YOU WANT, CONDOR?
WAIT, IS THAT? YOU BROUGHT HIM HERE!! ARE YOU INSANE?!?
HE'S NO BONE NO MORE. LOOK AT HIM, HE'S GOT THE SCARS TO PROVE IT.
DON'T MOVE AN INCH.
DROP YOUR WEAPONS.
LITTLE OVERBOARD, GUYS.
BRING HIM TO WIZARD.

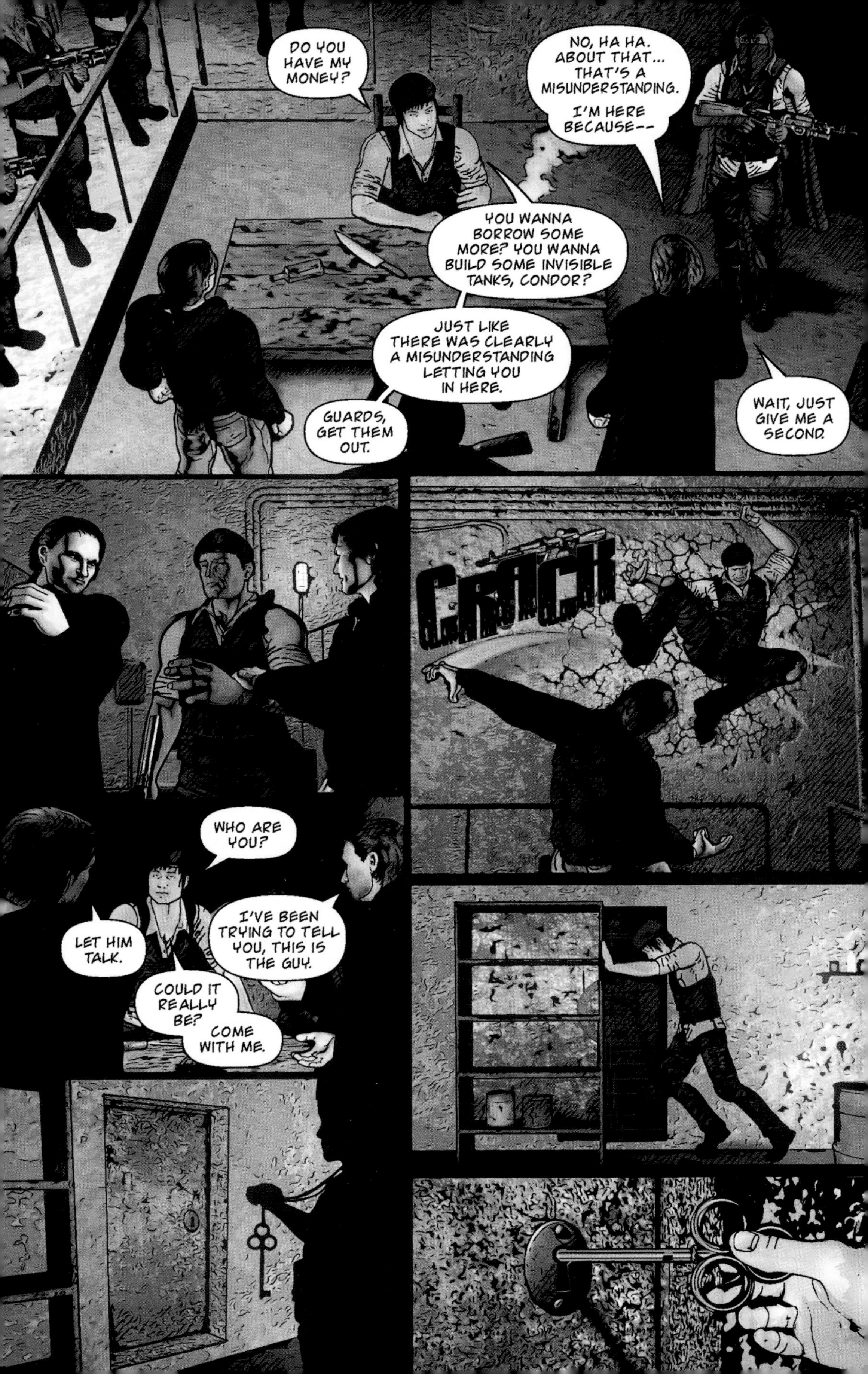
DO YOU HAVE MY MONEY?
NO, HA HA. ABOUT THAT... THAT'S A MISUNDERSTANDING.
I'M HERE BECAUSE--
YOU WANNA BORROW SOME MORE? YOU WANNA BUILD SOME INVISIBLE TANKS, CONDOR?
JUST LIKE THERE WAS CLEARLY A MISUNDERSTANDING LETTING YOU IN HERE.
GUARDS, GET THEM OUT.
WAIT, JUST GIVE ME A SECOND.
CRACK
WHO ARE YOU?
LET HIM TALK.
I'VE BEEN TRYING TO TELL YOU, THIS IS THE GUY.
COULD IT REALLY BE?
COME WITH ME.

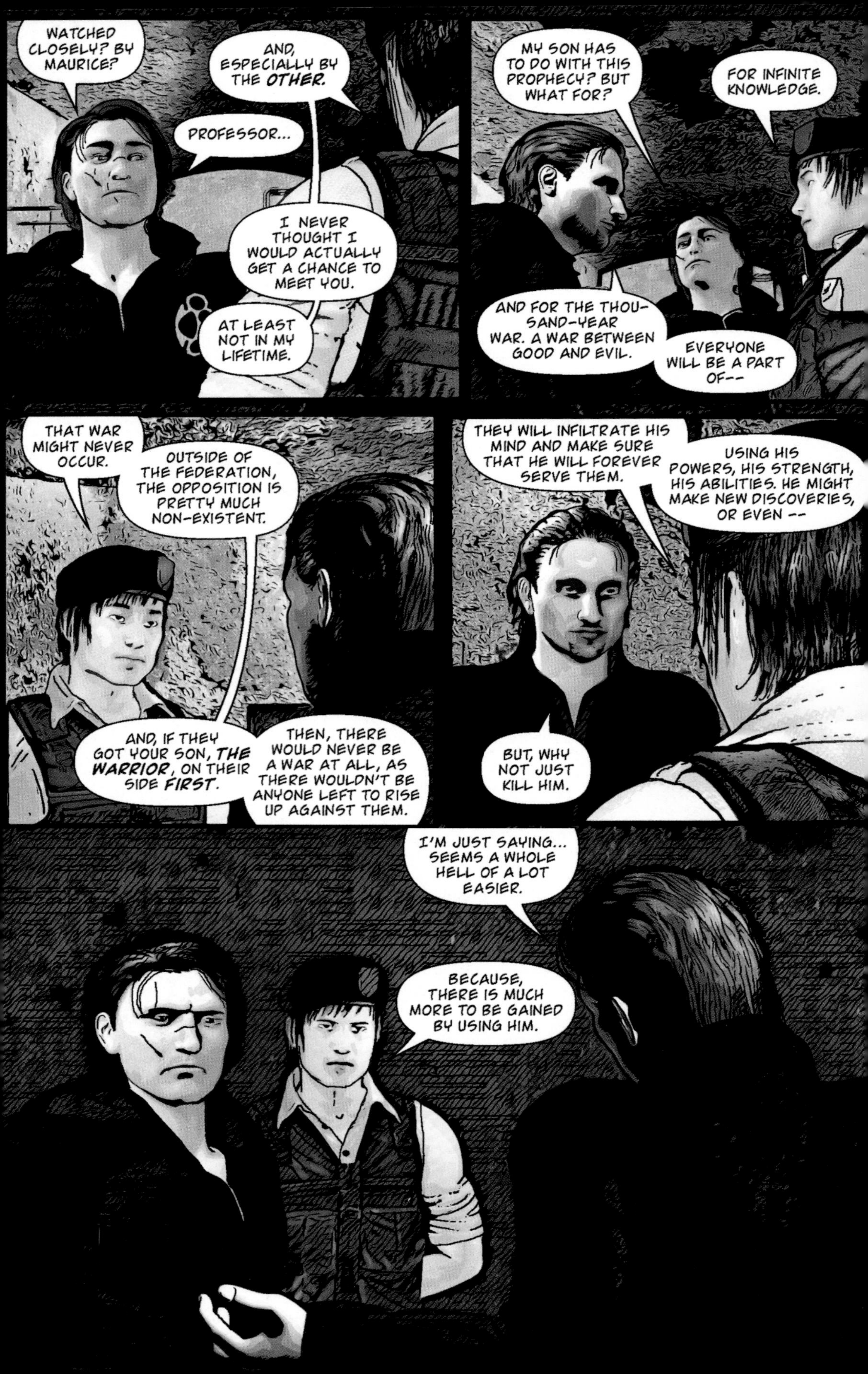
WATCHED CLOSELY? BY MAURICE?
AND, ESPECIALLY BY THE *OTHER.*
PROFESSOR...
I NEVER THOUGHT I WOULD ACTUALLY GET A CHANCE TO MEET YOU.
AT LEAST NOT IN MY LIFETIME.
MY SON HAS TO DO WITH THIS PROPHECY? BUT WHAT FOR?
FOR INFINITE KNOWLEDGE.
AND FOR THE THOUSAND-YEAR WAR. A WAR BETWEEN GOOD AND EVIL.
EVERYONE WILL BE A PART OF--
THAT WAR MIGHT NEVER OCCUR.
OUTSIDE OF THE FEDERATION, THE OPPOSITION IS PRETTY MUCH NON-EXISTENT.
AND, IF THEY GOT YOUR SON, ***THE WARRIOR***, ON THEIR SIDE ***FIRST***.
THEN, THERE WOULD NEVER BE A WAR AT ALL, AS THERE WOULDN'T BE ANYONE LEFT TO RISE UP AGAINST THEM.
THEY WILL INFILTRATE HIS MIND AND MAKE SURE THAT HE WILL FOREVER SERVE THEM.
USING HIS POWERS, HIS STRENGTH, HIS ABILITIES. HE MIGHT MAKE NEW DISCOVERIES, OR EVEN --
BUT, WHY NOT JUST KILL HIM.
I'M JUST SAYING... SEEMS A WHOLE HELL OF A LOT EASIER.
BECAUSE, THERE IS MUCH MORE TO BE GAINED BY USING HIM.

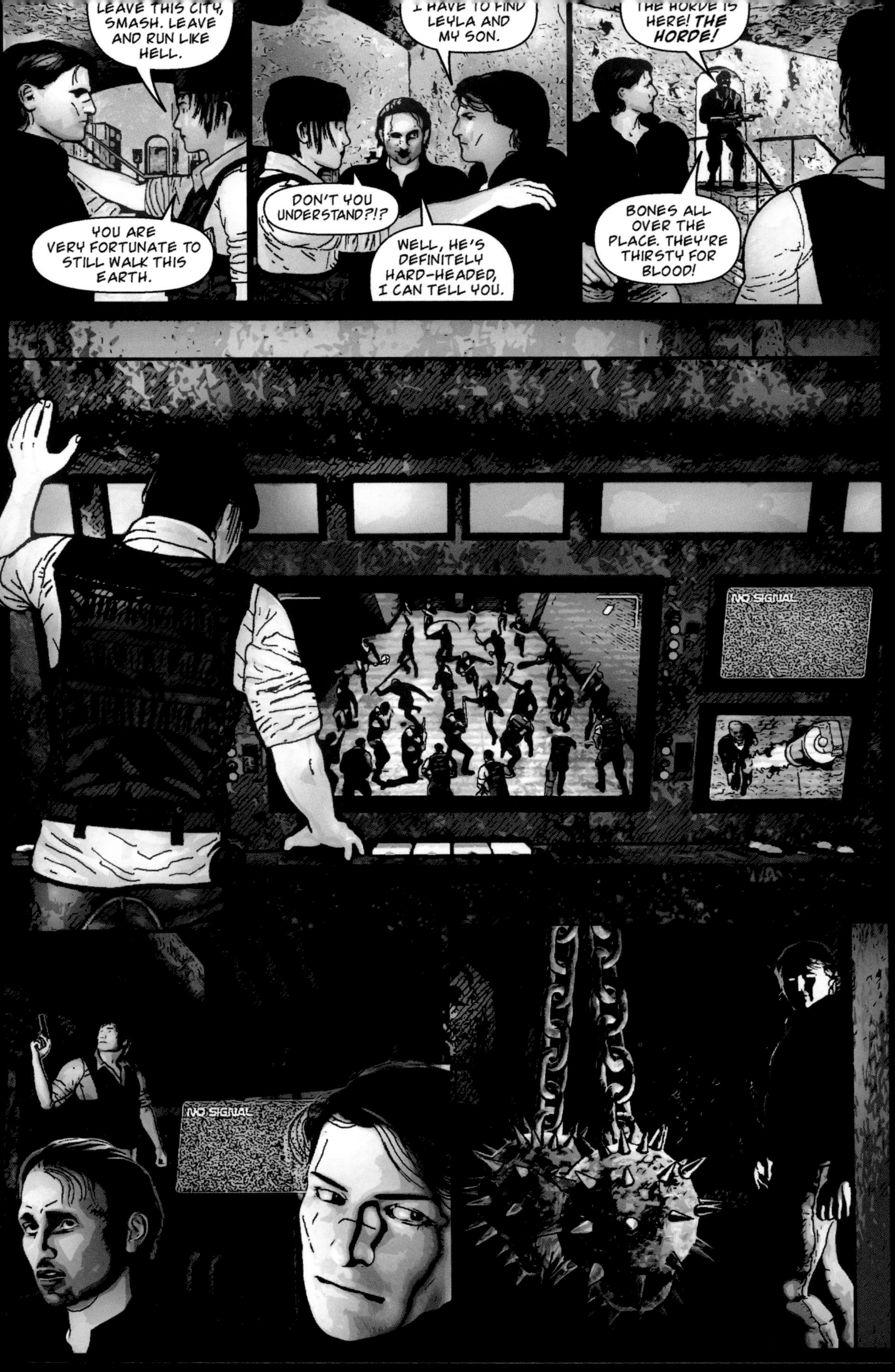
LEAVE THIS CITY, SMASH. LEAVE AND RUN LIKE HELL.
YOU ARE VERY FORTUNATE TO STILL WALK THIS EARTH.
I HAVE TO FIND LEYLA AND MY SON.
DON'T YOU UNDERSTAND?!?
WELL, HE'S DEFINITELY HARD-HEADED, I CAN TELL YOU.
THE HORDE IS HERE! THE HORDE!
BONES ALL OVER THE PLACE. THEY'RE THIRSTY FOR BLOOD!
NO SIGNAL
NO SIGNAL

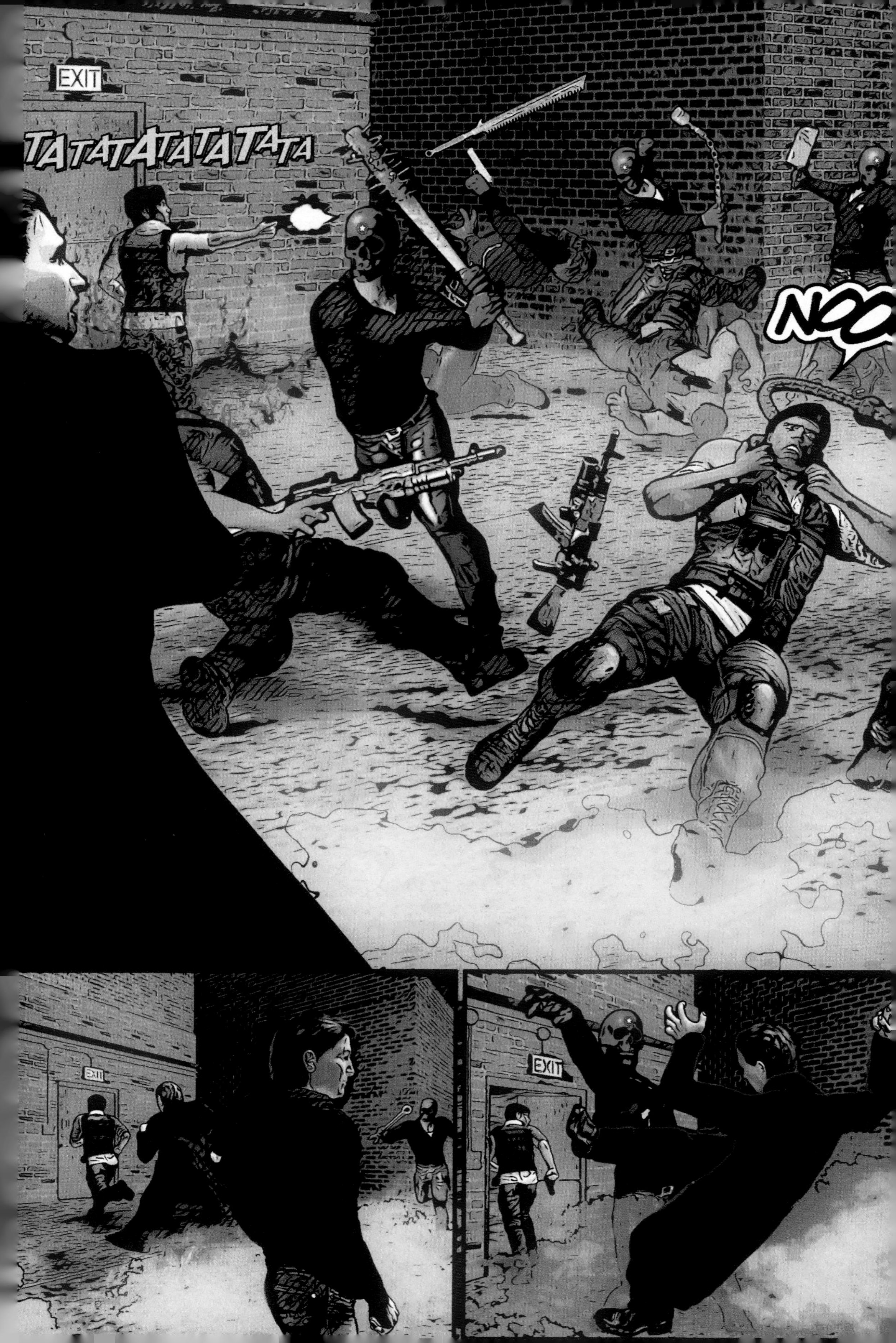
EXIT
TATATATATATATATA
NOO
EXIT
EXIT

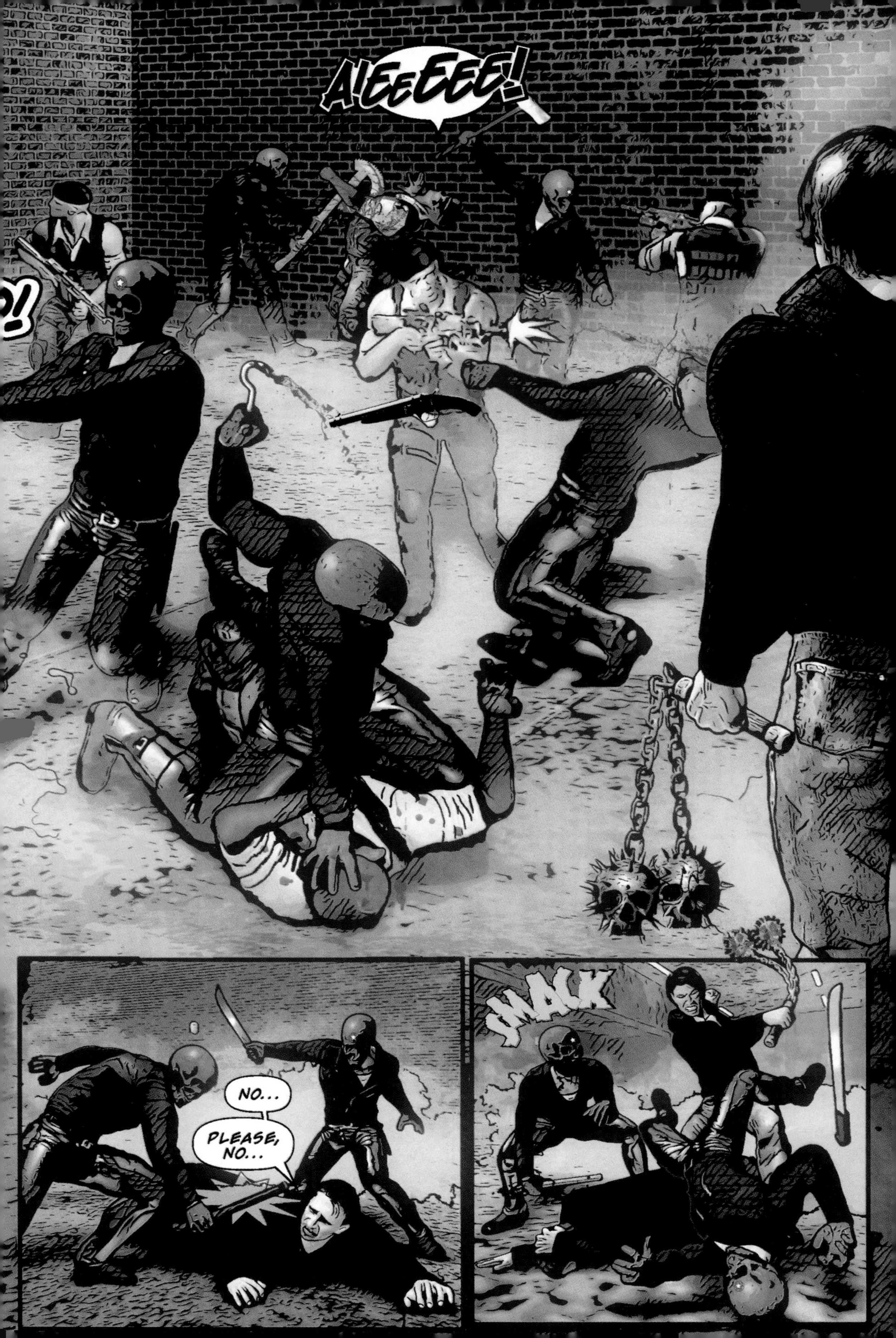
AIEEEEE!
NO...
PLEASE, NO...
SMACK

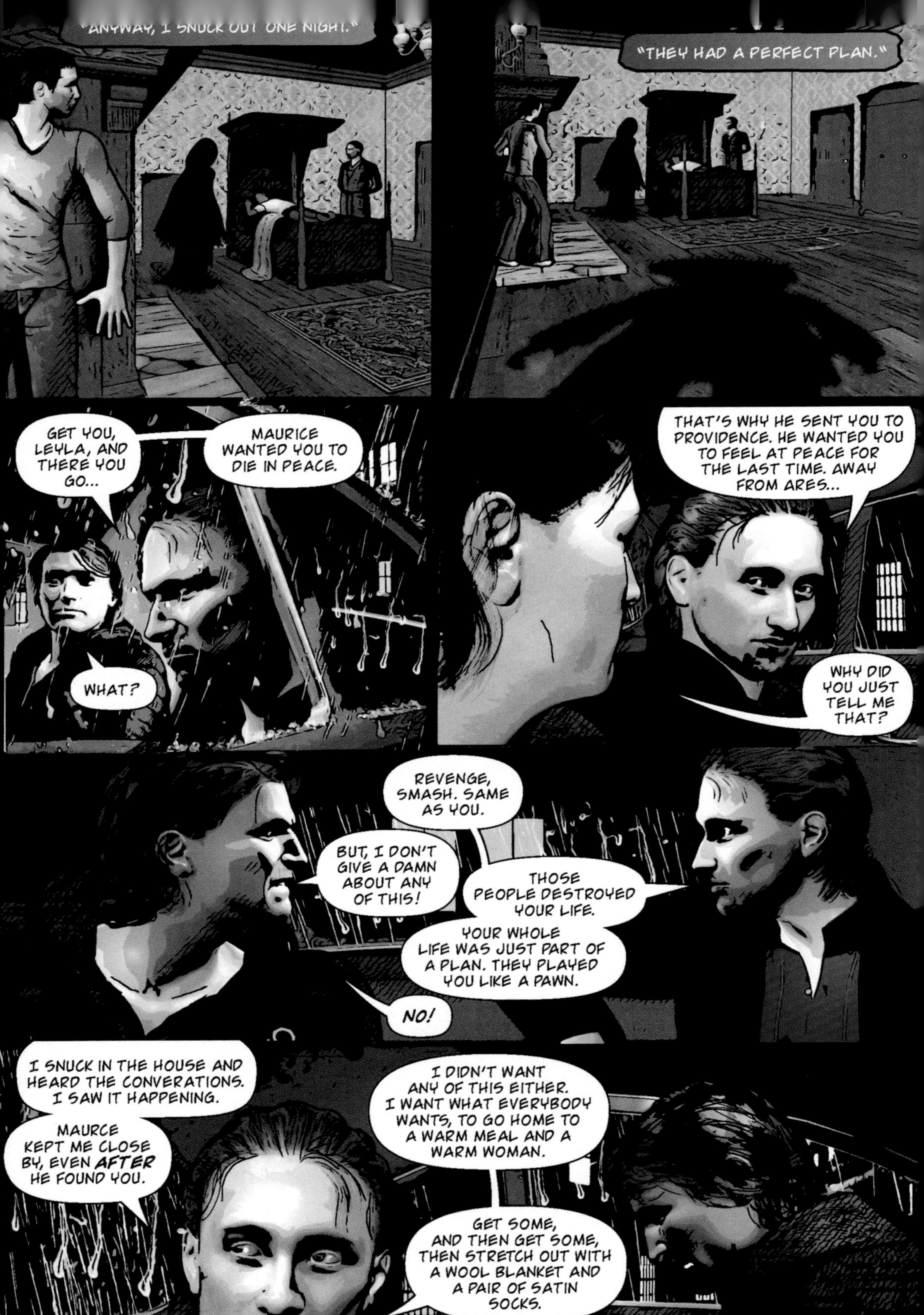
"ANYWAY, I SNUCK OUT ONE NIGHT."
"THEY HAD A PERFECT PLAN."
GET YOU, LEYLA, AND THERE YOU GO...
MAURICE WANTED YOU TO DIE IN PEACE.
WHAT?
THAT'S WHY HE SENT YOU TO PROVIDENCE. HE WANTED YOU TO FEEL AT PEACE FOR THE LAST TIME. AWAY FROM ARES...
WHY DID YOU JUST TELL ME THAT?
REVENGE, SMASH. SAME AS YOU.
BUT, I DON'T GIVE A DAMN ABOUT ANY OF THIS!
THOSE PEOPLE DESTROYED YOUR LIFE.
YOUR WHOLE LIFE WAS JUST PART OF A PLAN. THEY PLAYED YOU LIKE A PAWN.
NO!
I SNUCK IN THE HOUSE AND HEARD THE CONVERATIONS. I SAW IT HAPPENING.
MAURCE KEPT ME CLOSE BY, EVEN AFTER HE FOUND YOU.
I DIDN'T WANT ANY OF THIS EITHER. I WANT WHAT EVERYBODY WANTS, TO GO HOME TO A WARM MEAL AND A WARM WOMAN.
GET SOME, AND THEN GET SOME, THEN STRETCH OUT WITH A WOOL BLANKET AND A PAIR OF SATIN SOCKS.

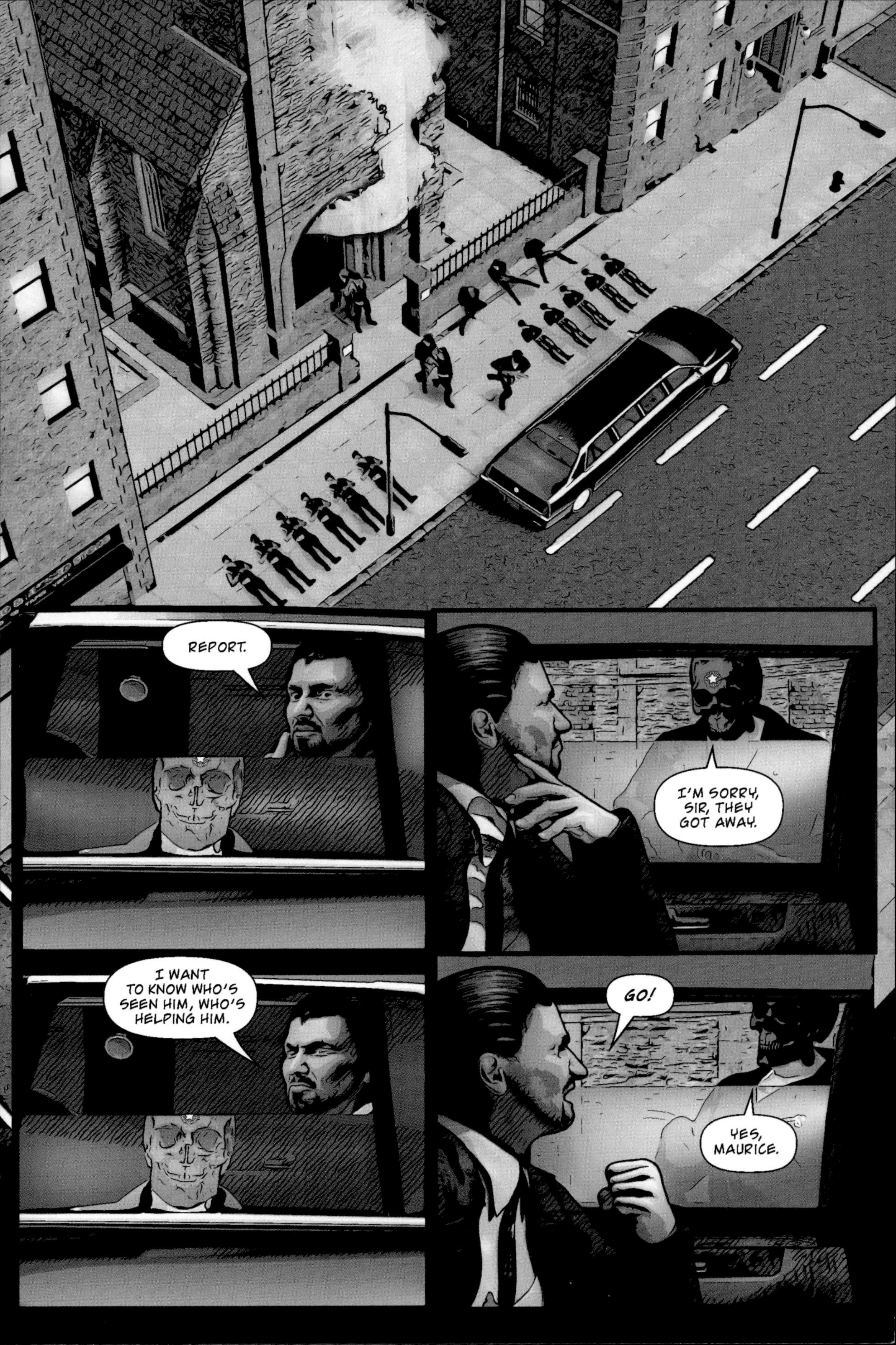
REPORT.
I'M SORRY, SIR, THEY GOT AWAY.
I WANT TO KNOW WHO'S SEEN HIM, WHO'S HELPING HIM.
GO!
YES, MAURICE.

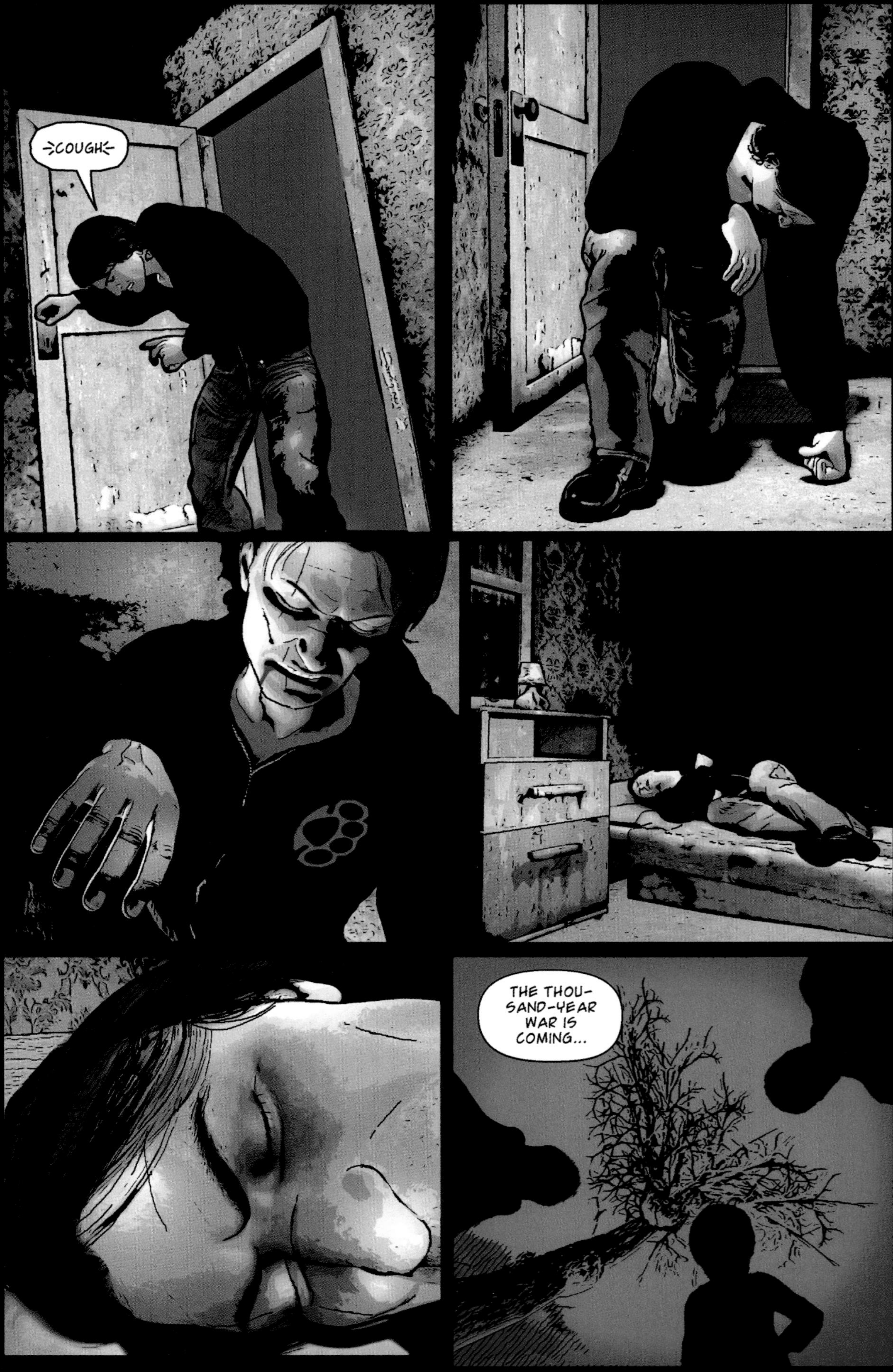
COUGH
THE THOUSAND-YEAR WAR IS COMING...

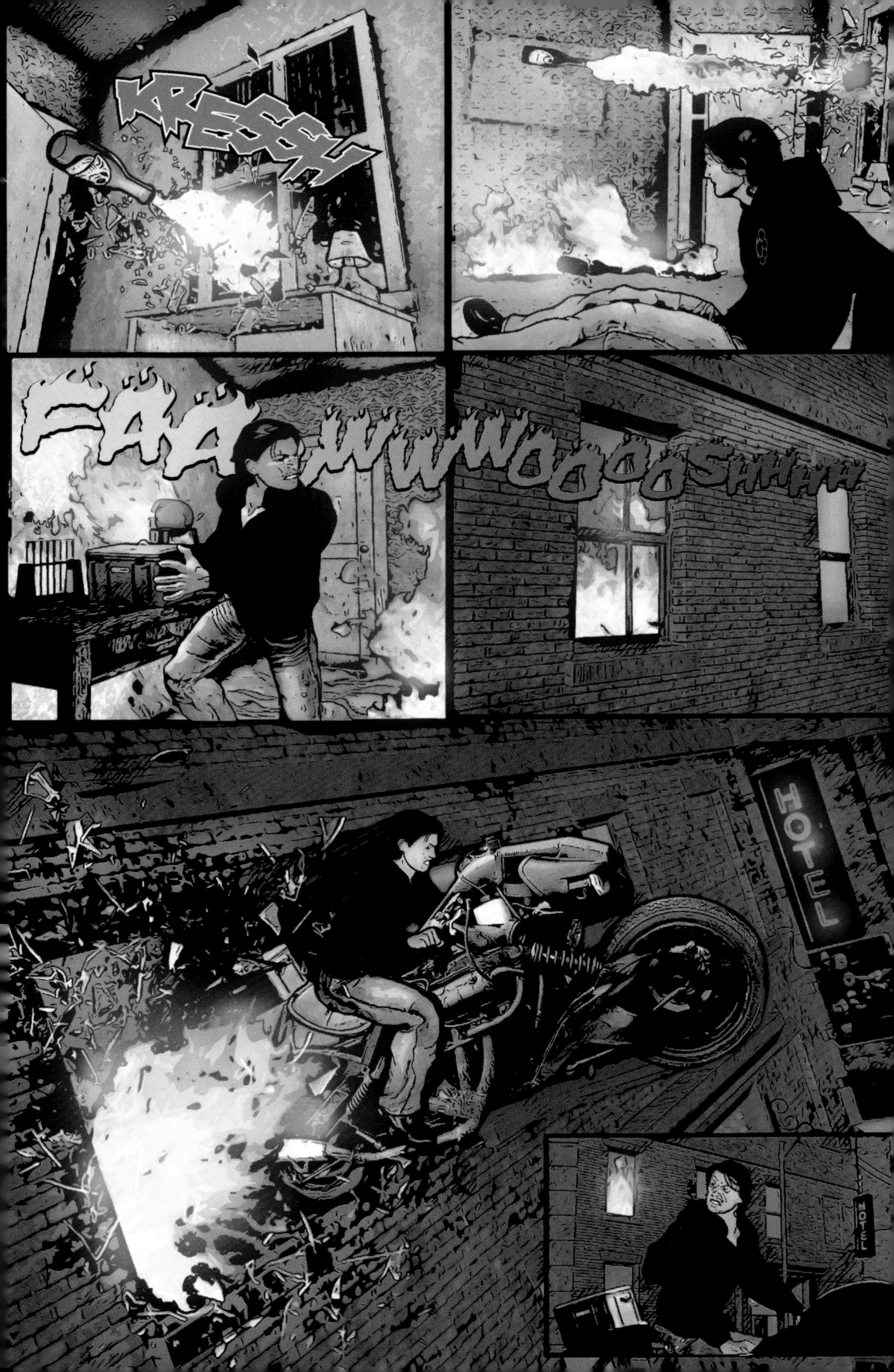
KRESSH
FAAWWWOOOOSHHHH
HOTEL
HOTEL

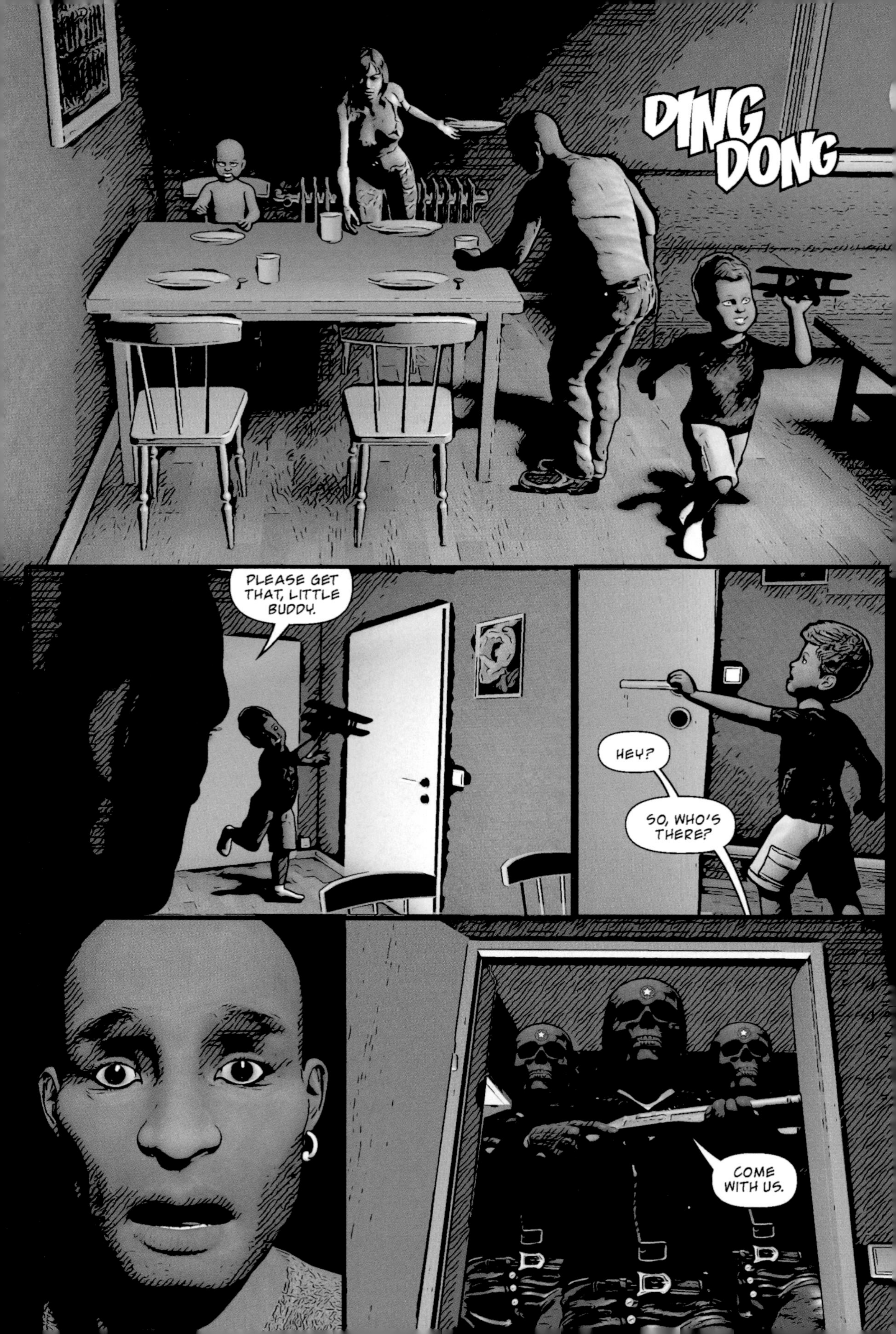
DING DONG
PLEASE GET THAT, LITTLE BUDDY.
HEY?
SO, WHO'S THERE?
COME WITH US.

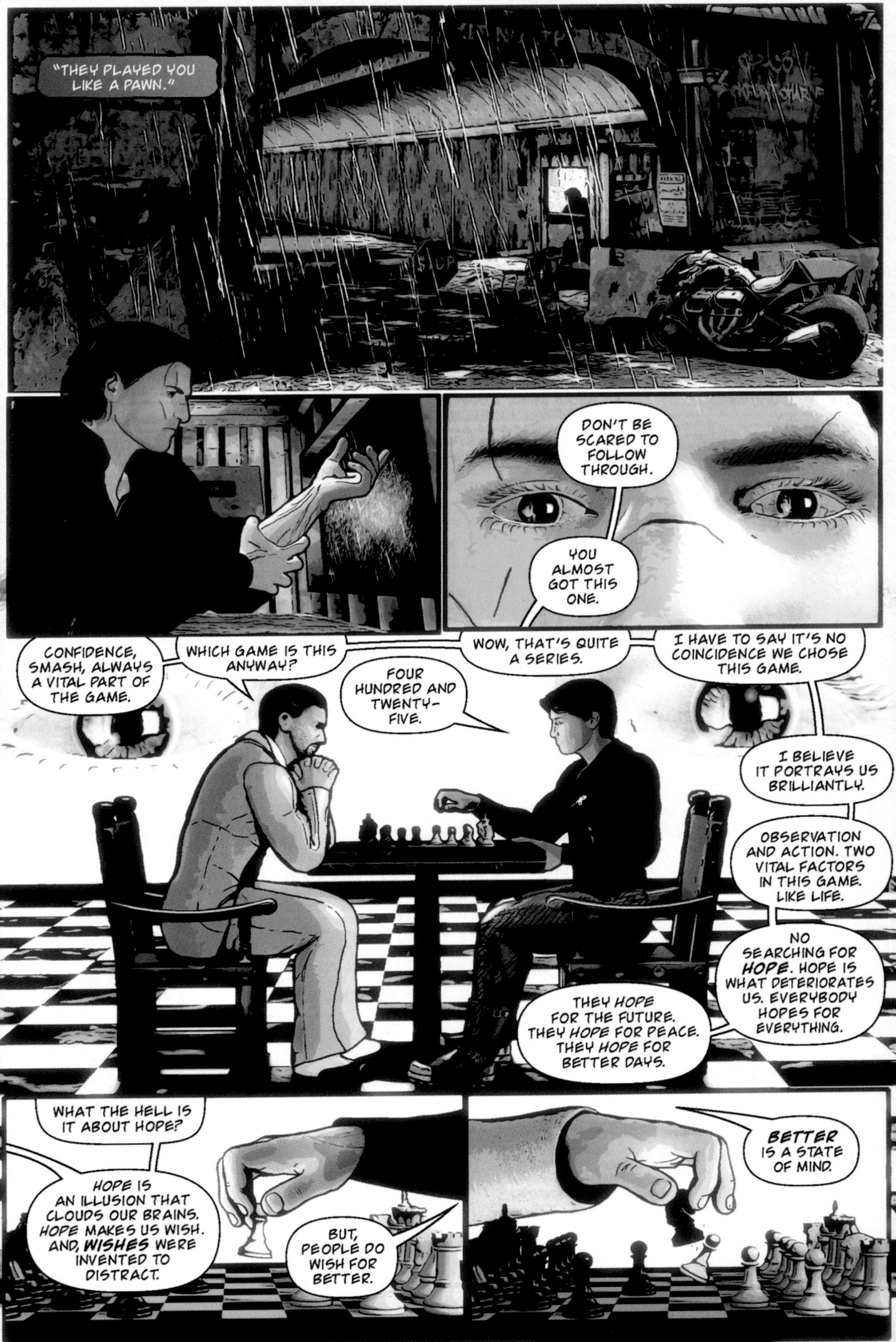
"THEY PLAYED YOU LIKE A PAWN."
DON'T BE SCARED TO FOLLOW THROUGH.
YOU ALMOST GOT THIS ONE.
CONFIDENCE, SMASH, ALWAYS A VITAL PART OF THE GAME.
WHICH GAME IS THIS ANYWAY?
FOUR HUNDRED AND TWENTY-FIVE.
WOW, THAT'S QUITE A SERIES.
I HAVE TO SAY IT'S NO COINCIDENCE WE CHOSE THIS GAME.
I BELIEVE IT PORTRAYS US BRILLIANTLY.
OBSERVATION AND ACTION. TWO VITAL FACTORS IN THIS GAME. LIKE LIFE.
NO SEARCHING FOR HOPE. HOPE IS WHAT DETERIORATES US. EVERYBODY HOPES FOR EVERYTHING.
THEY HOPE FOR THE FUTURE. THEY HOPE FOR PEACE. THEY HOPE FOR BETTER DAYS.
WHAT THE HELL IS IT ABOUT HOPE?
HOPE IS AN ILLUSION THAT CLOUDS OUR BRAINS. HOPE MAKES US WISH. AND, WISHES WERE INVENTED TO DISTRACT.
BUT, PEOPLE DO WISH FOR BETTER.
BETTER IS A STATE OF MIND.

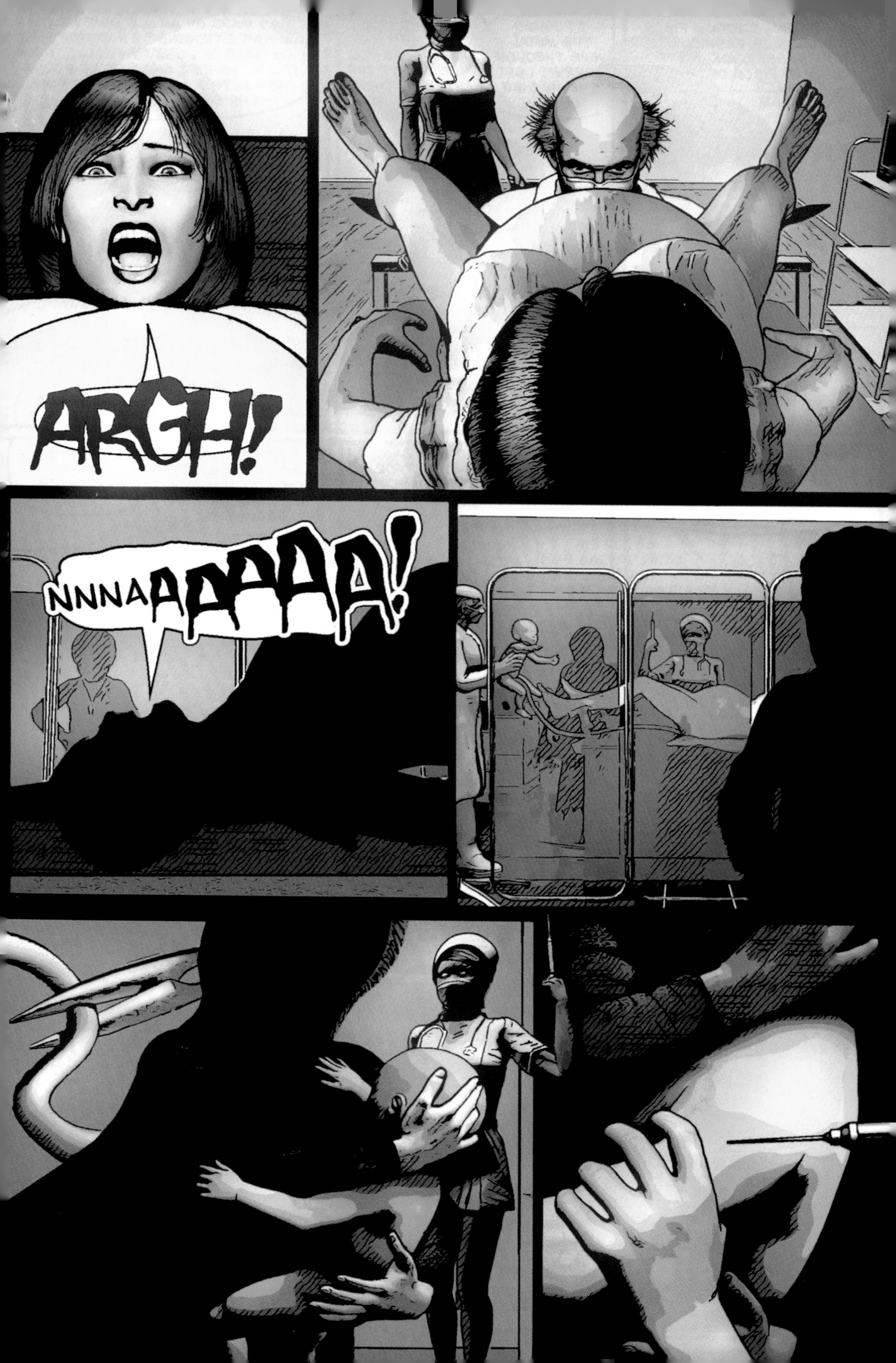
ARGH!
NNNAAAAAA!

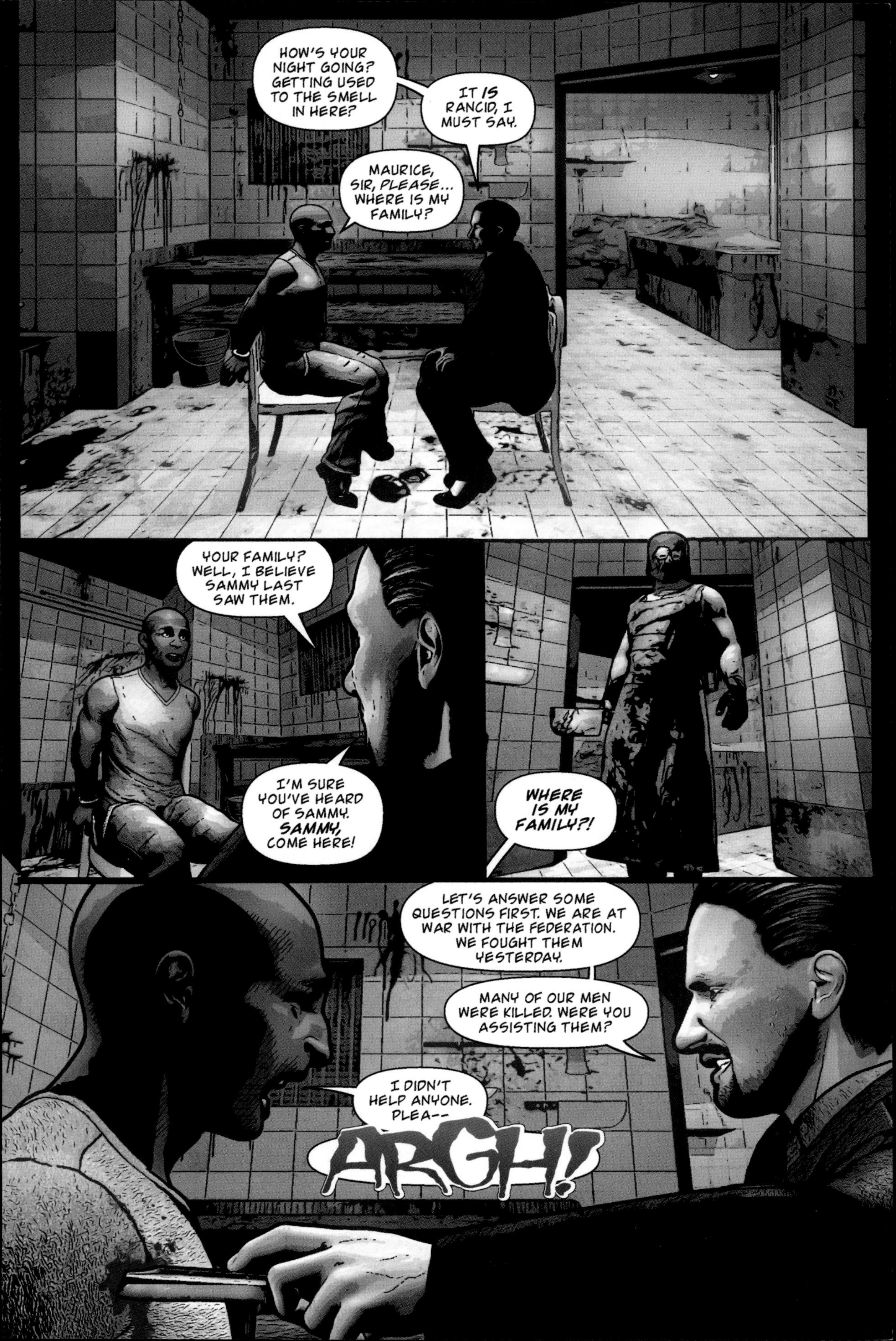
HOW'S YOUR NIGHT GOING? GETTING USED TO THE SMELL IN HERE?
IT *IS* RANCID, I MUST SAY.
MAURICE, SIR, *PLEASE*... WHERE IS MY FAMILY?
YOUR FAMILY? WELL, I BELIEVE SAMMY LAST SAW THEM.
I'M SURE YOU'VE HEARD OF SAMMY. **SAMMY,** COME HERE!
WHERE IS MY FAMILY?!
LET'S ANSWER SOME QUESTIONS FIRST. WE ARE AT WAR WITH THE FEDERATION. WE FOUGHT THEM YESTERDAY.
MANY OF OUR MEN WERE KILLED. WERE YOU ASSISTING THEM?
I DIDN'T HELP ANYONE. PLEA--
ARGH!

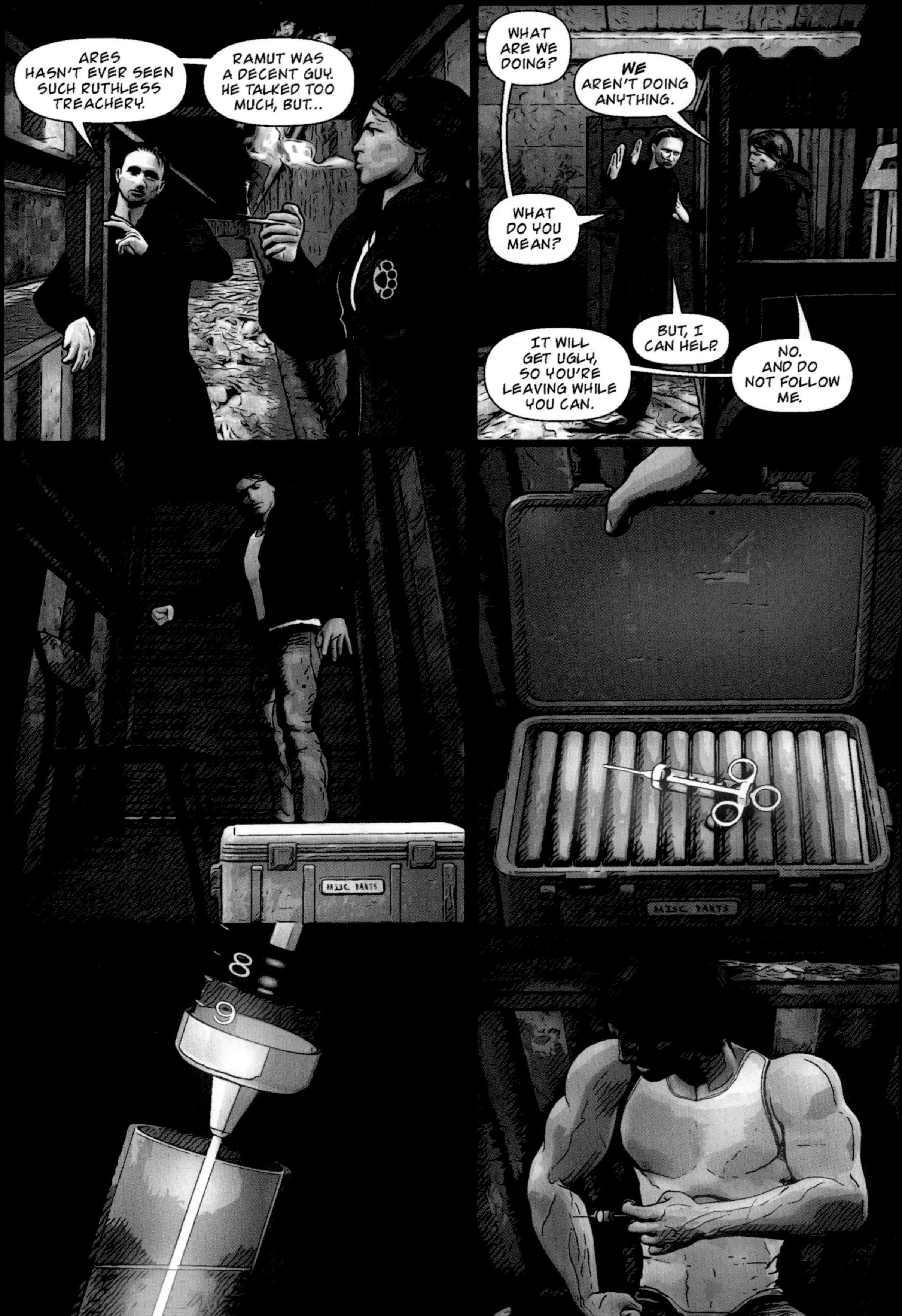

ARES HASN'T EVER SEEN SUCH RUTHLESS TREACHERY.
RAMUT WAS A DECENT GUY. HE TALKED TOO MUCH, BUT...
WHAT ARE WE DOING?
WE AREN'T DOING ANYTHING.
WHAT DO YOU MEAN?
BUT, I CAN HELP.
IT WILL GET UGLY, SO YOU'RE LEAVING WHILE YOU CAN.
NO. AND DO NOT FOLLOW ME.
MISC. PARTS
MISC. PARTS

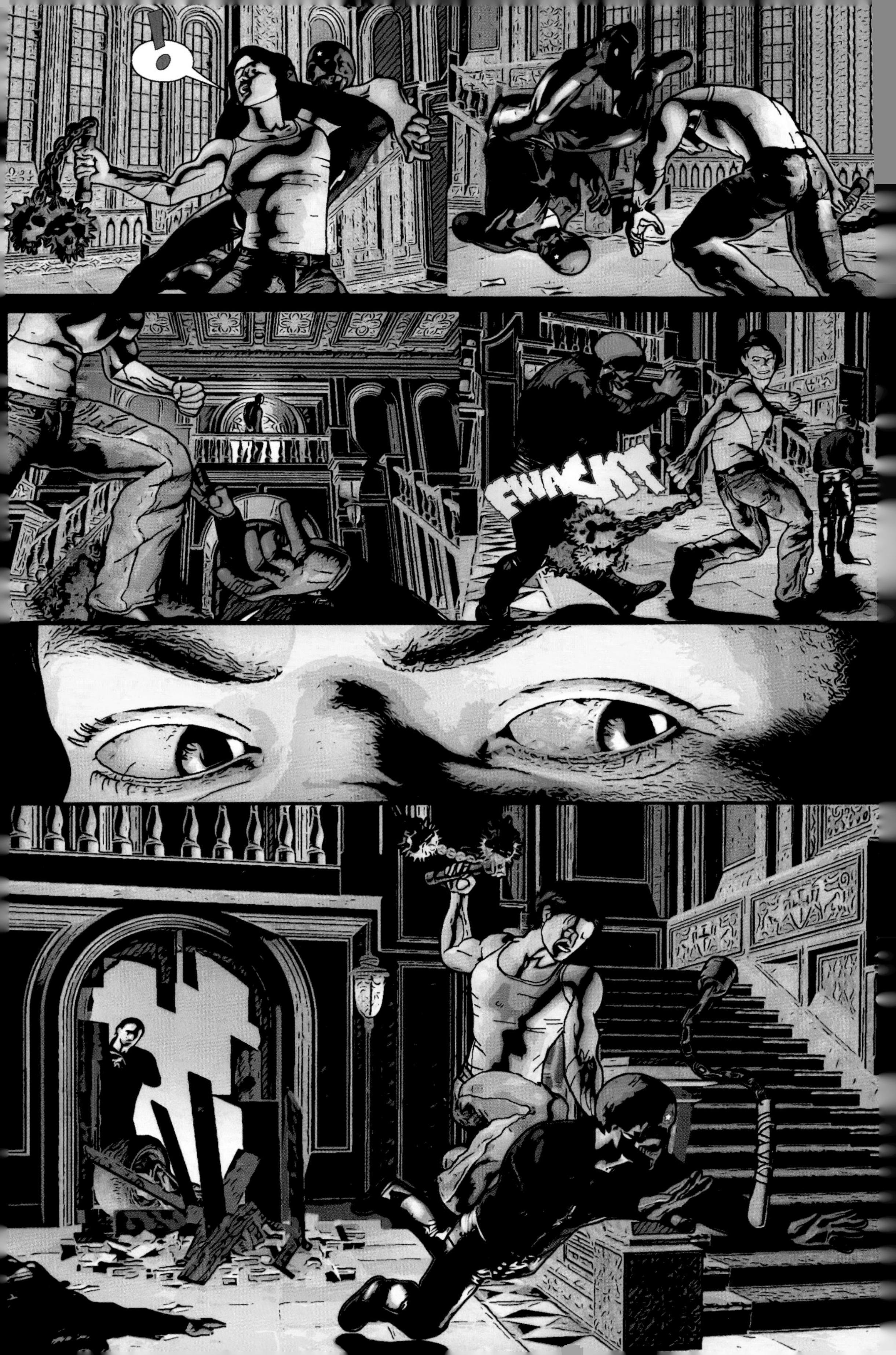
!
FWAKT

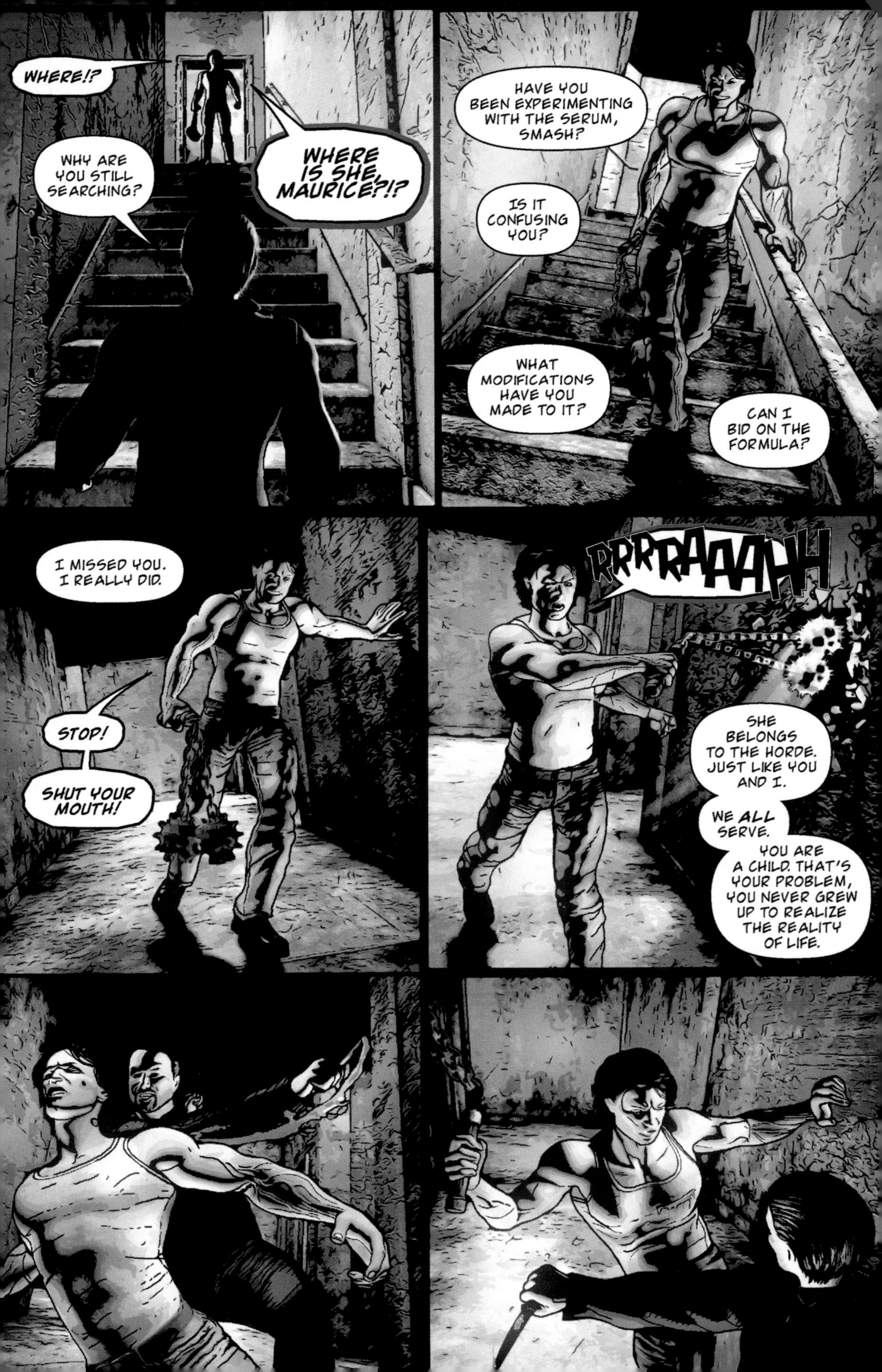
WHERE!?
WHY ARE YOU STILL SEARCHING?
WHERE IS SHE, MAURICE?!?
HAVE YOU BEEN EXPERIMENTING WITH THE SERUM, SMASH?
IS IT CONFUSING YOU?
WHAT MODIFICATIONS HAVE YOU MADE TO IT?
CAN I BID ON THE FORMULA?
I MISSED YOU. I REALLY DID.
STOP!
SHUT YOUR MOUTH!
RRRRAAAAHH
SHE BELONGS TO THE HORDE. JUST LIKE YOU AND I.
WE ALL SERVE.
YOU ARE A CHILD. THAT'S YOUR PROBLEM, YOU NEVER GREW UP TO REALIZE THE REALITY OF LIFE.

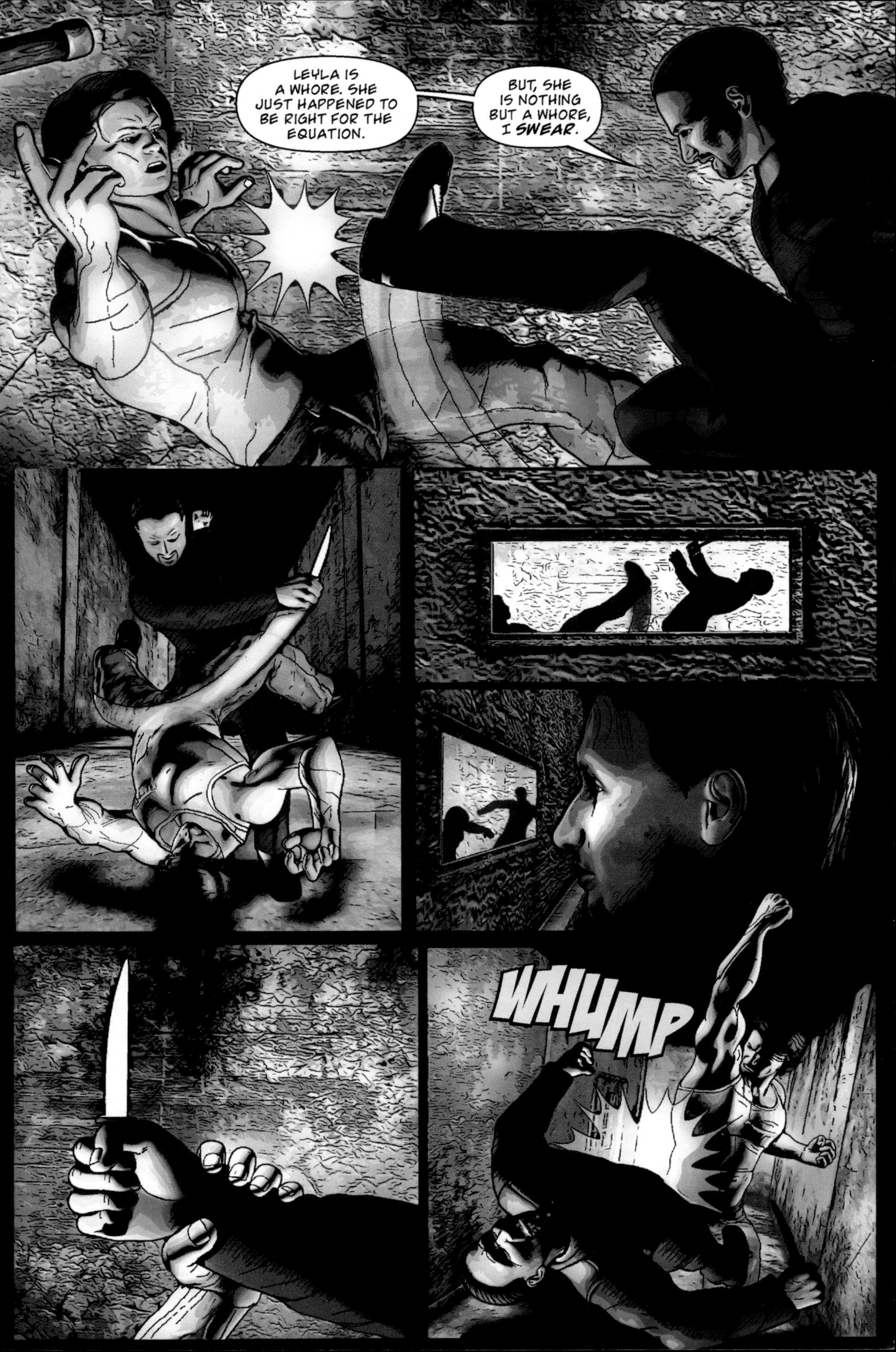
LEYLA IS A WHORE. SHE JUST HAPPENED TO BE RIGHT FOR THE EQUATION.
BUT, SHE IS NOTHING BUT A WHORE, I SWEAR.
WHUMP

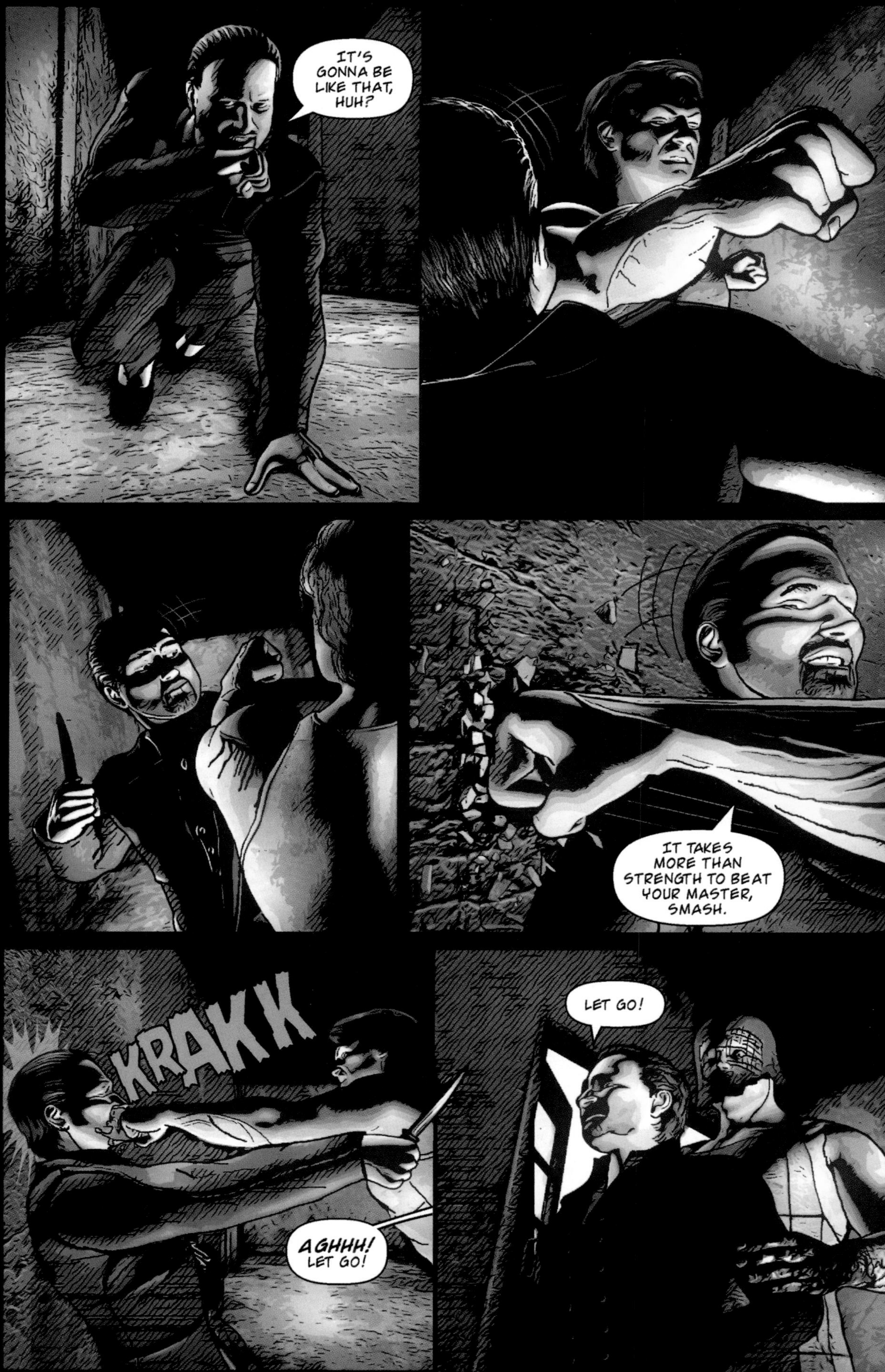
IT'S GONNA BE LIKE THAT, HUH?
IT TAKES MORE THAN STRENGTH TO BEAT YOUR MASTER, SMASH.
KRAKK
AGHHH! LET GO!
LET GO!

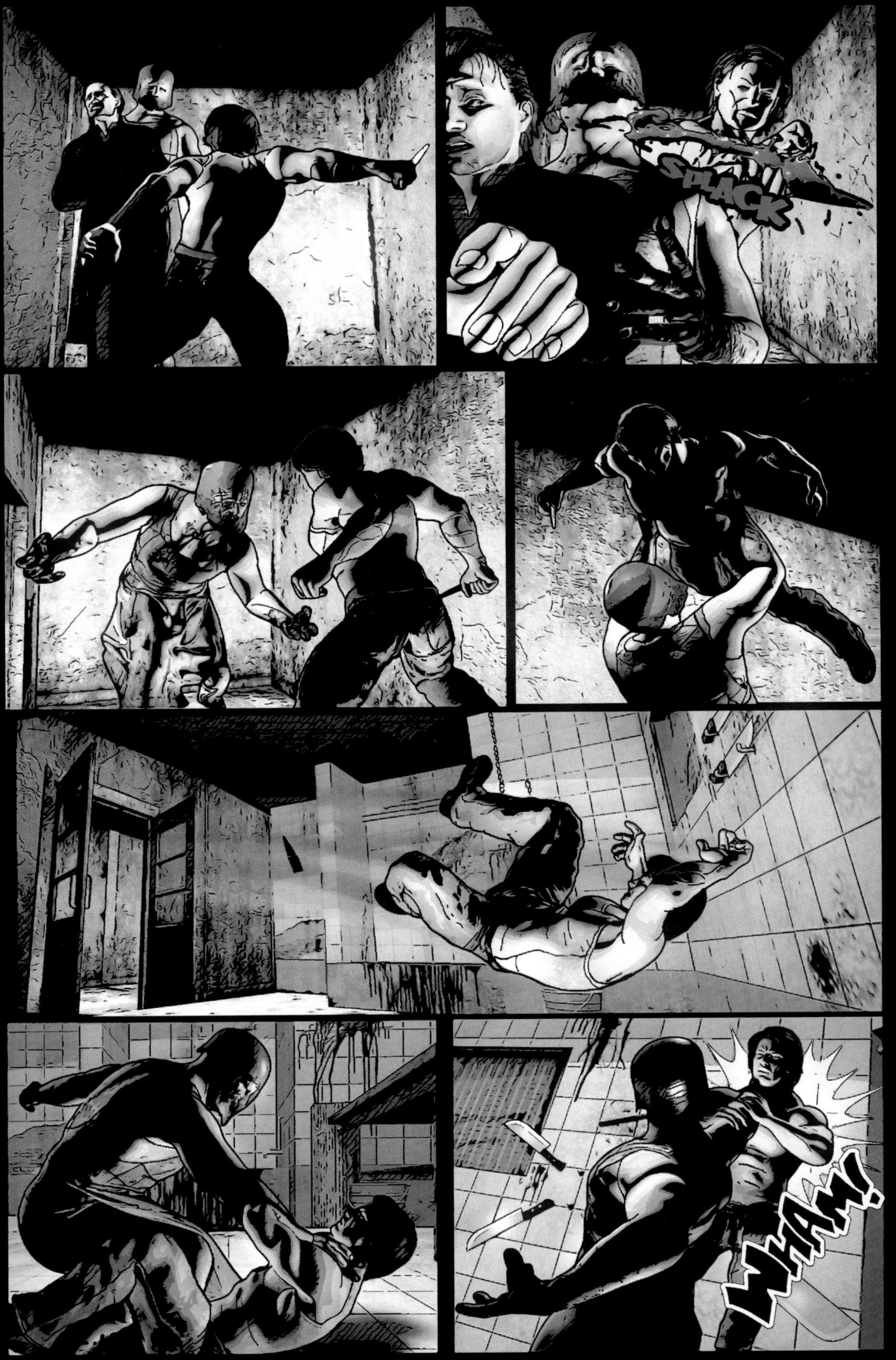
SPLACK
WHAM!

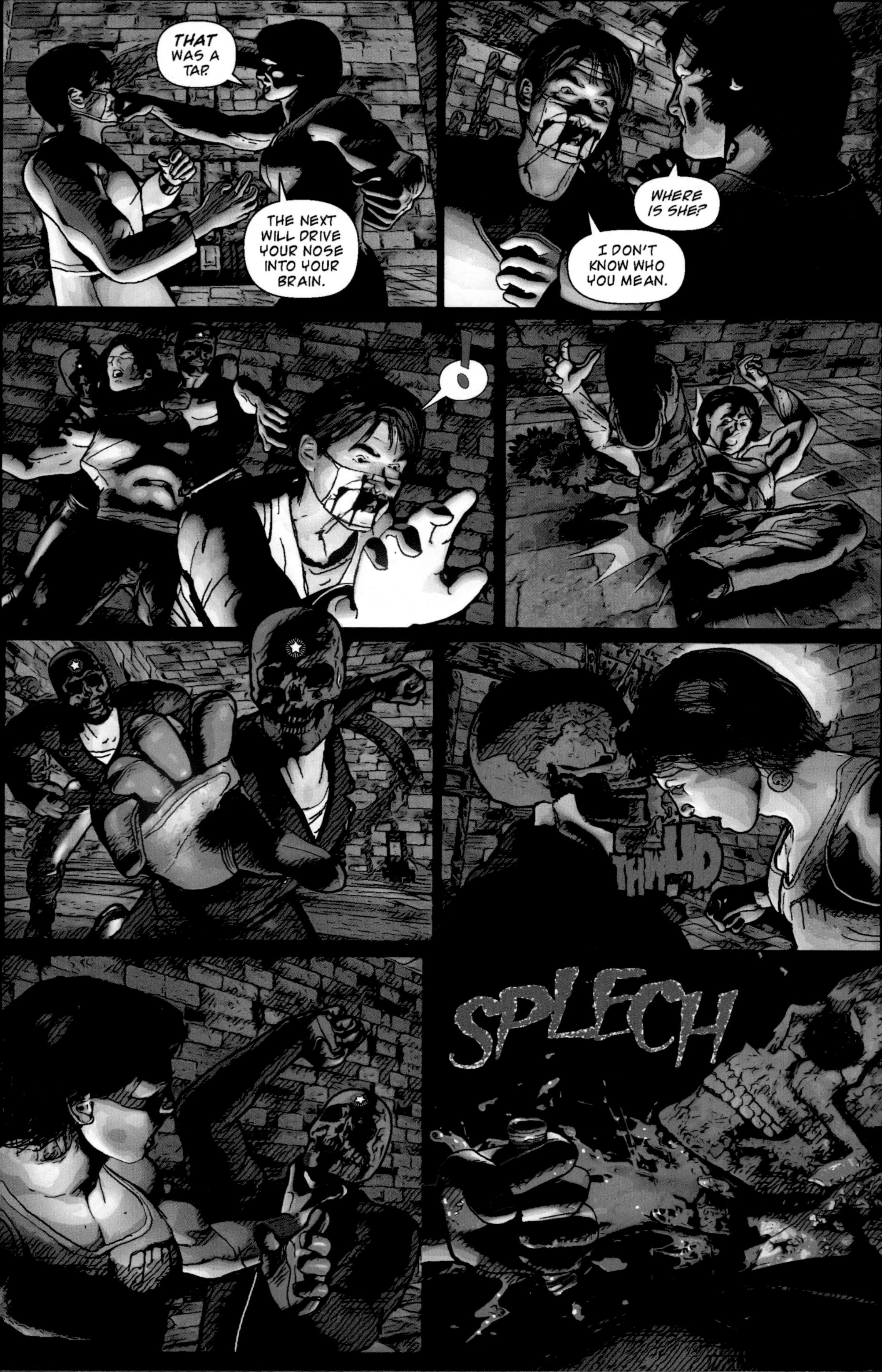
THAT WAS A TAP.
THE NEXT WILL DRIVE YOUR NOSE INTO YOUR BRAIN.
WHERE IS SHE?
I DON'T KNOW WHO YOU MEAN.
!
SPLECH

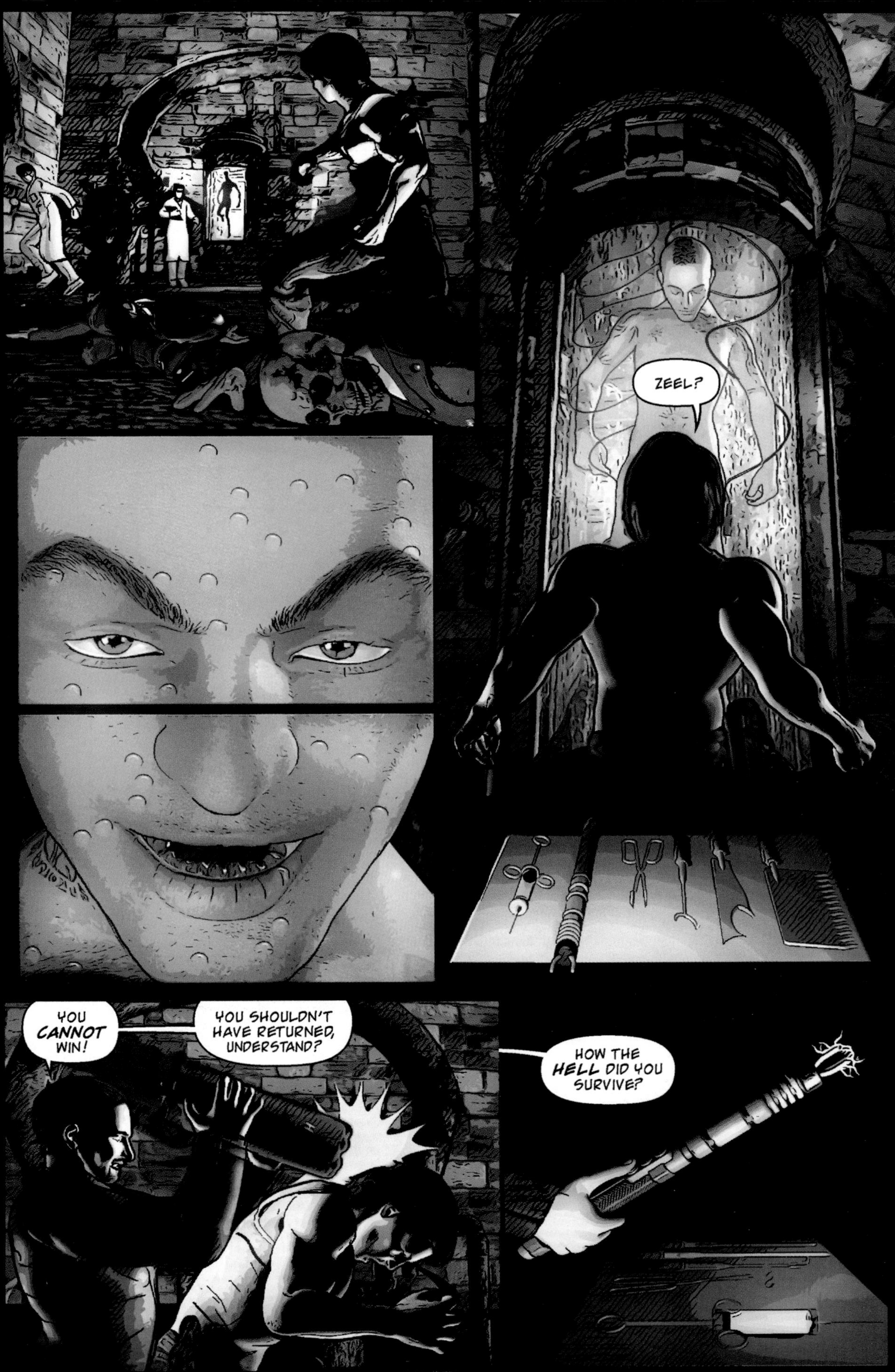
ZEEL?
YOU CANNOT WIN!
YOU SHOULDN'T HAVE RETURNED, UNDERSTAND?
HOW THE HELL DID YOU SURVIVE?

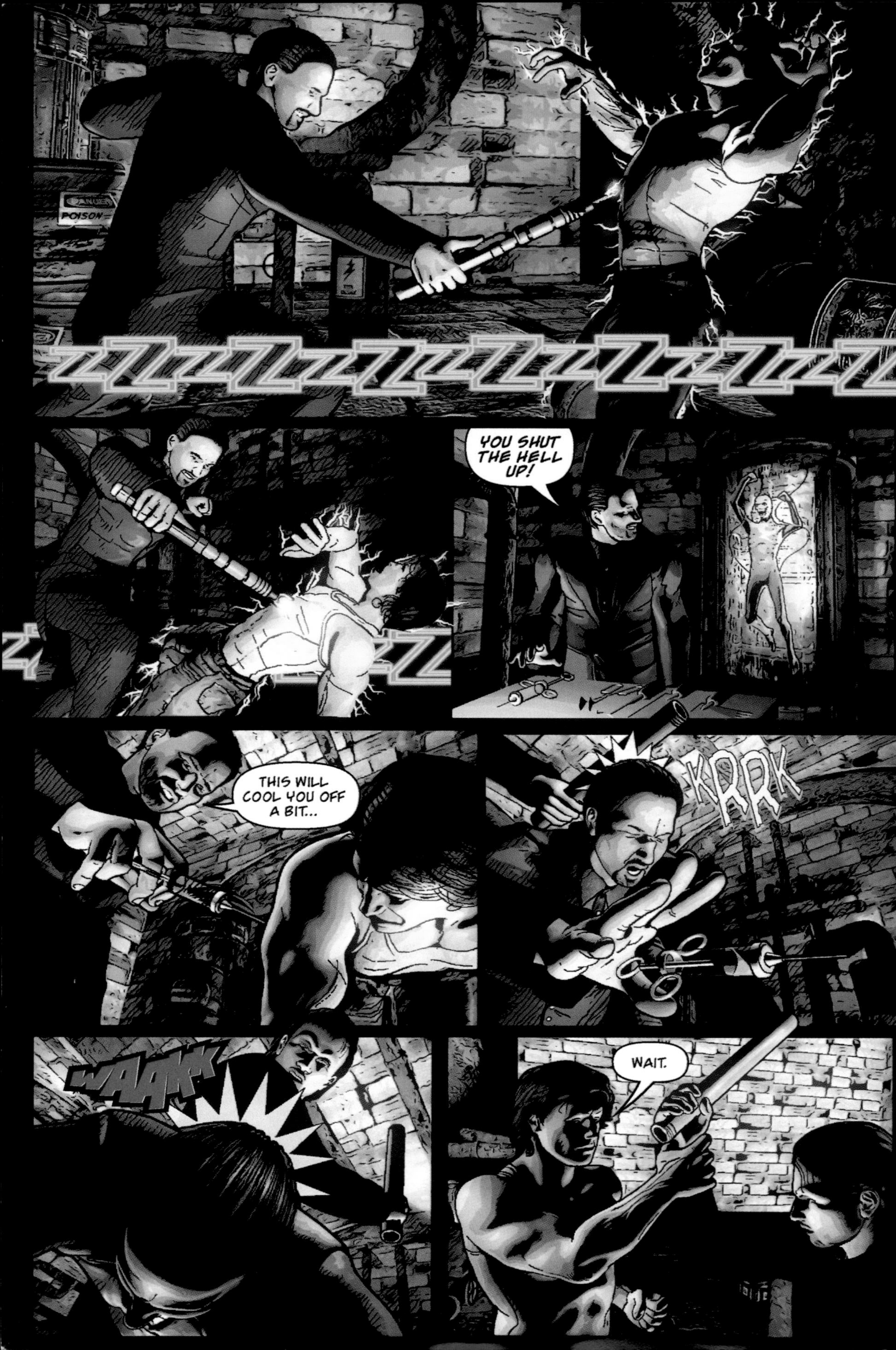
DANGER
POISON
YOU SHUT THE HELL UP!
THIS WILL COOL YOU OFF A BIT...
KRRK
WAAKK
WAIT.

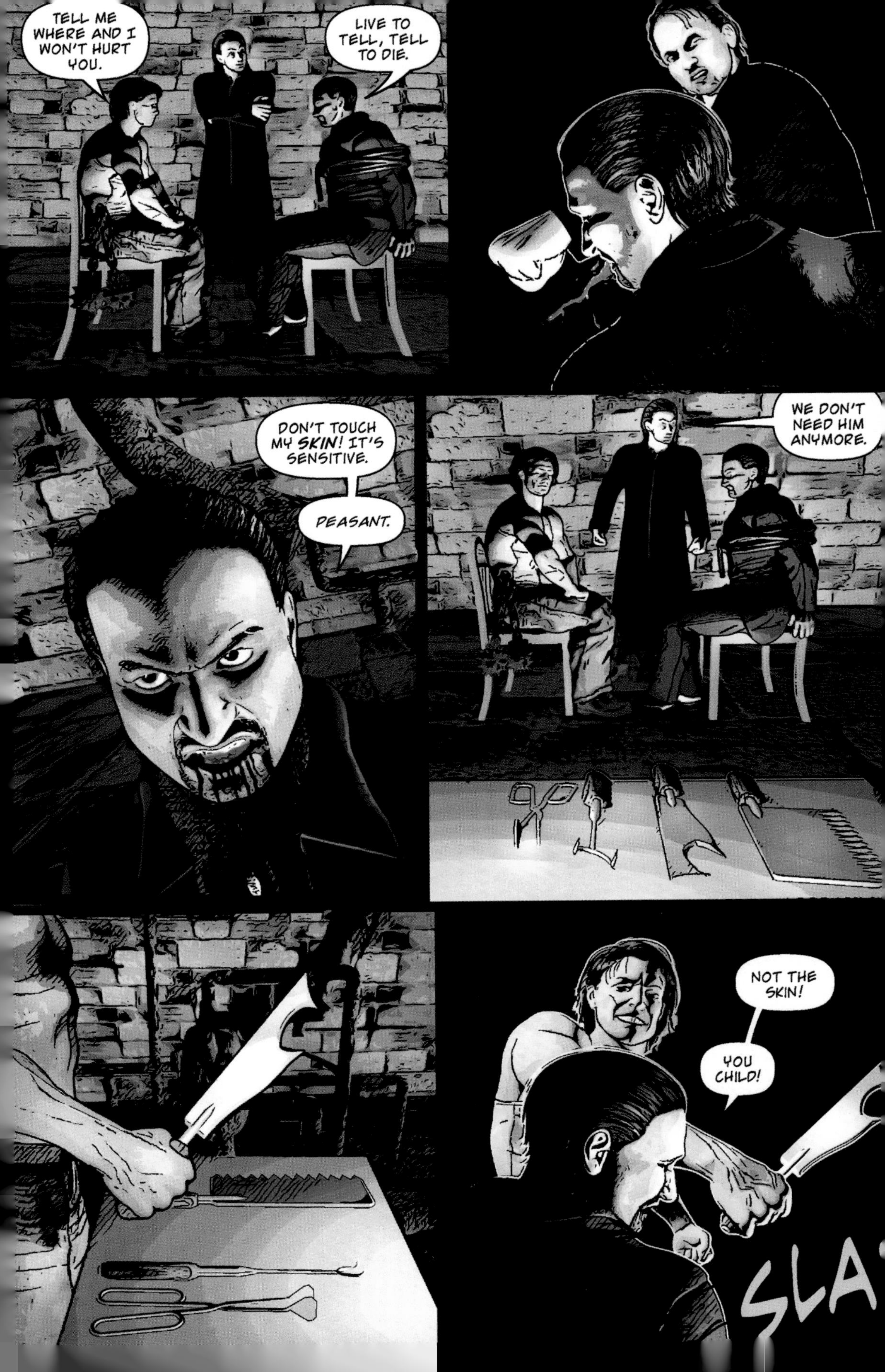
TELL ME WHERE AND I WON'T HURT YOU.
LIVE TO TELL, TELL TO DIE.
DON'T TOUCH MY SKIN! IT'S SENSITIVE.
PEASANT.
WE DON'T NEED HIM ANYMORE.
NOT THE SKIN!
YOU CHILD!
SLA

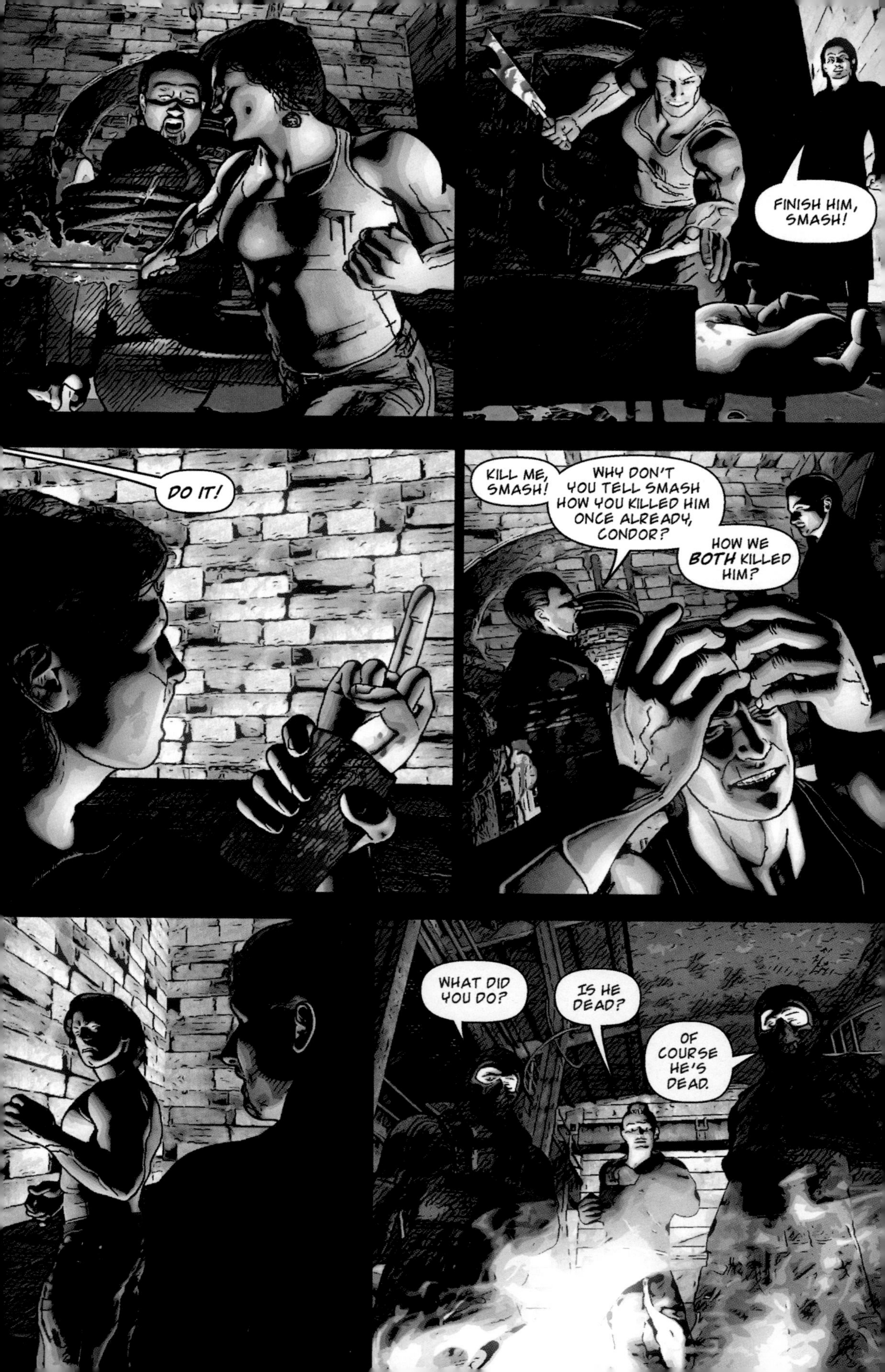
FINISH HIM, SMASH!
DO IT!
KILL ME, SMASH!
WHY DON'T YOU TELL SMASH HOW YOU KILLED HIM ONCE ALREADY, CONDOR?
HOW WE BOTH KILLED HIM?
WHAT DID YOU DO?
IS HE DEAD?
OF COURSE HE'S DEAD.

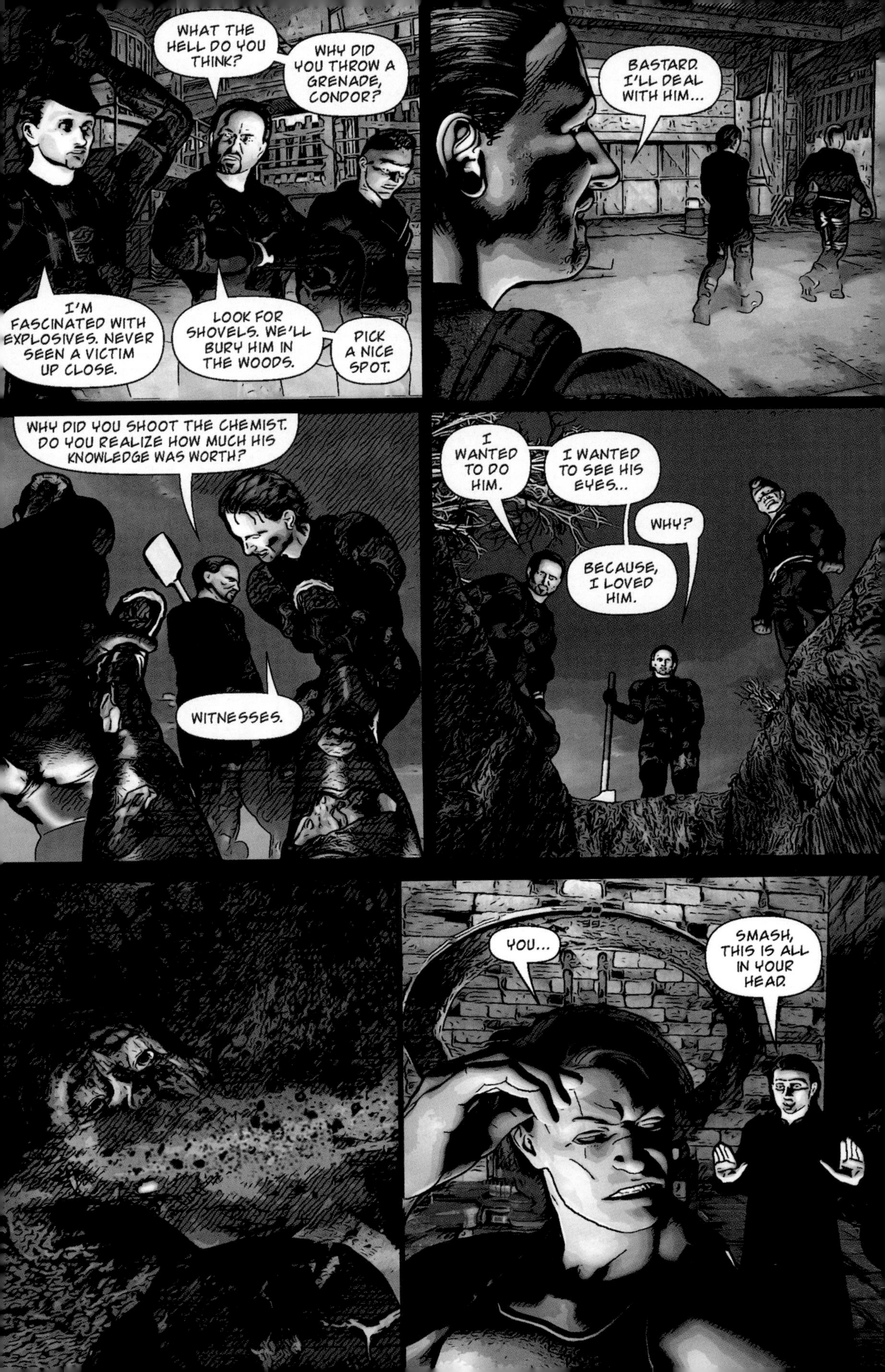
WHAT THE HELL DO YOU THINK?
WHY DID YOU THROW A GRENADE, CONDOR?
I'M FASCINATED WITH EXPLOSIVES. NEVER SEEN A VICTIM UP CLOSE.
LOOK FOR SHOVELS. WE'LL BURY HIM IN THE WOODS.
PICK A NICE SPOT.
BASTARD. I'LL DEAL WITH HIM...
WHY DID YOU SHOOT THE CHEMIST. DO YOU REALIZE HOW MUCH HIS KNOWLEDGE WAS WORTH?
WITNESSES.
I WANTED TO DO HIM.
I WANTED TO SEE HIS EYES...
WHY?
BECAUSE, I LOVED HIM.
YOU...
SMASH, THIS IS ALL IN YOUR HEAD.

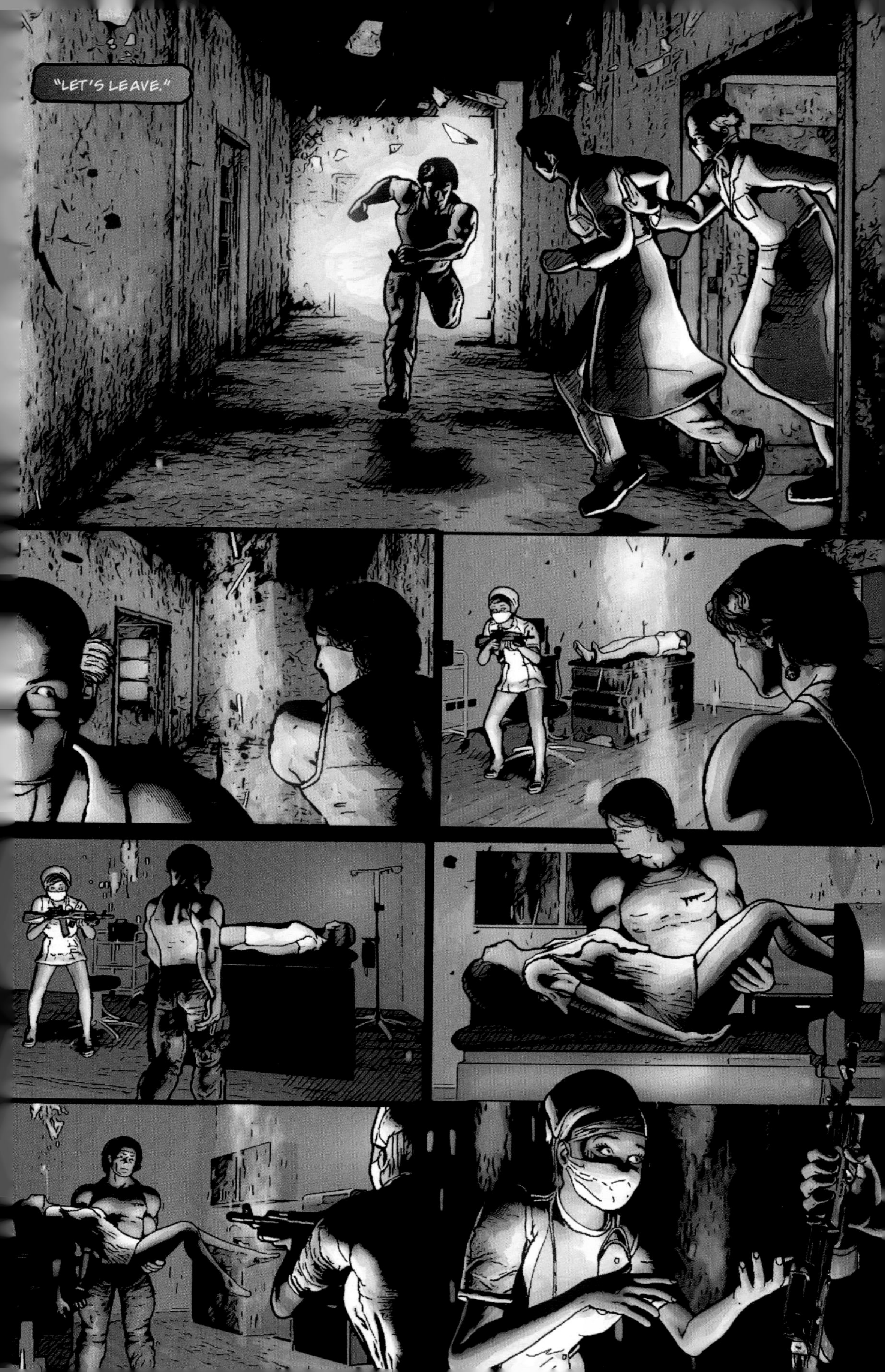
"LET'S LEAVE."

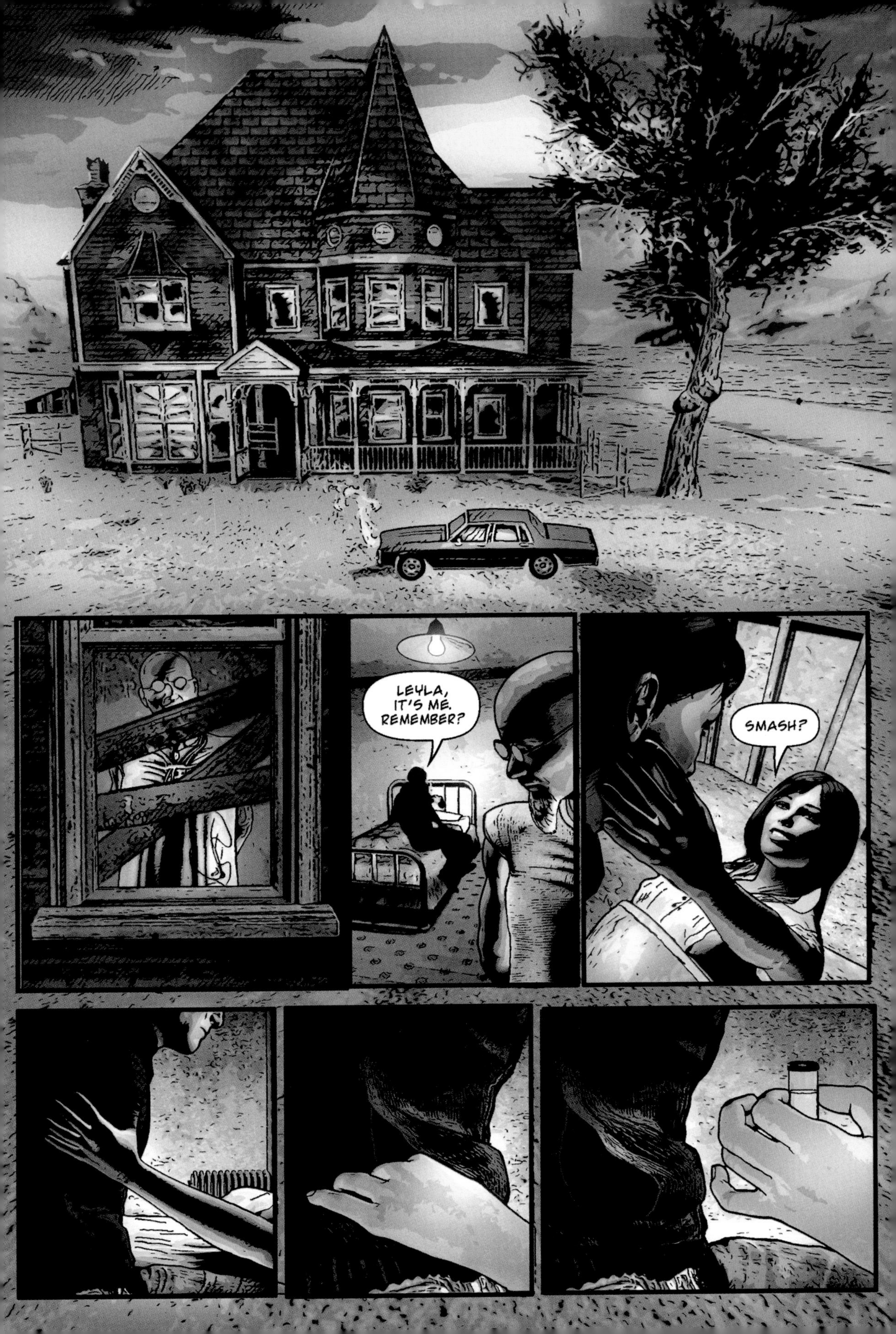
LEYLA, IT'S ME. REMEMBER?
SMASH?

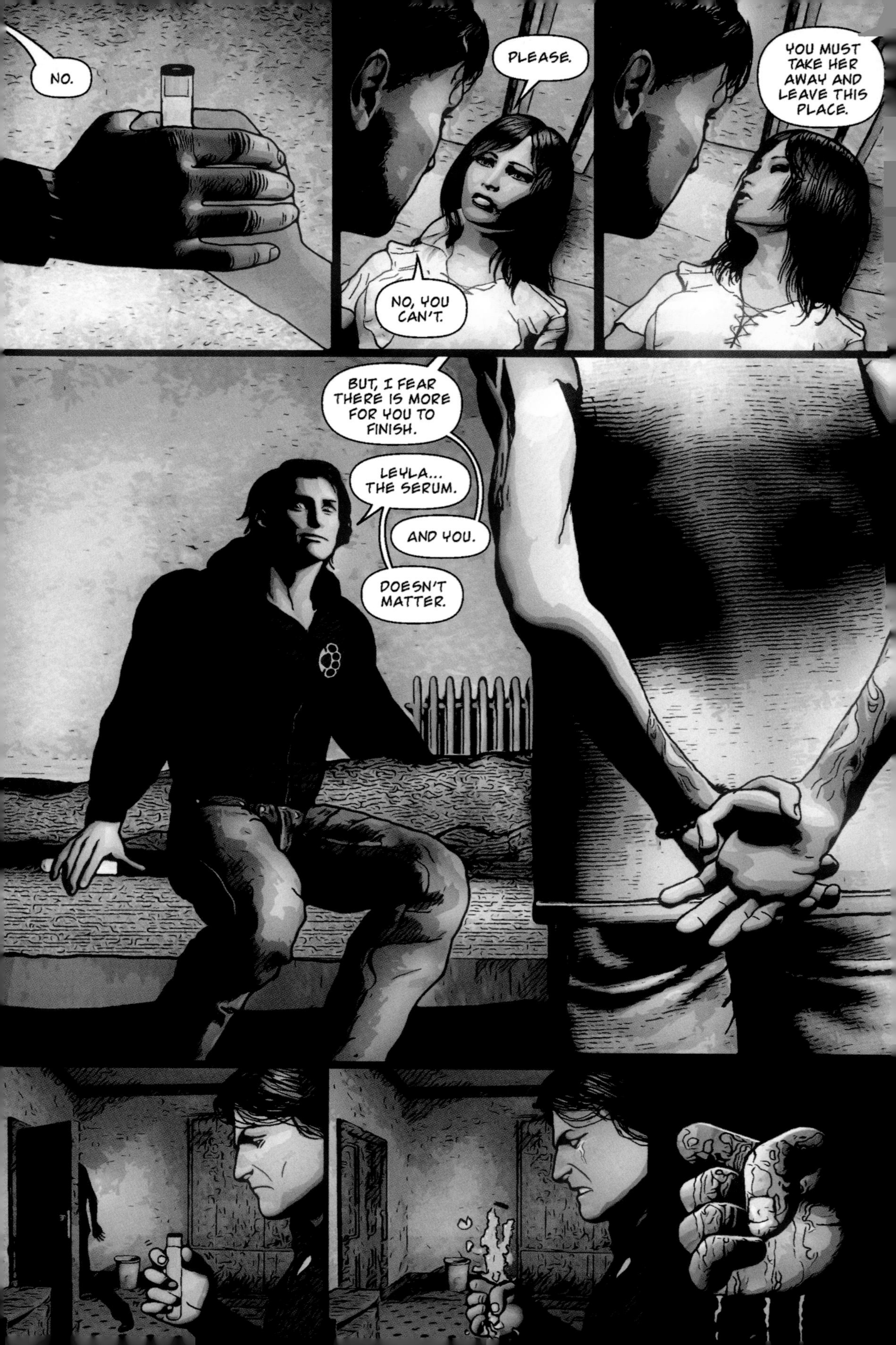
NO.
PLEASE.
NO, YOU CAN'T.
YOU MUST TAKE HER AWAY AND LEAVE THIS PLACE.
BUT, I FEAR THERE IS MORE FOR YOU TO FINISH.
LEYLA... THE SERUM.
AND YOU.
DOESN'T MATTER.

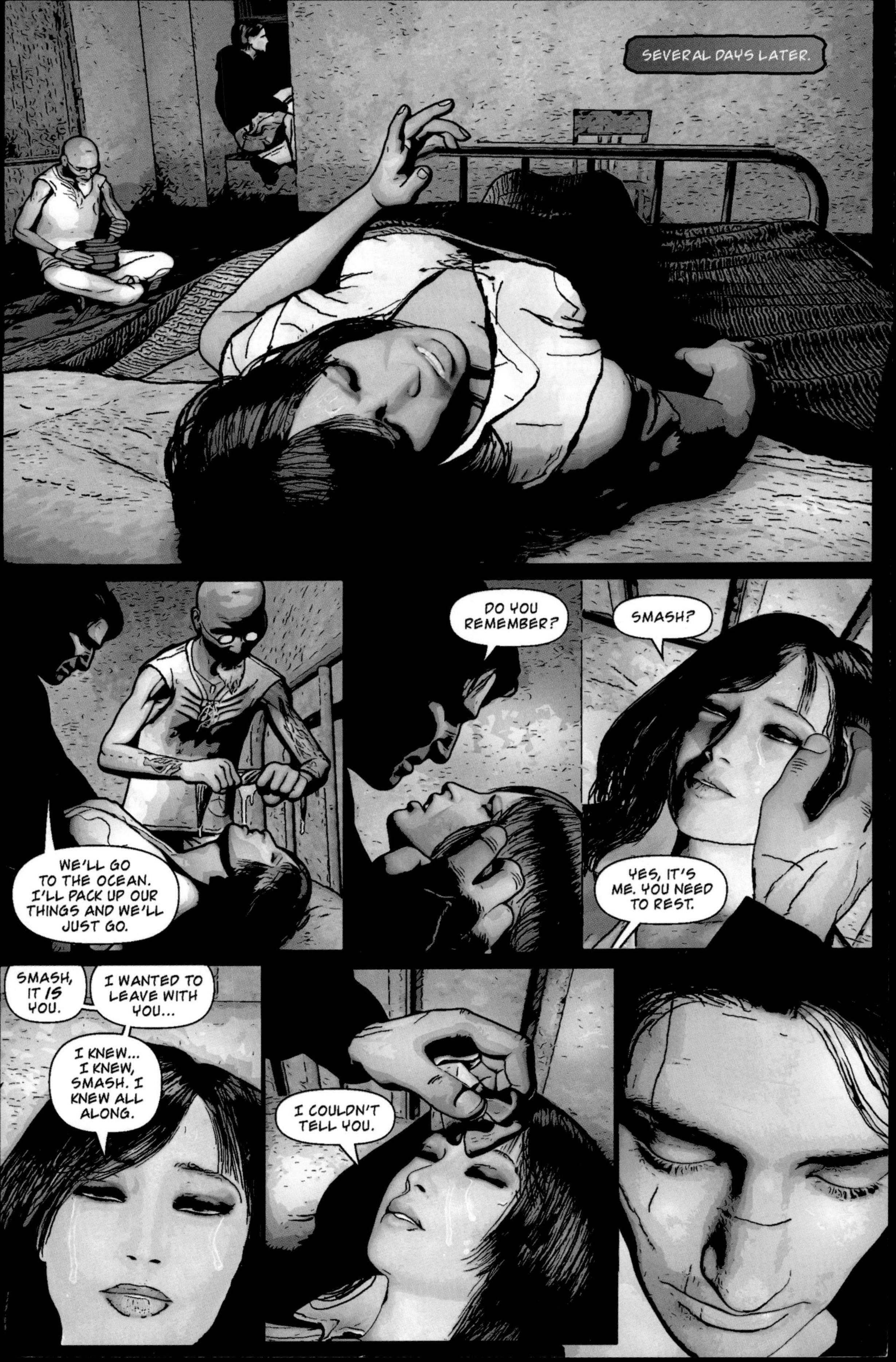
SEVERAL DAYS LATER.
WE'LL GO TO THE OCEAN. I'LL PACK UP OUR THINGS AND WE'LL JUST GO.
DO YOU REMEMBER?
SMASH?
YES, IT'S ME. YOU NEED TO REST.
SMASH, IT *IS* YOU.
I WANTED TO LEAVE WITH YOU...
I KNEW... I KNEW, SMASH. I KNEW ALL ALONG.
I COULDN'T TELL YOU.

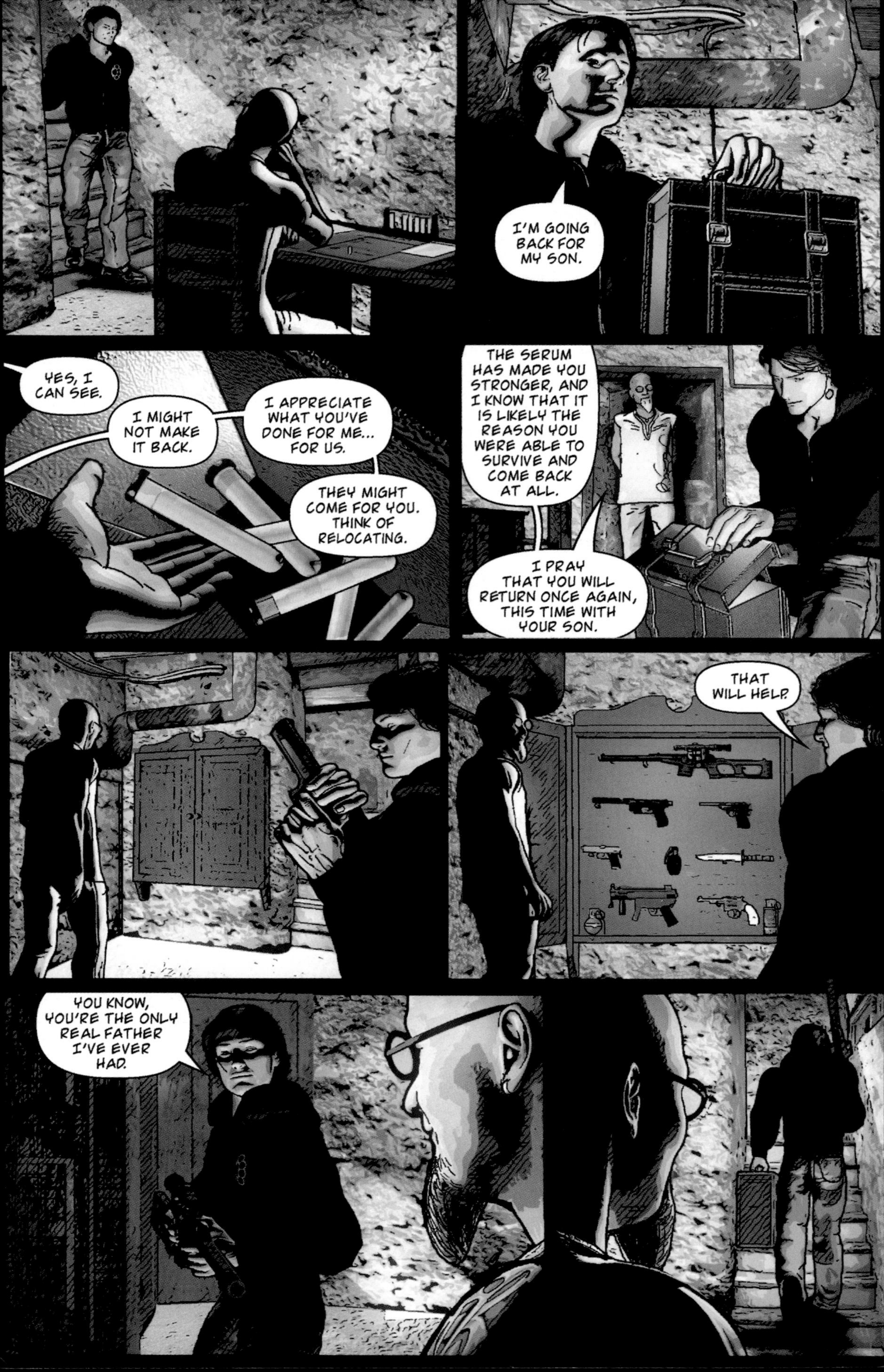
I'M GOING BACK FOR MY SON.
YES, I CAN SEE.
I MIGHT NOT MAKE IT BACK.
I APPRECIATE WHAT YOU'VE DONE FOR ME... FOR US.
THEY MIGHT COME FOR YOU. THINK OF RELOCATING.
THE SERUM HAS MADE YOU STRONGER, AND I KNOW THAT IT IS LIKELY THE REASON YOU WERE ABLE TO SURVIVE AND COME BACK AT ALL.
I PRAY THAT YOU WILL RETURN ONCE AGAIN, THIS TIME WITH YOUR SON.
THAT WILL HELP.
YOU KNOW, YOU'RE THE ONLY REAL FATHER I'VE EVER HAD.

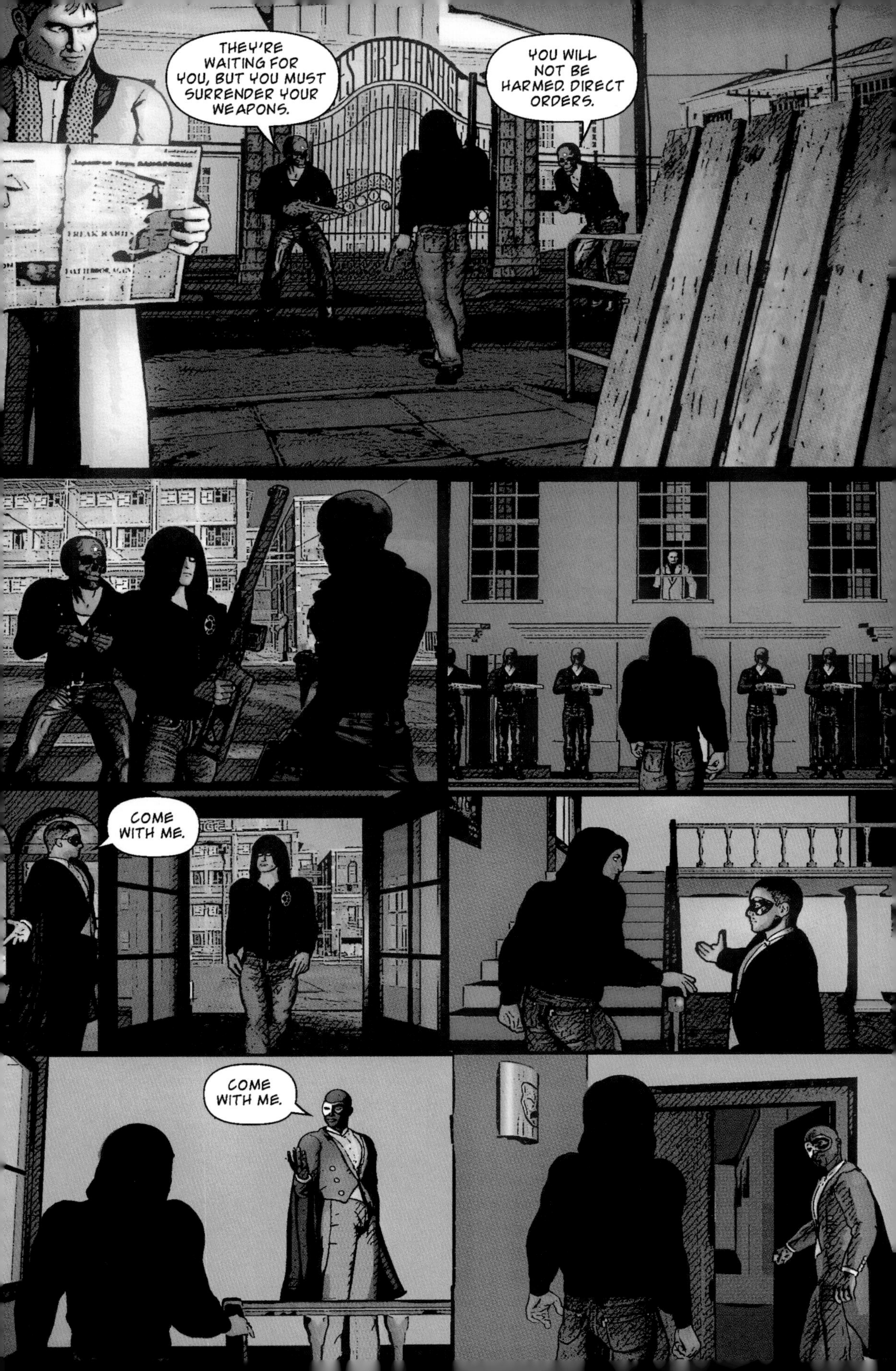
THEY'RE WAITING FOR YOU, BUT YOU MUST SURRENDER YOUR WEAPONS.
YOU WILL NOT BE HARMED. DIRECT ORDERS.
COME WITH ME.
COME WITH ME.

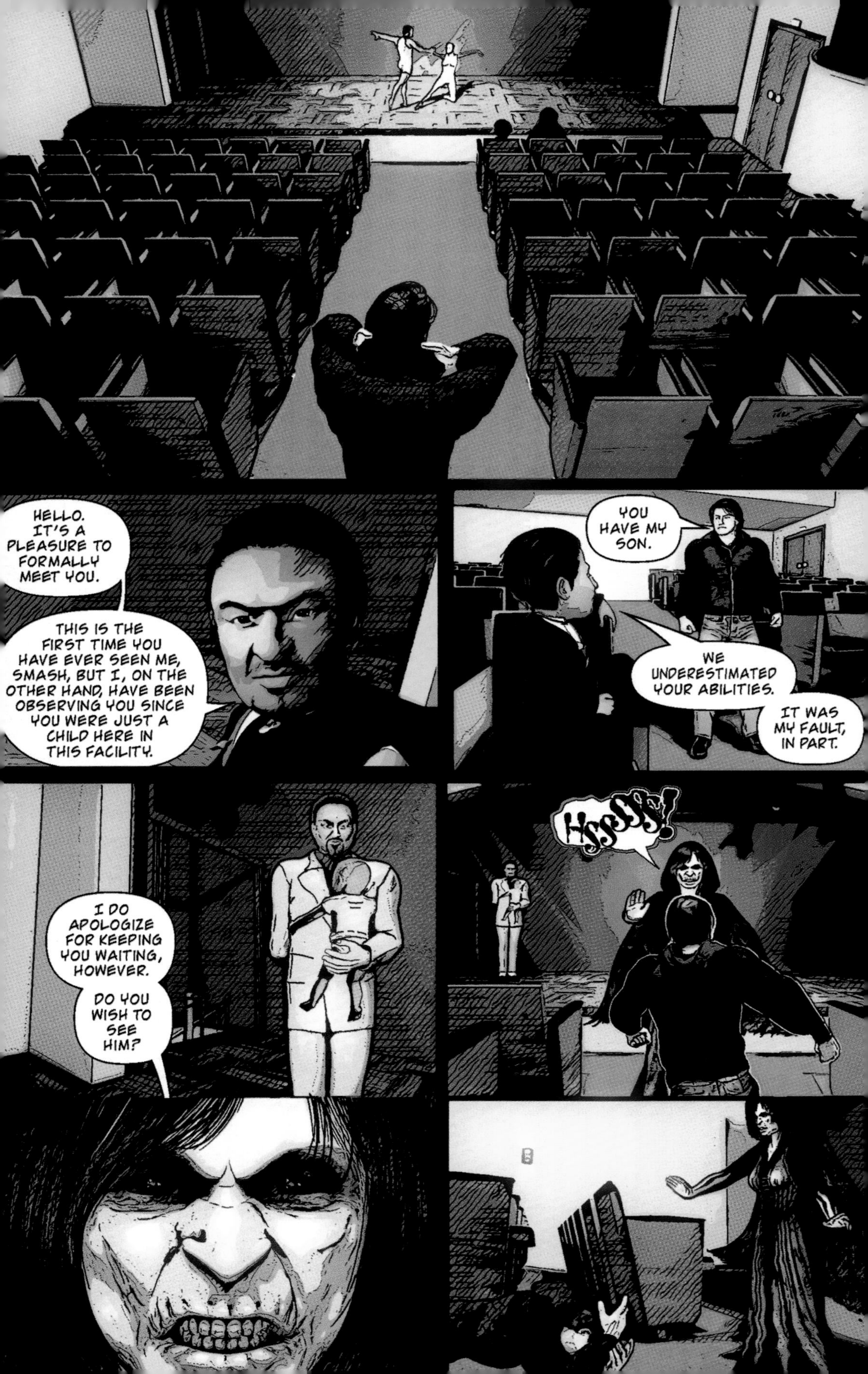
HELLO. IT'S A PLEASURE TO FORMALLY MEET YOU.
THIS IS THE FIRST TIME YOU HAVE EVER SEEN ME, SMASH, BUT I, ON THE OTHER HAND, HAVE BEEN OBSERVING YOU SINCE YOU WERE JUST A CHILD HERE IN THIS FACILITY.
YOU HAVE MY SON.
WE UNDERESTIMATED YOUR ABILITIES.
IT WAS MY FAULT, IN PART.
I DO APOLOGIZE FOR KEEPING YOU WAITING, HOWEVER.
DO YOU WISH TO SEE HIM?
HSSSSS!

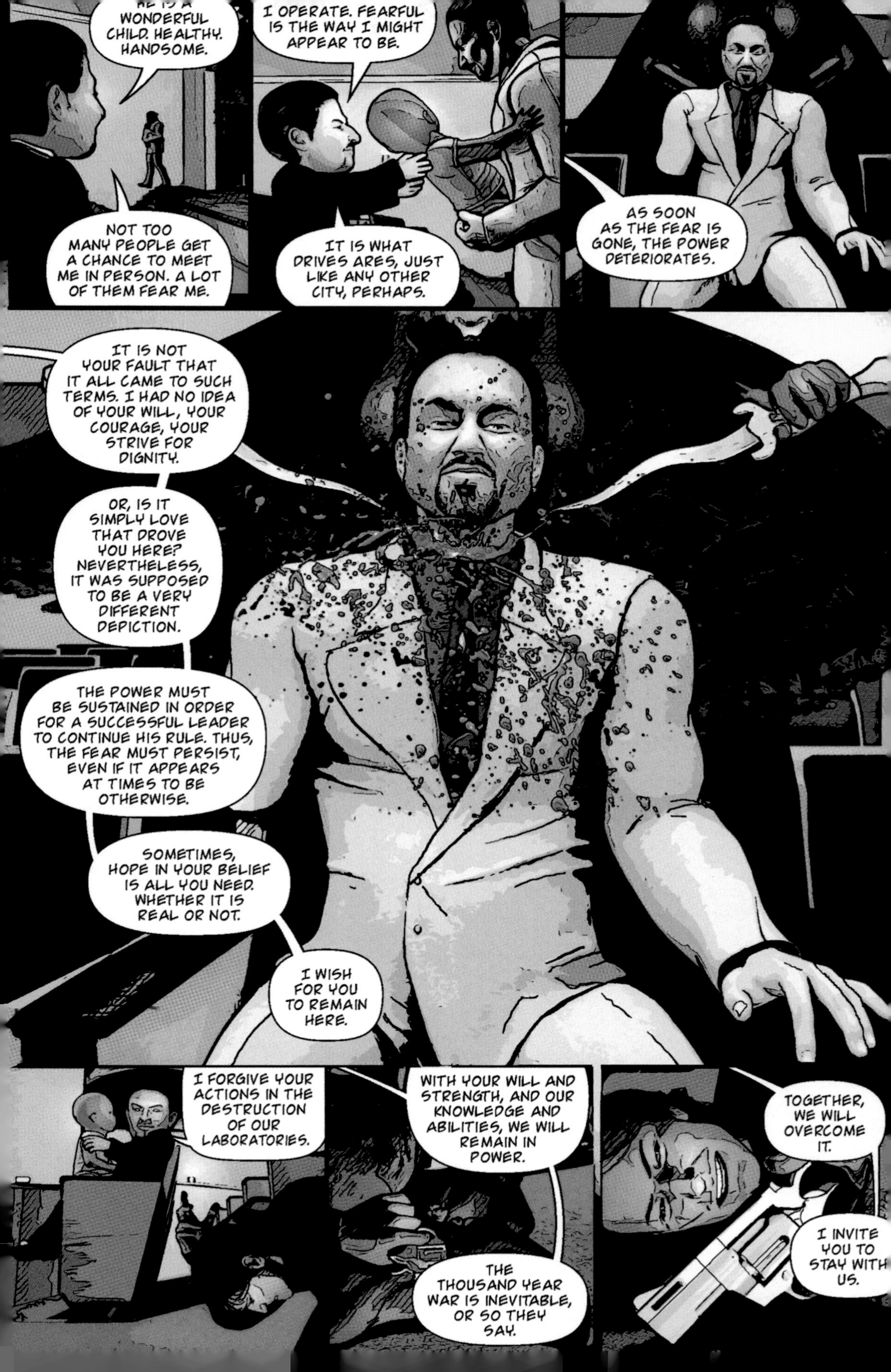
WONDERFUL CHILD. HEALTHY. HANDSOME.
NOT TOO MANY PEOPLE GET A CHANCE TO MEET ME IN PERSON. A LOT OF THEM FEAR ME.
I OPERATE. FEARFUL IS THE WAY I MIGHT APPEAR TO BE.
IT IS WHAT DRIVES ARES, JUST LIKE ANY OTHER CITY, PERHAPS.
AS SOON AS THE FEAR IS GONE, THE POWER DETERIORATES.
IT IS NOT YOUR FAULT THAT IT ALL CAME TO SUCH TERMS. I HAD NO IDEA OF YOUR WILL, YOUR COURAGE, YOUR STRIVE FOR DIGNITY.
OR, IS IT SIMPLY LOVE THAT DROVE YOU HERE? NEVERTHELESS, IT WAS SUPPOSED TO BE A VERY DIFFERENT DEPICTION.
THE POWER MUST BE SUSTAINED IN ORDER FOR A SUCCESSFUL LEADER TO CONTINUE HIS RULE. THUS, THE FEAR MUST PERSIST, EVEN IF IT APPEARS AT TIMES TO BE OTHERWISE.
SOMETIMES, HOPE IN YOUR BELIEF IS ALL YOU NEED. WHETHER IT IS REAL OR NOT.
I WISH FOR YOU TO REMAIN HERE.
I FORGIVE YOUR ACTIONS IN THE DESTRUCTION OF OUR LABORATORIES.
WITH YOUR WILL AND STRENGTH, AND OUR KNOWLEDGE AND ABILITIES, WE WILL REMAIN IN POWER.
THE THOUSAND YEAR WAR IS INEVITABLE, OR SO THEY SAY.
TOGETHER, WE WILL OVERCOME IT.
I INVITE YOU TO STAY WITH US.

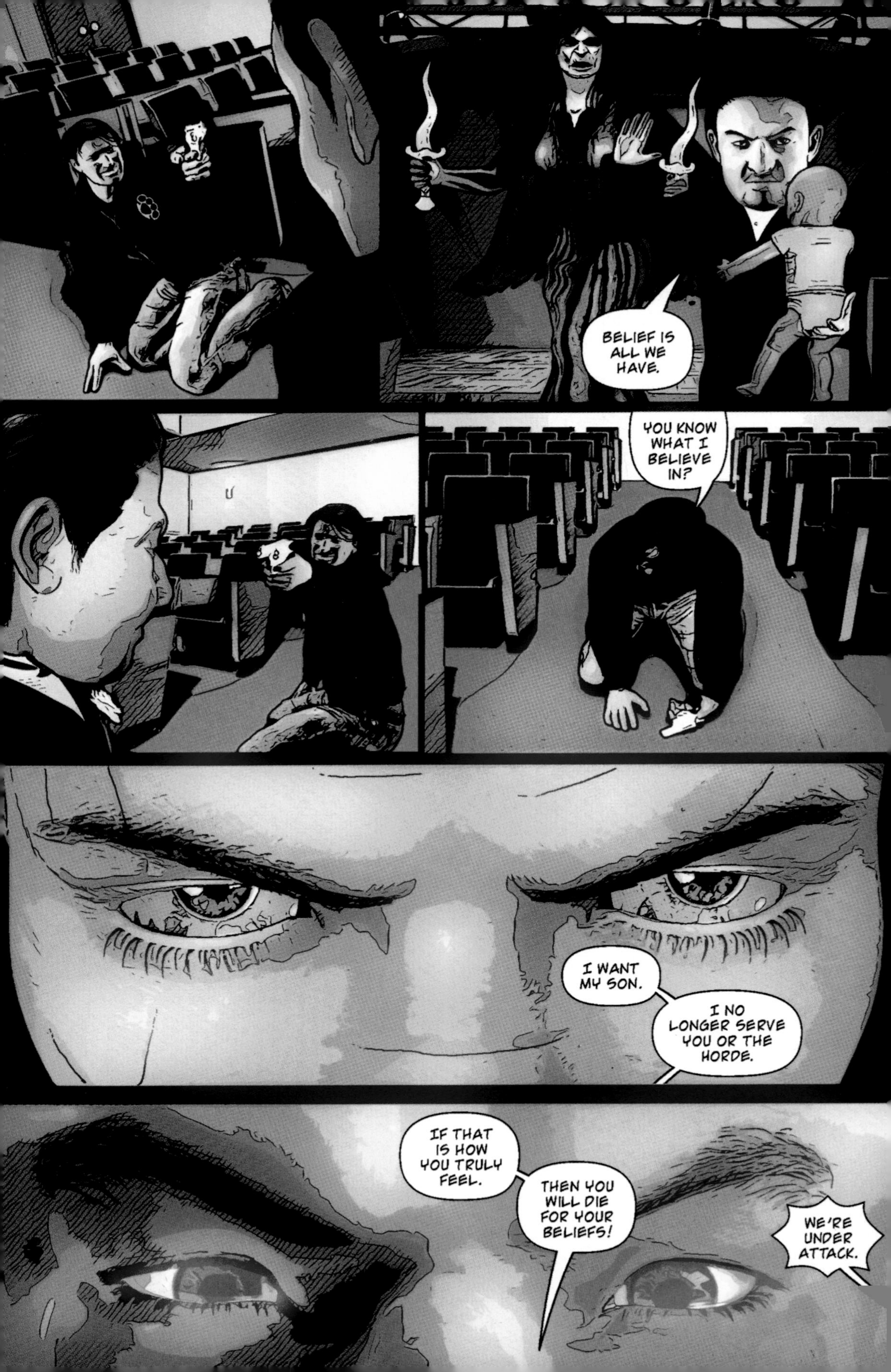
BELIEF IS ALL WE HAVE.
YOU KNOW WHAT I BELIEVE IN?
I WANT MY SON.
I NO LONGER SERVE YOU OR THE HORDE.
IF THAT IS HOW YOU TRULY FEEL.
THEN YOU WILL DIE FOR YOUR BELIEFS!
WE'RE UNDER ATTACK.

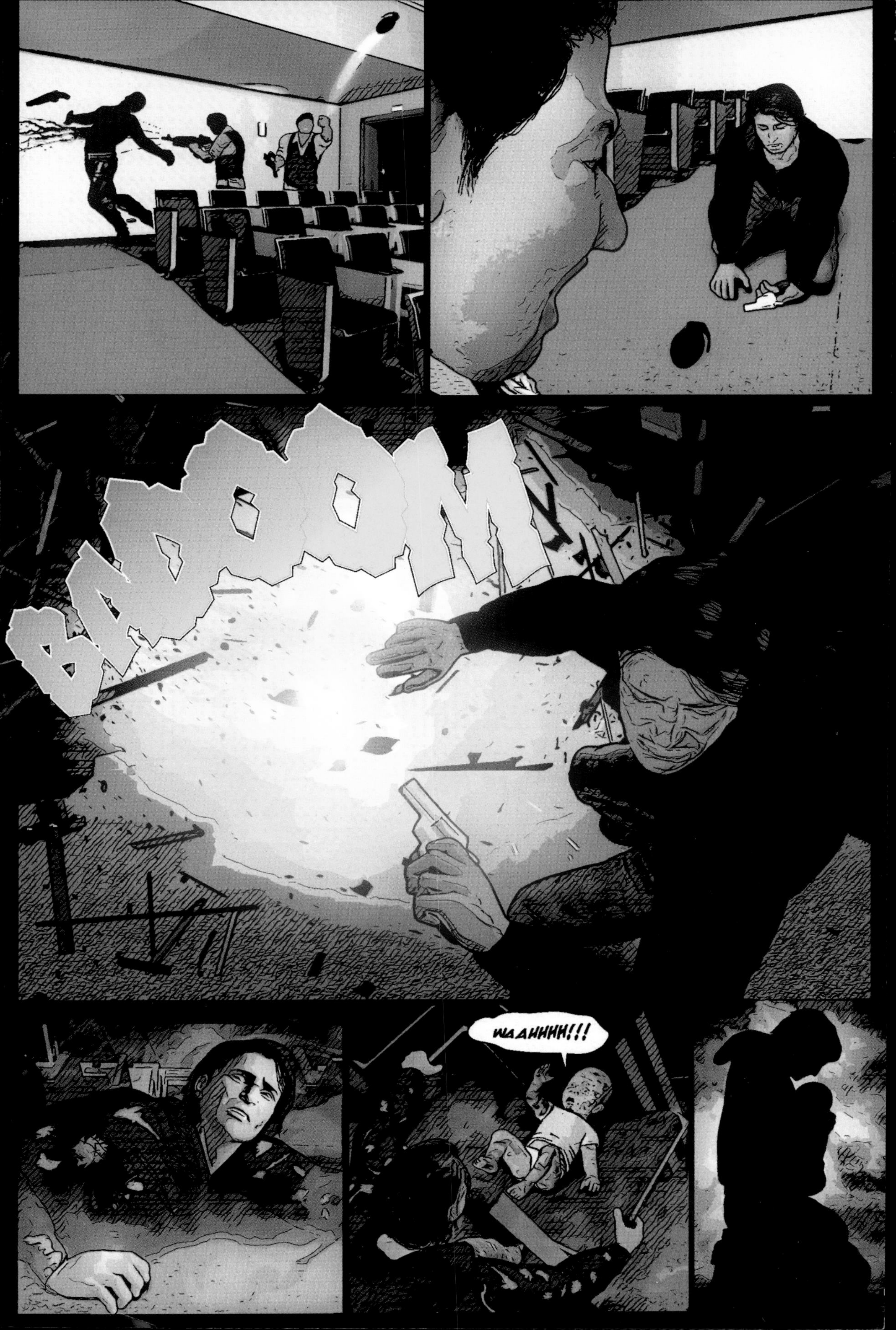
BADOOM
WAAHHHH!!!

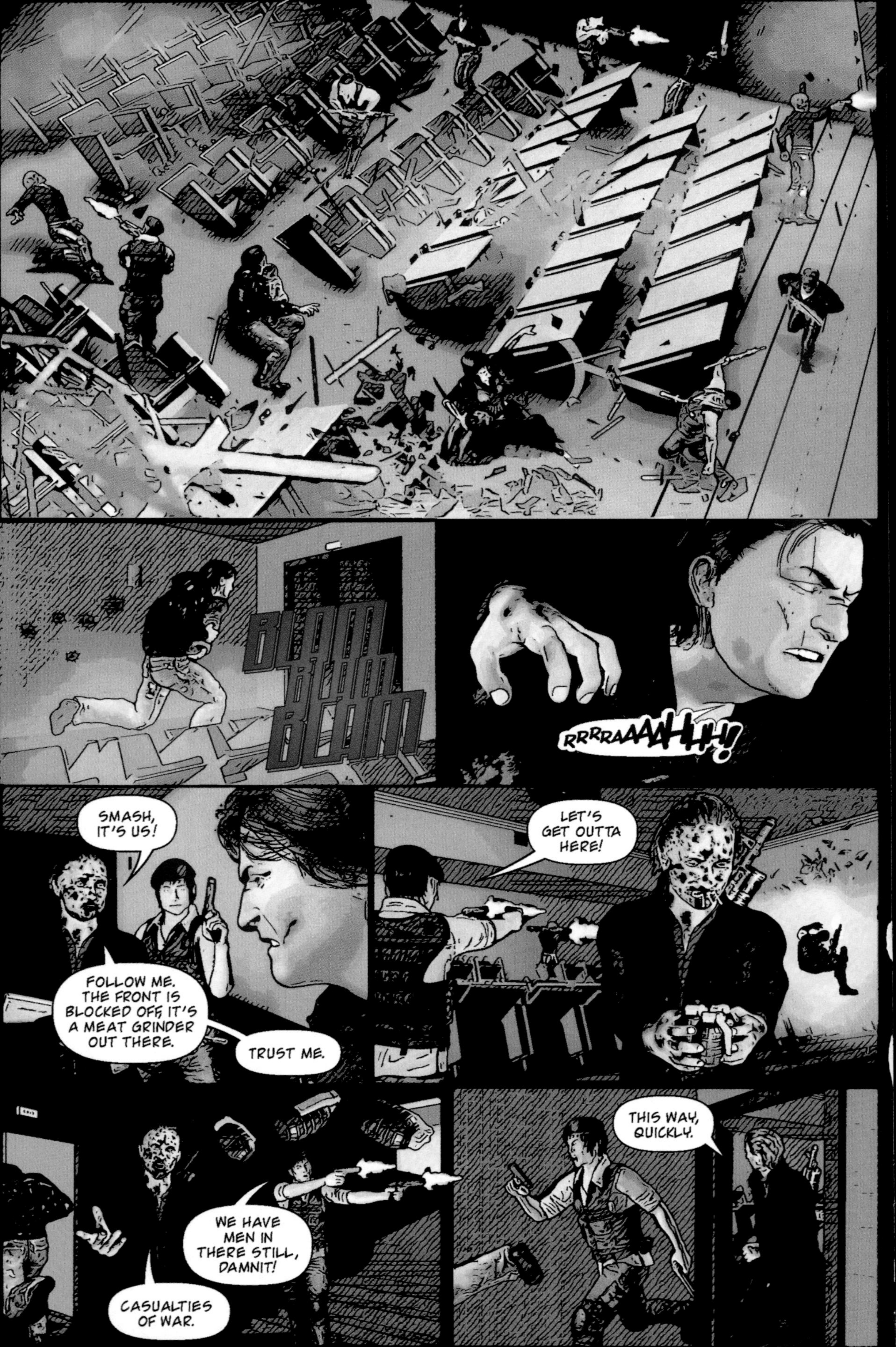
BLAM
BLAM
BLAM
RRRRAAAAHHH!
SMASH, IT'S US!
FOLLOW ME. THE FRONT IS BLOCKED OFF IT'S A MEAT GRINDER OUT THERE.
TRUST ME.
LET'S GET OUTTA HERE!
WE HAVE MEN IN THERE STILL, DAMNIT!
CASUALTIES OF WAR.
THIS WAY, QUICKLY.

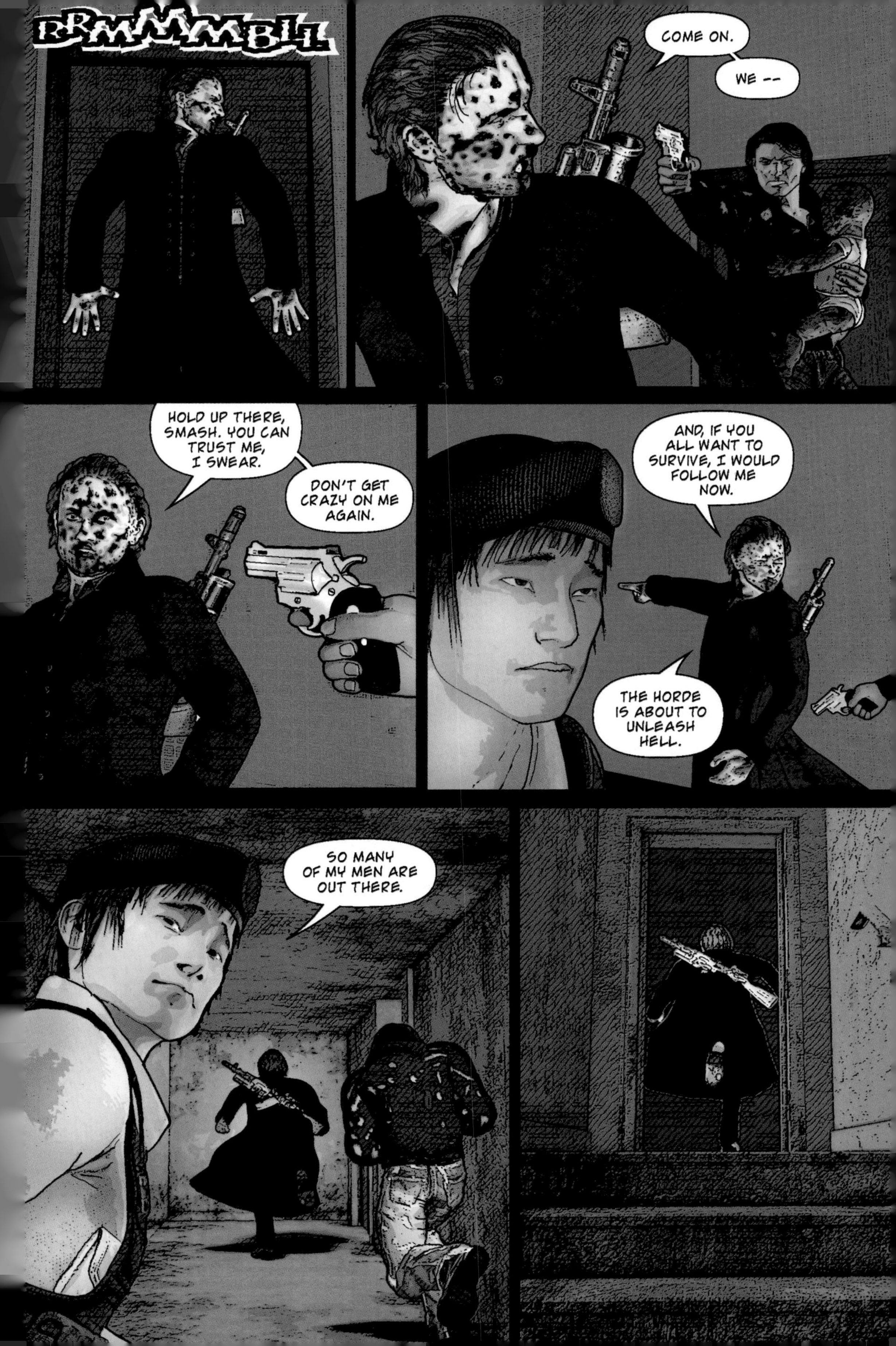
BRMMMMBILL
COME ON.
WE --
HOLD UP THERE, SMASH. YOU CAN TRUST ME, I SWEAR.
DON'T GET CRAZY ON ME AGAIN.
AND, IF YOU ALL WANT TO SURVIVE, I WOULD FOLLOW ME NOW.
THE HORDE IS ABOUT TO UNLEASH HELL.
SO MANY OF MY MEN ARE OUT THERE.

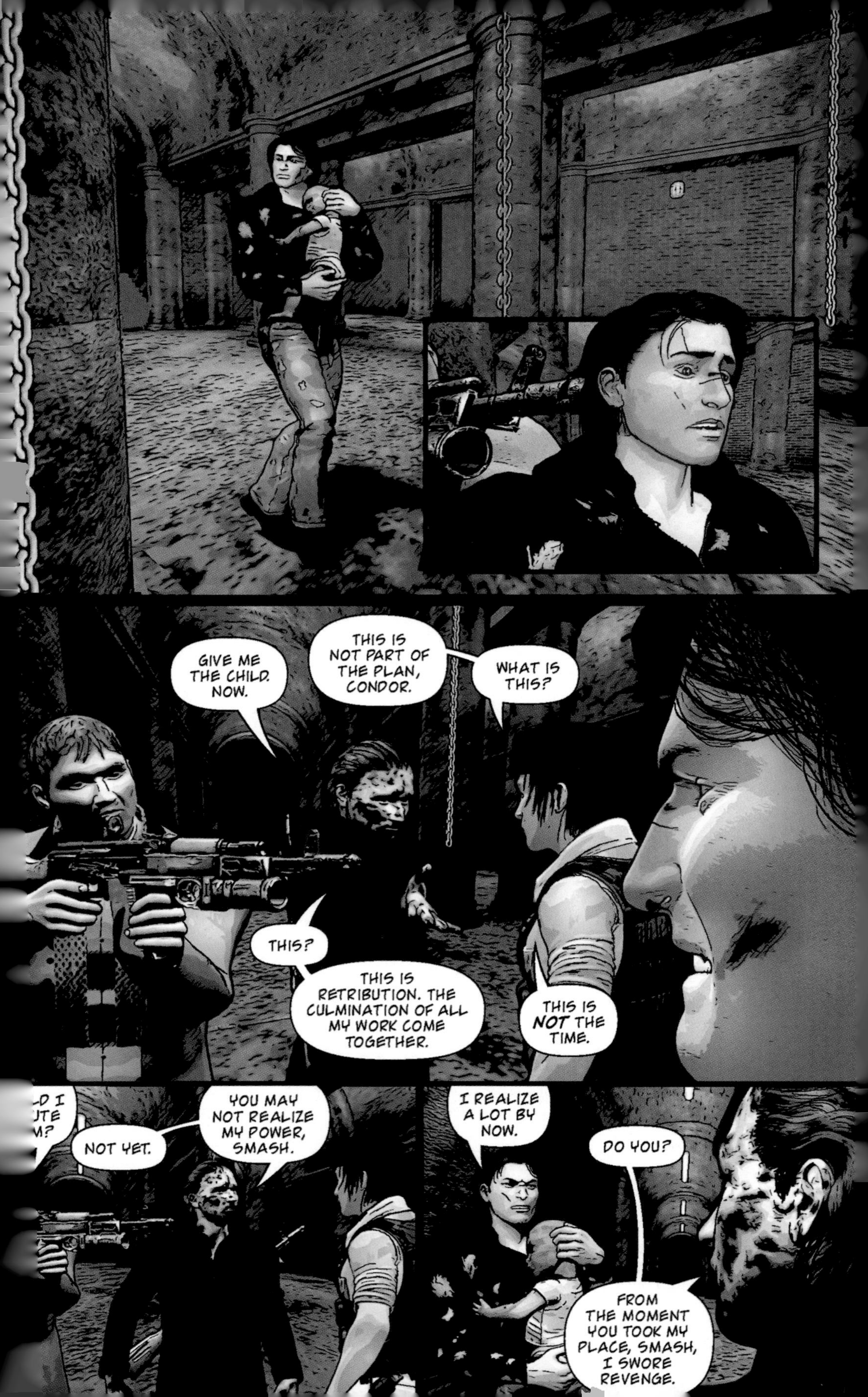
GIVE ME THE CHILD. NOW.
THIS IS NOT PART OF THE PLAN, CONDOR.
WHAT IS THIS?
THIS?
THIS IS RETRIBUTION. THE CULMINATION OF ALL MY WORK COME TOGETHER.
THIS IS **NOT** THE TIME.
NOT YET.
YOU MAY NOT REALIZE MY POWER, SMASH.
I REALIZE A LOT BY NOW.
DO YOU?
FROM THE MOMENT YOU TOOK MY PLACE, SMASH, I SWORE REVENGE.

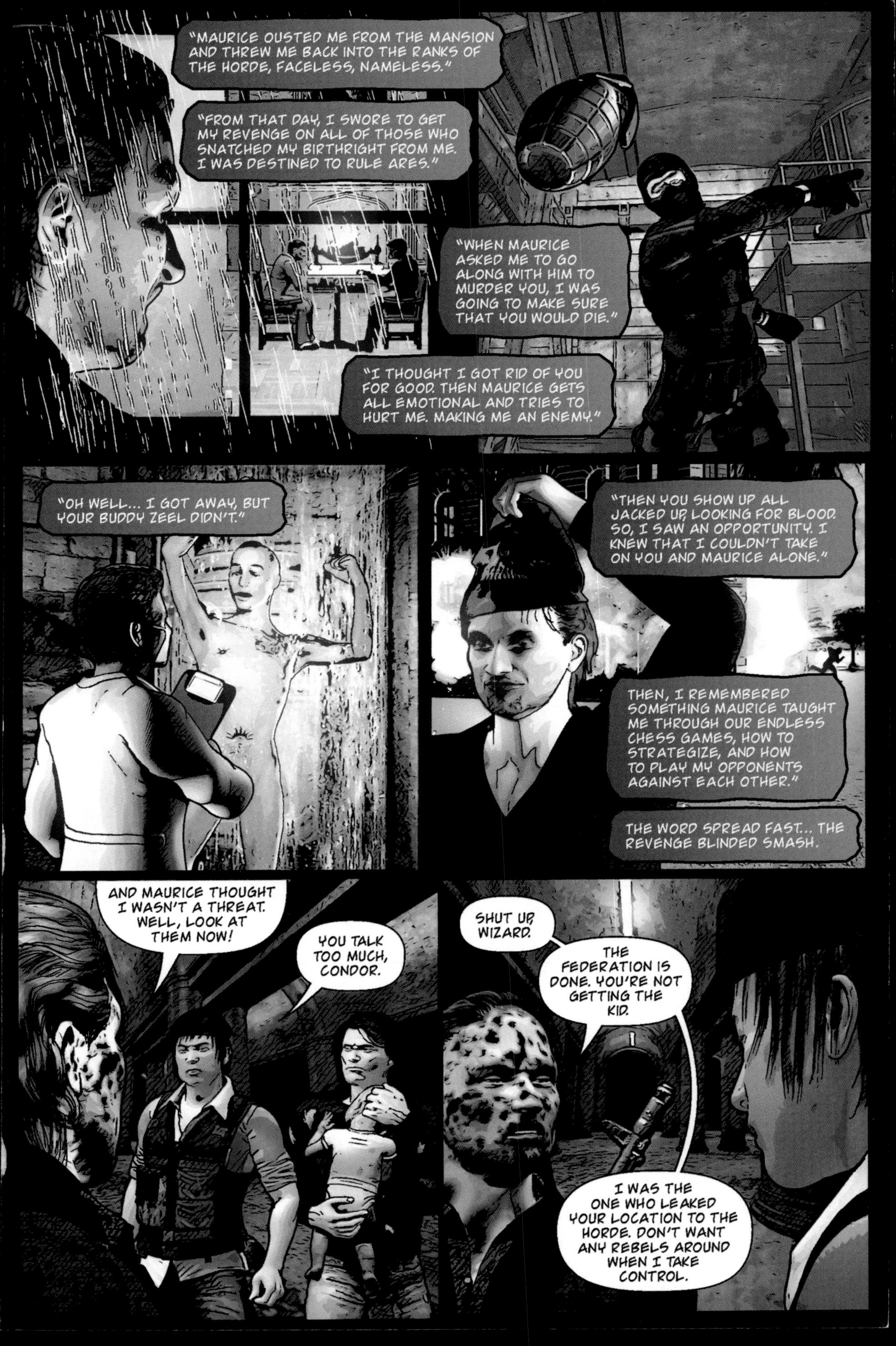
"MAURICE OUSTED ME FROM THE MANSION AND THREW ME BACK INTO THE RANKS OF THE HORDE, FACELESS, NAMELESS."
"FROM THAT DAY, I SWORE TO GET MY REVENGE ON ALL OF THOSE WHO SNATCHED MY BIRTHRIGHT FROM ME. I WAS DESTINED TO RULE ARES."
"WHEN MAURICE ASKED ME TO GO ALONG WITH HIM TO MURDER YOU, I WAS GOING TO MAKE SURE THAT YOU WOULD DIE."
"I THOUGHT I GOT RID OF YOU FOR GOOD. THEN MAURICE GETS ALL EMOTIONAL AND TRIES TO HURT ME. MAKING ME AN ENEMY."
"OH WELL... I GOT AWAY, BUT YOUR BUDDY ZEEL DIDN'T."
"THEN YOU SHOW UP ALL JACKED UP, LOOKING FOR BLOOD. SO, I SAW AN OPPORTUNITY. I KNEW THAT I COULDN'T TAKE ON YOU AND MAURICE ALONE."
THEN, I REMEMBERED SOMETHING MAURICE TAUGHT ME THROUGH OUR ENDLESS CHESS GAMES, HOW TO STRATEGIZE, AND HOW TO PLAY MY OPPONENTS AGAINST EACH OTHER."
THE WORD SPREAD FAST... THE REVENGE BLINDED SMASH.
AND MAURICE THOUGHT I WASN'T A THREAT. WELL, LOOK AT THEM NOW!
YOU TALK TOO MUCH, CONDOR.
SHUT UP, WIZARD.
THE FEDERATION IS DONE. YOU'RE NOT GETTING THE KID.
I WAS THE ONE WHO LEAKED YOUR LOCATION TO THE HORDE. DON'T WANT ANY REBELS AROUND WHEN I TAKE CONTROL.

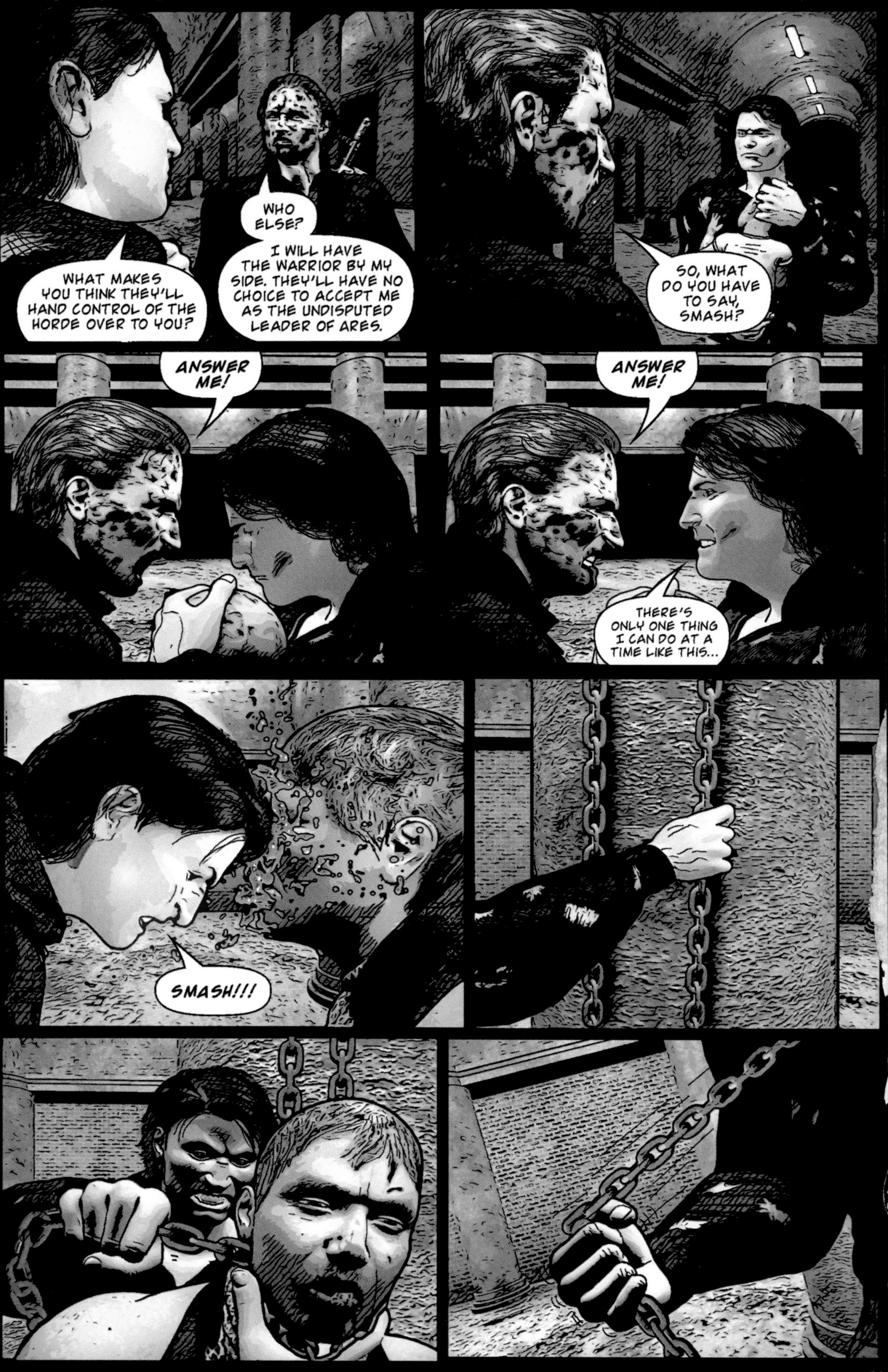
WHAT MAKES YOU THINK THEY'LL HAND CONTROL OF THE HORDE OVER TO YOU?
WHO ELSE?
I WILL HAVE THE WARRIOR BY MY SIDE. THEY'LL HAVE NO CHOICE TO ACCEPT ME AS THE UNDISPUTED LEADER OF ARES.
SO, WHAT DO YOU HAVE TO SAY, SMASH?
ANSWER ME!
ANSWER ME!
THERE'S ONLY ONE THING I CAN DO AT A TIME LIKE THIS...
SMASH!!!

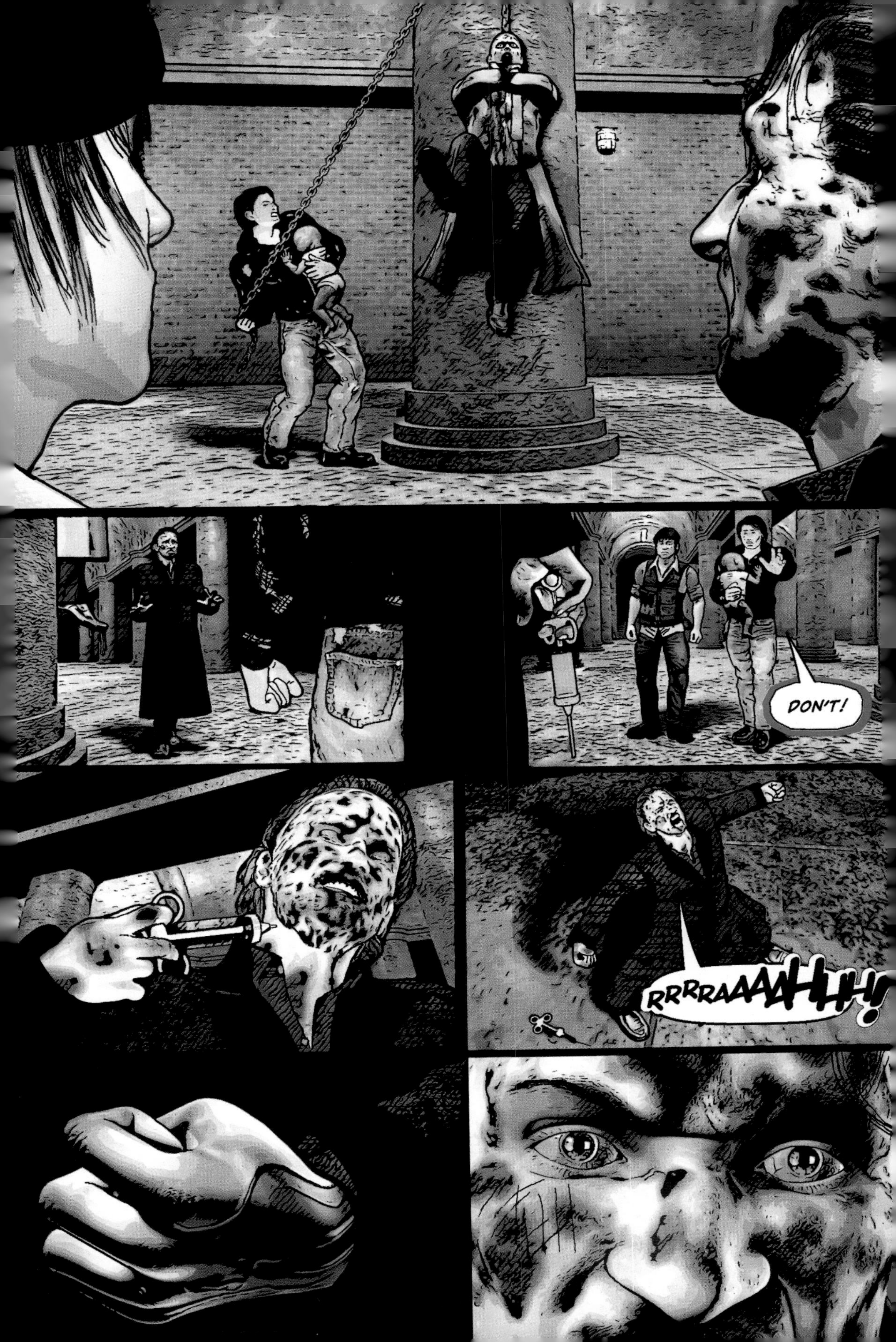
DON'T!
RRRRAAAAHHH!

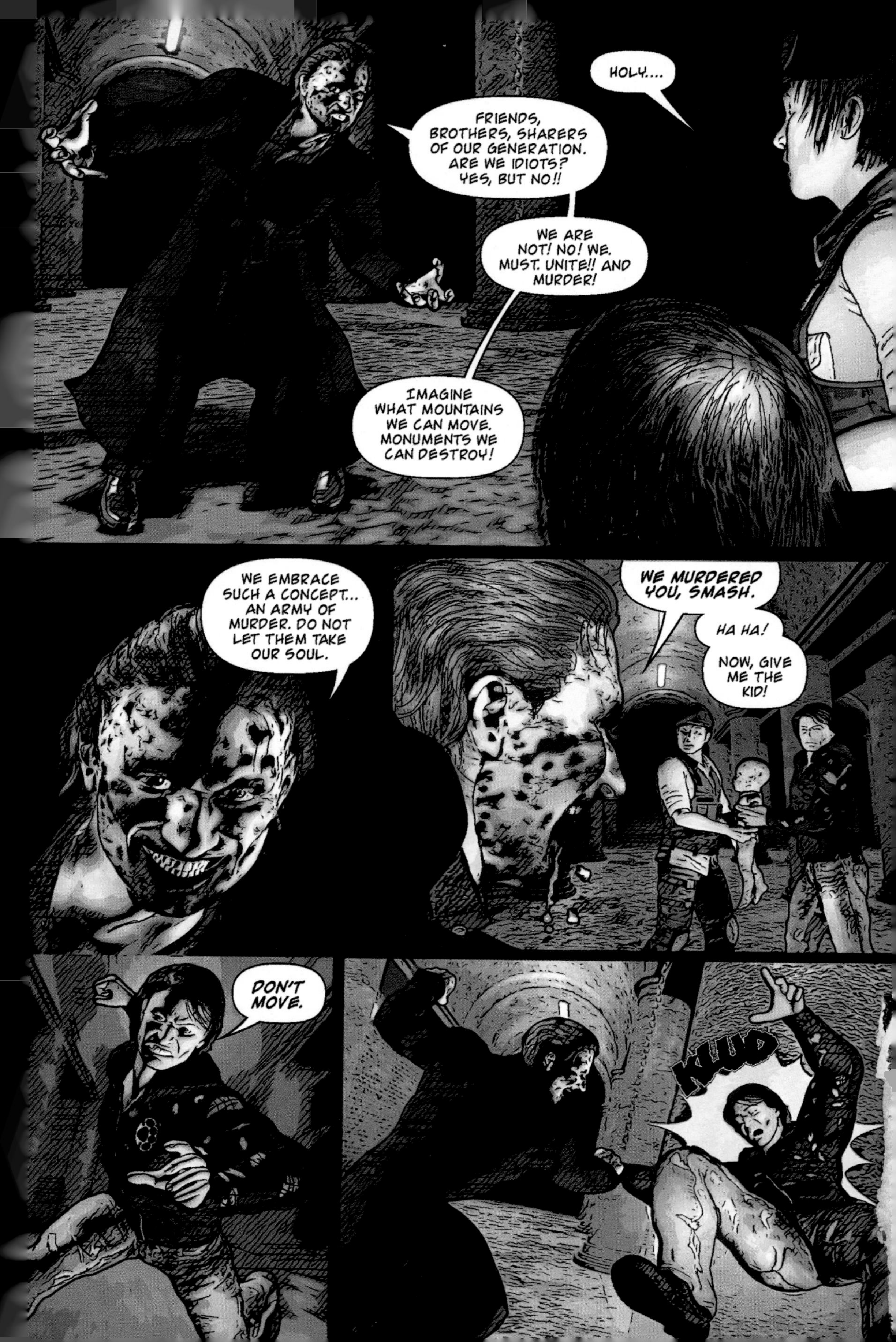
FRIENDS, BROTHERS, SHARERS OF OUR GENERATION. ARE WE IDIOTS? YES, BUT NO!!
HOLY....
WE ARE NOT! NO! WE. MUST. UNITE!! AND MURDER!
IMAGINE WHAT MOUNTAINS WE CAN MOVE. MONUMENTS WE CAN DESTROY!
WE EMBRACE SUCH A CONCEPT... AN ARMY OF MURDER. DO NOT LET THEM TAKE OUR SOUL.
WE MURDERED YOU, SMASH.
HA HA!
NOW, GIVE ME THE KID!
DON'T MOVE.
KLUUD

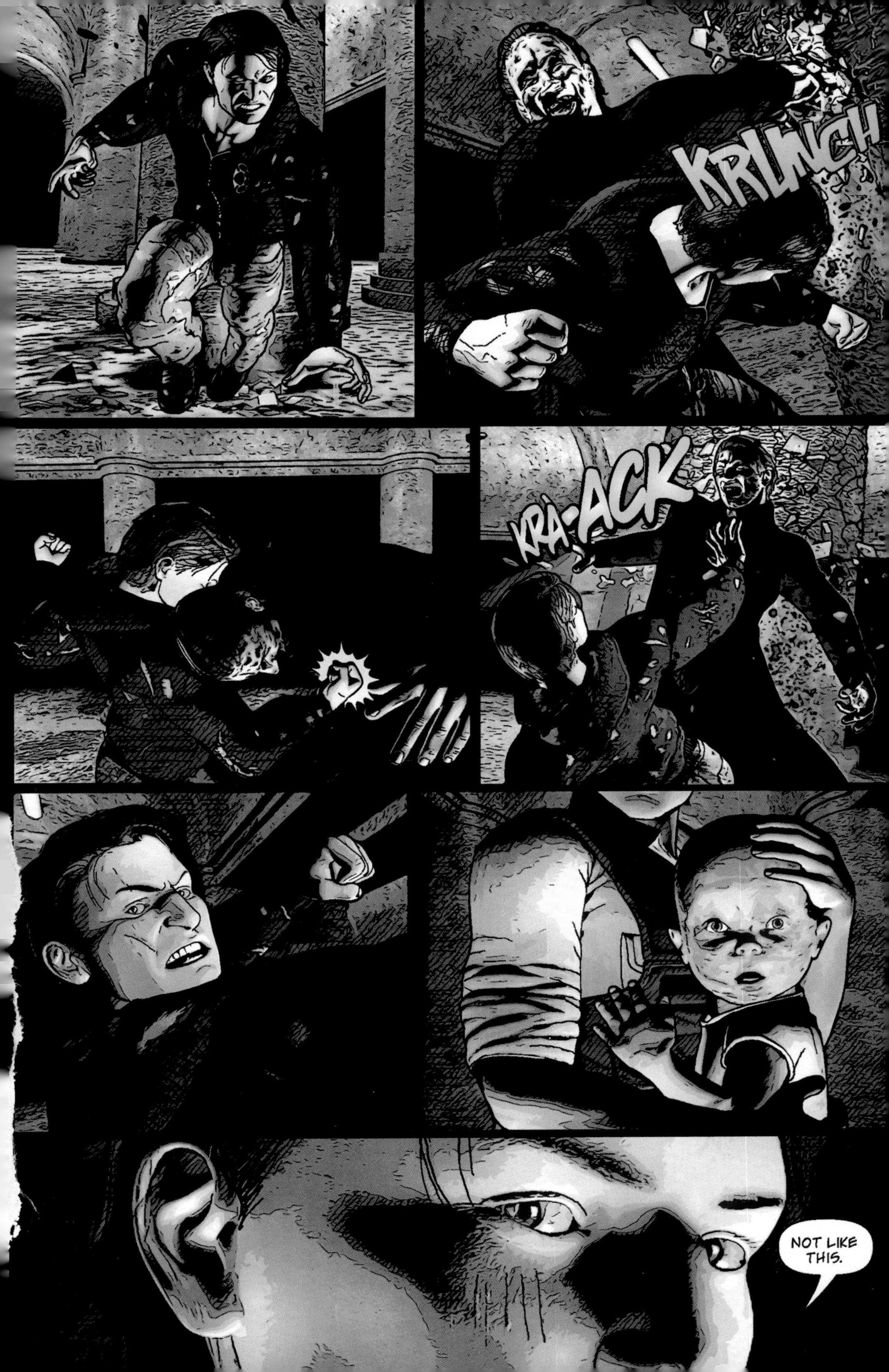
KRUNCH
KRA-ACK
NOT LIKE THIS.

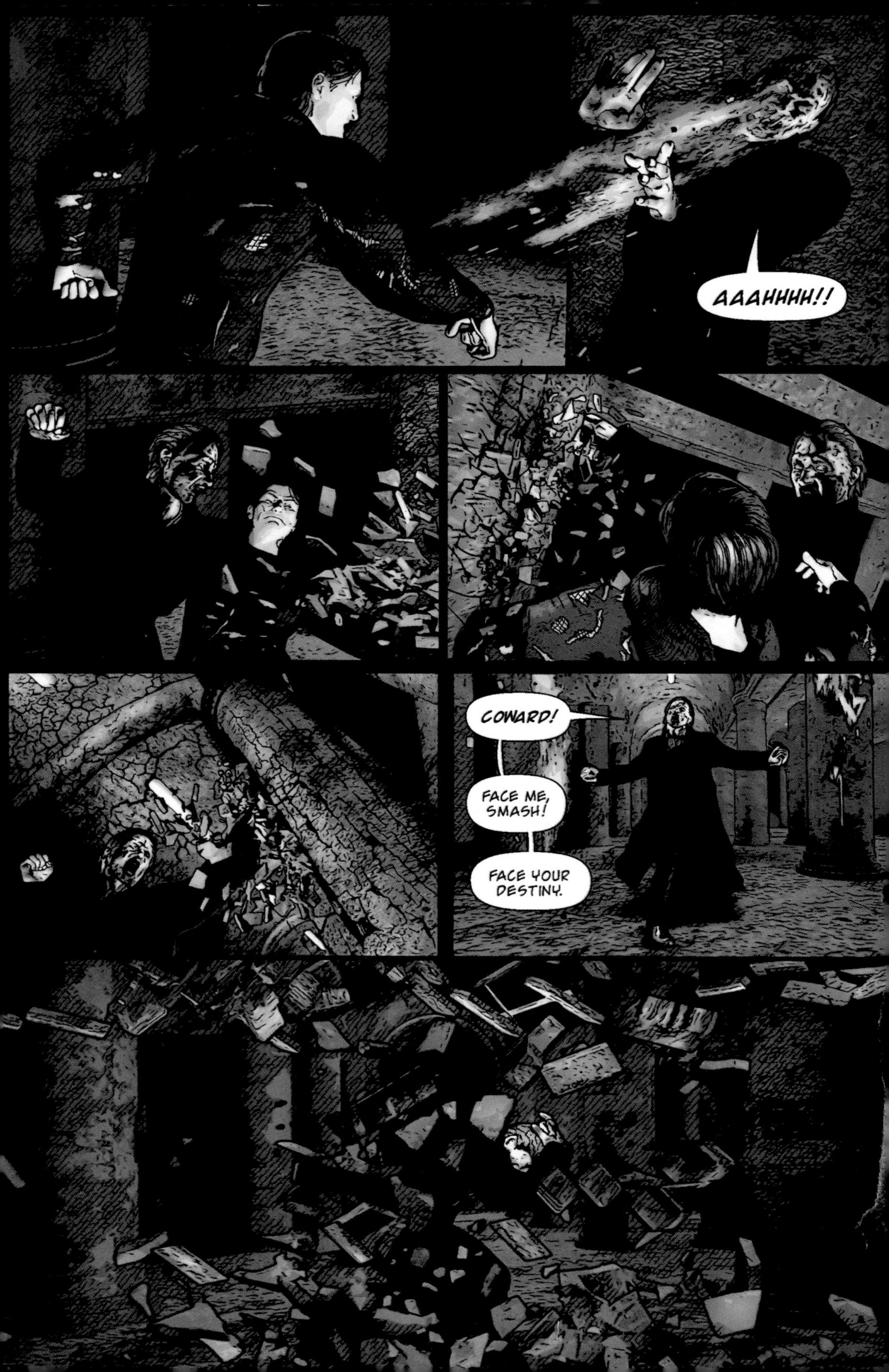
AAAHHHH!!
COWARD!
FACE ME, SMASH!
FACE YOUR DESTINY.

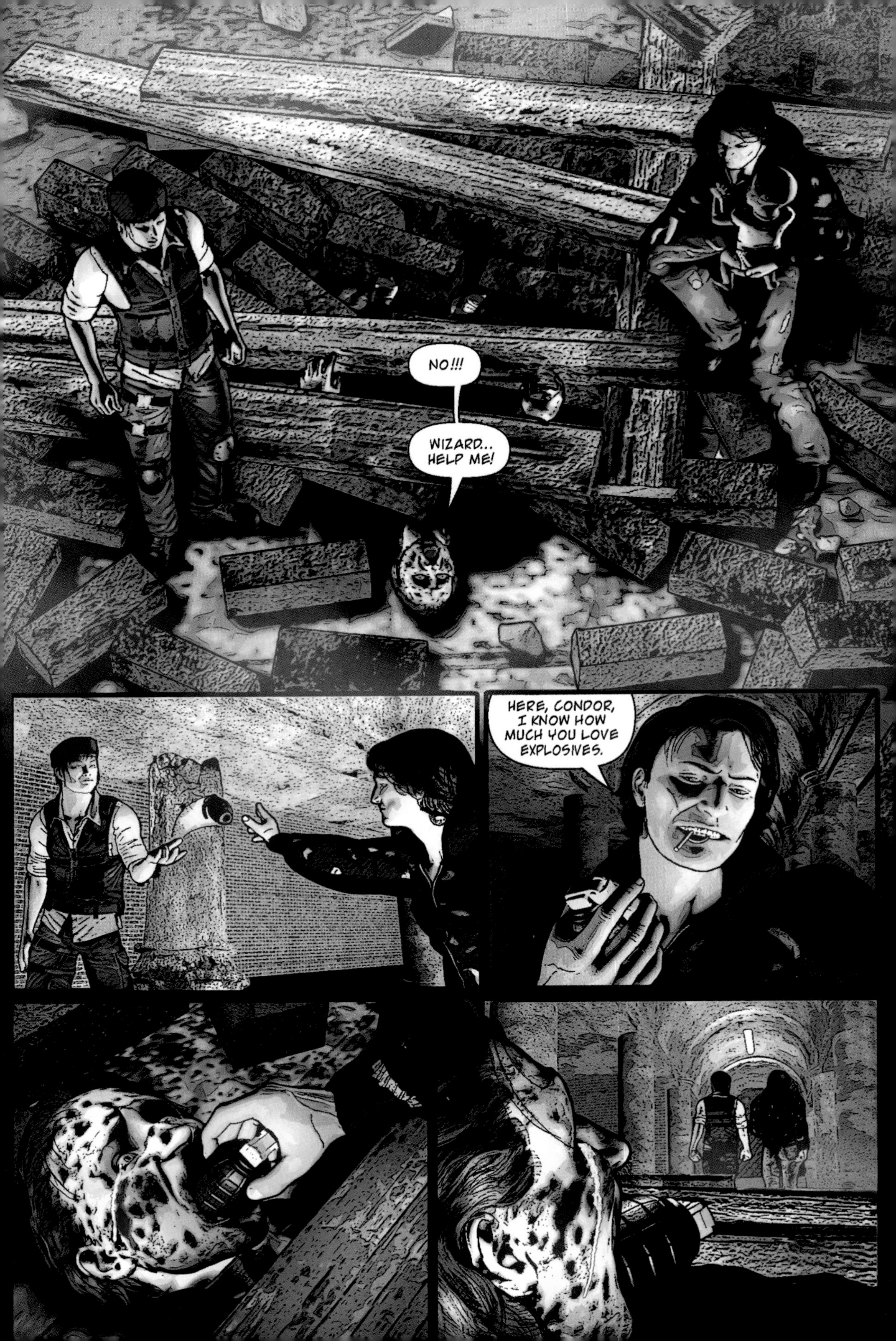
NO!!!
WIZARD... HELP ME!
HERE, CONDOR, I KNOW HOW MUCH YOU LOVE EXPLOSIVES.

FROM THE CREATOR

VLAD YUDIN

The origins of Head Smash are deceptively simple: a man out for revenge and a quest to save his family. But what emerged through the writing process was something much more monumental, a super-hero, but one unlike any I had ever encountered. Smash seemed to fit his time perfectly. He stood up for his beliefs in the face of a brutal totalitarian regime; he faced his oppressors with absolute abandon. I saw a parallel in his story with the people fighting for their freedom around the world.

I knew that to bring this story to life, to really create an entire world and style I would need the help of not just great, but visionary artists. Working with Tim Bradstreet and Dwayne Harris was an incredible experience. Their ability to bring the city of Ares to life was truly inspiring.

This is only the beginning for Head Smash. The seeds are sown throughout this story for a much grander tale that will play out over two more installments. Smash isn't a god, he isn't an alien with incredible powers; he is a man with strengths and weaknesses, with problems that you and I face everyday. His only supernatural tool is the mysterious serum that gives him extraordinary strength, but with that gift comes a terrible curse.

I am mostly known for writing and directing films, and Head Smash is no different. Stay tuned because we're heading to the big screen too. And remember: